DATE DUE			

Studies in Modern History

The Cold War, Hugh Higgins
Vietnam, Hugh Higgins
Cold War to Détente 1945–80, Colin Bown and Peter J. Mooney
China 1949–76, Colin Bown
America Since 1920, Daniel Snowman
The Soviet Superpower, Peter J. Mooney

Eastern Europe Since 1945

L P Morris

HEINEMANN EDUCATIONAL BOOKS
LONDON · EXETER

Heinemann Educational Books Ltd
22 Bedford Square, London WC1B 3HH

Heinemann Educational Books Inc.
4 Front Street, Exeter, NH 03833, USA

LONDON EDINBURGH MELBOURNE AUCKLAND
HONG KONG SINGAPORE KUALA LUMPUR NEW DELHI
IBADAN NAIROBI JOHANNESBURG
EXETER (NH) KINGSTON PORT OF SPAIN

British Library Cataloguing in Publication Data

Morris L.P.
Eastern Europe since 1945.
1. Europe, Eastern–History
I. Title
947.084   DK38
ISBN 0-435-31611-7

Typeset by The Castlefield Press of Moulton, Northampton
Printed in Great Britain by Biddles Ltd.

CONTENTS

MAPS

PREFACE

Anyone acquainted with eastern Europe will be familiar with the ground covered and the material contained in this book, which is intended to serve as an introduction to the subject. It does not cover developments in the USSR, the subject of P.J. Mooney's *The Soviet Superpower*, nor international politics, the subject of C. Bown and P.J. Mooney's *Cold War to Détente*, both of which are companion volumes in this series. Neither does it concentrate on relations between the USSR and eastern Europe, which are covered in K. Dawisha and P. Hanson (eds), *Soviet–East European Dilemmas* (Heinemann/RIIA, 1981). Solely concerned with internal eastern European developments, this volume is based on the premise that there have been close similarities and parallels between the evolution of the DDR, Poland, Czechoslovakia, Hungary, Romania, Yugoslavia and Bulgaria. It does not extend to Albania. The suggestion for the volume came from Janice Brown, and my colleagues Mike Duffy, Bob Lewis, Gerald Opie and Bill Tupman gave much helpful advice which greatly improved the final draft. To Hilary Tolley, who made sense of the typescript, and Sean Goddard, who drew the maps, I owe an especial debt. I alone am responsible for the weaknesses and errors.

L.P. Morris
May 1983

ACKNOWLEDGEMENTS

The author and publishers wish to thank the following for permission to reproduce copyright material:

George Allen & Unwin for Table 5.1 from J. Triska and C. Gati, *Blue Collar Workers in Eastern Europe*.

Harper & Row for Table 1.1 from G.H.N. Seton-Watson, *Eastern Europe Between the Wars, 1918–1941*.

NOTE ON SPELLING, STATISTICAL INFORMATION AND FURTHER READING

Accents and diacritical markings are an integral part of German, Hungarian, Polish, Romanian, Serbo-Croat and Czechoslovak. In this book they have been omitted. Those cognizant with the languages of the region will recognise where they should be added. The author trusts that those who are not familiar with the languages – likely to form the majority of the readership – will not be inconvenienced by their absence. Bulgarian and Serbian use Cyrillic alphabets, which have been transliterated into Latin script. Place names are given in the form most likely to be familiar to Western readers. Except where otherwise stated, all statistics come from *Whitaker's Almanack*, the United Nations annual *Economic Survey of Europe* or annual *Yearbooks* or from the UK Central Statistical Office's *Annual Abstract of Statistics*. Because of variations in definitions and periodic recasting of bases, they are not necessarily directly comparable and should be used with caution. They do, however, reflect trends and make possible rough comparisons.

At the end of each section is a list of further reading of works in English. These contain their own bibliographies of works in a wide range of languages. Many of them cover more than one aspect of the subject. At the end there is a short list of general works.

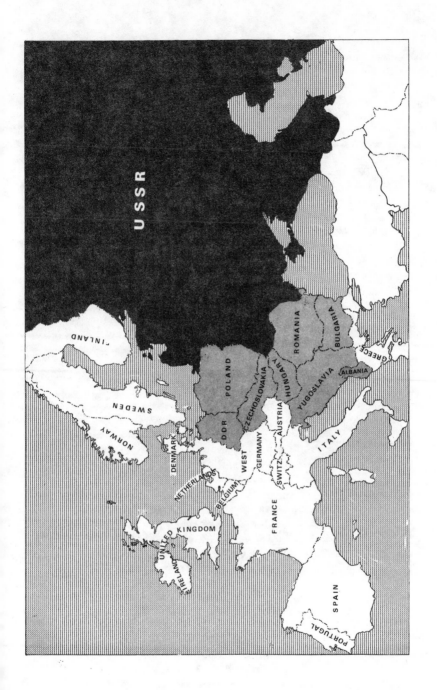

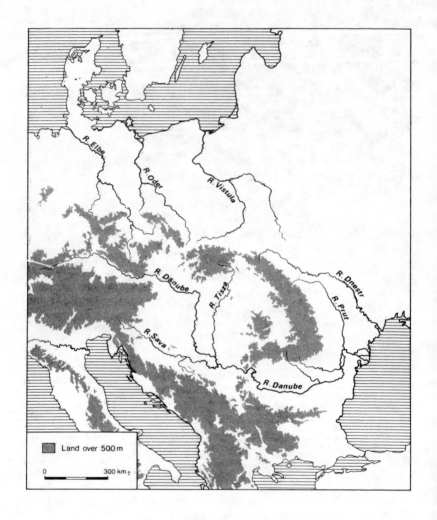

Map 1   *Topography of eastern Europe.*

1

EASTERN EUROPE BEFORE 1939

Before 1945 eastern and east central Europe had a chequered and blood-stained history. Frontier territory where neighbouring empires contended, throughout recorded history there were few periods when it was not the scene of political and military conflict. Its peoples had long been accustomed to the threat of war, to the devastations of invasion and the pressures of alien rulers. The problems of the area were compounded by the absence of clear-cut geographical features. The amorphous character of the countryside and the deeply contentious issues of national identity combined to deprive the area of precise political frontiers. It could have been said of all states in the region, as it was of Poland, that they were countries having neighbours rather than histories. It was, moreover, an area traditionally dominated by one or more great powers. During the seventeenth century the great medieval state of Poland–Lithuania had been briefly rivalled by Sweden and during the eighteenth century steadily replaced by Russia. Three partitions between 1772 and 1795 divided its territories between Russia, the Habsburg Empire and the developing state of Prussia. A similar development occurred in the Balkans. Ottoman conquest there brought Turkish armies to the gates of Vienna, besieged for the last time in 1683, and incorporated Hungary, the southern steppe lands of the modern Ukraine and the whole littoral of the Black Sea into the Sultan's Empire. Turkish power began to decline simultaneously with that of Poland, though it was a much slower process. By 1718 Habsburg armies had liberated Hungary and freed the northern fringes of the Balkans. They were then incorporated into the Habsburg Empire. Russia too made steady progress at Ottoman expense. By 1774 its armies had reached the north and east coasts of the Black Sea.

The relatively rapid collapse of the Polish state and the amicable partition among its neighbours was renewed in 1815 and effectively fixed the political pattern there until 1918. Polish revolts in 1830–1 and between 1863 and 1865 disturbed but did not seriously threaten the political order, although the Polish community in exile in France and, later, the USA kept before world opinion the ideal of a re-born independent Poland. A similar role was played in the areas comprised within Russia and Prussia by the Roman Catholic Church and by Polish creative artists. Further south Habsburg control over the Czech lands of Bohemia and Moravia and over Slovakia was not seriously endangered despite the 1848 uprising in Prague. Between 1870 and 1914 the sense of Czech national identity grew steadily. Czech politicians took part in the electoral system and obstructed parliamentary business in Vienna, but they were deeply divided over their preferred political future. Failing any convincing alternative they accepted the Habsburgs to whom they looked to defend them from German political, cultural and economic domination. The Hungarians, however, were not so docile. They had not been especially grateful for Habsburg liberation from Turkish rule and looked back nostalgically to the great days of Hungary under King Stephen I and his successors in the eleventh and twelfth centuries before the Ottoman victory at Mohacs in 1526. During every eighteenth- and nineteenth-century crisis they sought to wring concessions from the embattled Habsburgs. Maria Theresa, Joseph II, Ferdinand and Franz Joseph in 1848 and Franz Joseph in 1866 all encountered Hungarian intransigence. Finally in 1867 the Austrian Empire was converted into the Dual Monarchy, with a separate Hungarian government at Budapest controlling the territories east of the River Leithe, including the Croat, Slovak and Romanian populations of the Monarchy. There was no evidence that Hungarian appetites had been satisfied. They continued to whittle away at the links with the other lands of the Habsburgs, to which they were joined by a personal union through the Habsburg King of Hungary, by a Delegation comprising equal representation of both parts of the Dual Monarchy and by an unofficial common Cabinet based on the Imperial Crown Council.

Further south still the Ottoman Empire gave ground slowly to the emerging forces of Balkan nationalism. Its long rearguard action drew in the other powers who at each stage consulted on mutually acceptable frontiers and ensured satisfactory monarchs for the new states. It rapidly became clear that as neighbours, Russia and the Habsburg state were the two most directly affected. By 1880 Serbs, Greeks, Romanians and Bulgars had asserted or were in the process of asserting their independence. The ensuing wars involved the other European powers and exacerbated relations and deepened the mutual suspicions of Russia and the Dual Monarchy. The newly independent Balkan states had their own ambitions and aspirations and were very willing to associate themselves with rival great powers. While they inspired the Ruritania of Anthony Hope and the comedy of Bernard Shaw's *Arms and the Man* the Balkan states themselves were in deadly earnest. Serbian territorial ambitions extended to Habsburg-administered Bosnia and

Hercegovina, annexed by the Dual Monarchy in 1908, where Serbian nationalist terrorists achieved the assassination at Sarajevo in 1914, and to Macedonia, where they came into conflict with Bulgarian claims, upheld by the terrorist IMRO (International Macedonian Revolutionary Organisation) movement. It was relatively easy for the Balkan states to sink their common differences in a united fight against the Turks – as they showed in the First Balkan War of 1912. Once it was over, however, the Second Balkan War immediately followed as the victors' conflicting ambitions could not be reconciled. Bulgarian aspirations in Macedonia brought it into conflict with both Serbia and Greece, and disagreements over the Dobrudja brought war with Romania. There was no reason to think that independence and the disappearance of the Ottoman Empire had ended the strife and conflict hitherto characteristic of the region.

The First World War wrought an extraordinary change. In an historically unparalleled development the great states dominating the region either disintegrated, as did the Dual Monarchy, collapsed in enfeebled disarray, like the rump of the Ottoman Empire, or suffered revolution and eclipse, as was the case with both Russia and Germany. Not only was there an opportunity for a thorough re-casting: such a re-organisation was unavoidable. The hopes and dreams of eastern European political leaders seemed to be realised. It was the more startling for being almost totally unexpected. Only in 1917 had the entente powers begun to accept the principle of national self-determination as a war aim, and it was not until the summer of 1918 that the essential features of the post-war settlement became discernible. Agreement was reached by nationalist political leaders in exile, claiming to speak on behalf of their peoples. In the USA Czech and Slovak politicians under the leadership of Masaryk agreed to the fusion of their respective peoples in a new Czecho-Slovak state. In August 1917 the allies recognised the Czecho-Slovak National Council as a belligerent ally, in effect acknowledging the break-up of the Dual Monarchy as a war aim. Although proposals for the creation of a south Slav state had been mooted by exiled Croat, Serb and Slovene politicians in 1914, it was not until spring 1918 that the Serbian government and the Yugoslav Committee secured allied commitment to a south Slav state. Early in 1917 allied support for the liberation of the Romanians was announced. Finally, the collapse of tsarist Russia permitted the acceptance of the re-creation of a separate Polish state. Despite the tsarist declaration of a free Poland as a Russian war aim, made in December 1916, only after the February Revolution could real progress be made. In January 1918 President Wilson had committed himself to the creation of an independent Poland, and finally in June 1918 the entente powers formally endorsed this. Bolshevik annulment of the partition treaties in August placed the matter beyond dispute. The Paris-based Polish National

Committee became the medium of entente co-operation with the Poles. Parallel to this the central powers had also accepted the creation of a Polish state. After occupying all the Polish lands they formally announced their commitment in November 1916 and permitted the recruitment of a Polish Legion. The subsequent chequered history of this body cast serious doubts on the unity of will and good intentions of the German and Austro–Hungarian governments. Despite this, in autumn 1918 there was a military force active under Pilsudski and an administrative and political structure was rapidly emerging among Poles in eastern Europe.

As it was an article of faith in 1918 that conditions in eastern Europe had created the atmosphere leading to war, the peacemakers were intent on removing these once and for all. Typical was the conviction of President Wilson, whose intention to satisfy all 'well-defined national elements' was optimistically linked to an undertaking to do so without causing discord between national groups and while ending existing ones. Inevitably such hopes were disappointed, for the realities of eastern Europe precluded neat, seemly solutions. By 1918 four years of war, and the hopes and fears aroused by profound political changes, had heightened national awareness. The resentments of former subject peoples against the dominant position of traditional governing nationalities had been supplemented by the growing anxieties of the latter as military defeat foreshadowed political eclipse. There was no reason to believe that the resolution of these antagonisms would be easy. The expansionist aspirations of Serbia and Romania also brought their own difficulties. The incorporation of the new state of Yugoslavia required that Serbian ambitions be tempered to meet the sensitivities of the powerful Croat and Slovene communities, both of which enjoyed a proud history of superior economic and cultural achievement. Neither took kindly to Serbian political domination. Similar resentments occurred among the Hungarian and German population of Transylvania, incorporated into Romania in 1919. Such problems were vitiated by recollections of historical greatness, carefully polished during the nineteenth century and used to awaken national emotions. The memory of the Polish Commonwealth, of the prosperity and power of the Principality of Bohemia from the tenth to the early fifteenth centuries, of the achievements of the Serbian hero Stephen Dushan between 1331 and 1355 or of the great days of medieval Bulgaria between the late twelfth and mid-fourteenth centuries were inspirations to Polish, Czech, Serbian or Bulgarian nationalists. They were inclined to base their twentieth-century territorial ambitions on the achievements of their adopted progenitors. Inevitably such claims conflicted, for these erstwhile potentates had each governed the same areas at different historical periods. Particular points of contention after 1918 were Teschen, where Polish and Czechoslovak claims conflicted, southern

Slovakia, where a substantial Hungarian minority was disputed by Czechoslovakia and Hungary, the Dobruja province which Romanians and Bulgarians claimed, and Macedonia, an area of particular ethnic confusion where Serbian and Bulgarian suits clashed with each other and with that of Greece. To such demands were added those of defeated Hungarians unable to reconcile themselves to the narrow boundaries of post-war Hungary. After 1919 bad relations between the new, independent states of the region were normal. Over all loomed the problems of relations with the USSR and Germany. The former was unreconciled to territorial losses to Poland in the Russo-Polish war in 1919–20, confirmed by the Treaty of Riga in 1921, and of Bessarabia to Romania in 1918. Germany had its own grievances with Poland, whose territory divided East and West Prussia and constituted the 'Polish corridor', and with Czechoslovakia, where the north-western fringe of Bohemia had a substantial German population, known as the Sudeten Germans from the mountainous area that they occupied. The proclaimed intention to redraw frontiers in accordance with national considerations may have made things worse. After the Treaties of Versailles, St Germain and Trianon national groups included within states of predominantly different nationality could argue that they had been unjustly treated. Indeed the allies had hurried the demarcation of the new states and had given little time for careful statistical or local investigation. However, even if the process had been more painstaking it would have been impossible to avoid the inclusion of sizeable minorities within the new national states. As it was, with the exception of Hungary and Bulgaria, there were relatively large groups within each country that did not identify with it and whose allegiance was considered doubtful (see Table 1.1).

No government was free from anxieties over its internal cohesion and its neighbours' intentions and they sought security through alliances with each other and with the powers. A pattern strikingly reminiscent of pre-1914 Europe emerged as states solicited the friendship of their neighbours' enemies. Relations between Czechoslovakia and Yugoslavia were friendly, as were those between Romania and Yugoslavia and Romania and Czechoslavakia. Traditional Hungarian dislike of Russia was strengthened by the short-lived communist regime of Kun in 1919, while the behaviour of Romanian armed forces intervening to assist its supression did nothing to conciliate Hungarian anti-Romanian sentiment. Relations with Germany were, however, good and those with Bulgaria warm. Popular sentiment in Bulgaria was as well disposed to the USSR as it had formerly been to Imperial Russia though the government energetically repressed communist organisation and looked to Germany. Polish border disputes with her powerful neighbours reinforced a public feeling traditionally anti-German and anti-Russian. Poland enjoyed good relations with Romania and Yugoslavia. All three countries had close ties with France, as had Czechoslovakia. Between

Table 1.1   Ethnic composition of eastern European countries, pre Second World War: principal groups

1. Poland – 1921 census:		
Poles	18,814,239	69.2%
Ukrainians	3,898,431	14.3%
Jews	2,110,448	7.8%
White Russians	1,060,237	3.9%
Germans	1,059,194	3.9%
Total	27,176,717	

2. Czechoslovakia – 1921 census:		
Czechoslovaks*	8,760,937	65.5%
Germans	3,123,568	23.4%
Hungarians	745,431	5.6%
Ukrainians	461,849	3.5%
Total	13,374,364	

3. Hungary – 1920 census:		
Hungarians	7,147,053	89.6%
Germans	551,211	6.9%
Slovaks	141,882	1.8%
Total	7,980,143	

4. Romania – 1930 census:		
Romanians	12,980,033	72.9%
Hungarians	1,426,178	8.0%
Jews	725,318	4.0%
Germans	740,169	4.2%
Total	17,793,252	

5. Bulgaria – 1934 census:		
Bulgarians	5,274,854	86.8%
Turks and Tatars	618,268	10.2%
Gypsies	80,532	1.3%
Total	6,077,939	

6. Yugoslavia – 1921 census:		
Serbs and Croats	8,911,509	74.3%
Slovenes	1,019,907	8.5%
All Yugoslavs	9,931,416	82.8%
Germans	505,790	3.9%
Hungarians	467,479	3.9%
Albanians	439,657	3.6%
Total	11,894,911	

*No separate figures for Czechs and Slovaks were given.
Source: G.H.N. Seton-Watson, *Eastern Europe Between the Wars, 1918–1941*, 3rd edn (Harper & Row, 1968) appendix.

1920 and 1938 tension did not lessen and relations between the eastern European states were generally as poor as those between their predecessors had been. As first Soviet and subsequently Nazi power was re-established, the tension increased.

These external complications diverted attention from pressing internal problems and the expenditure of substantial sums on armaments drained already scarce financial resources. They also enhanced the position of the armed forces in national life, weakening still further the democratic basis of the states. The entente powers had been convinced that the activities of traditional governing classes and the monopoly of power in the hands of kings and aristocracies had been instrumental in bringing war in 1914. Victory for the entente in 1918 was a victory for the democratic system, and the new states acquired the full panoply of elected Parliaments, responsible governments and ministers and official oppositions. Party politics in eastern Europe were, however, built on sectional interests and institutionalised the most disruptive and divisive factors in national life. Nationalist parties emerged. Some espoused the same political doctrine while preaching it to different groups within a single state, as in the Agrarian Party in Czechoslovakia or the separate Serbian and Croatian Agrarian parties. Others became the mouthpieces of exclusively nationalist claims, as with the Slovak People's Party or the Serbian Radical Party. The worst case was Yugoslavia, which rapidly established a system of ineffectual parliamentary government tempered by assassination, the most distinguished victims of which were the Croat leader Radic, killed in 1928, and King Alexander, shot in 1934. Where stable parliamentary government was successful it was largely the result of the rapidly established tradition that governing parties did not lose elections, especially apparent in Hungary and Romania. Czechoslovakia apart, democracy did not command respect and struck no enduring roots. The most striking illustration of this ineffectiveness was the fate of the important peasant parties, significant everywhere after 1919. Originally the vehicle of peasant radicalism demanding land reform and government responsive to peasant economic and social needs, they enshrined traditional antagonism towards the ruling landed elites. During the 1920s, however, they became steadily more conservative as peasant parties came to be dominated by land-holding rather than landless peasants. Land redistribution, however partial, gave them an interest in the *status quo*. As landholders and pious Christians they felt threatened by atheistic socialism as represented by the USSR. Parliamentary comradeship too exerted its pull on peasant party deputies usually professional and provincial in background. Alarm at the socialist challenge and the flattery of acceptance by acknowledged social superiors combined to deradicalise them. Peasant party deputies in Czechoslovakia formed the essential nucleus of successive coalition governments. It became the establishment party and provided the stability that allowed democratic government to work there. Elsewhere they were incorporated into right-wing, authoritarian governments – the fate of the Smallholders' Party in Hungary, the Agrarian Party in Yugoslavia and the National Peasant Party in Romania. Only the Bulgarian Agrarian Union persisted in its commitment to sweeping radical reform, symbolised by its membership of the Moscow-based Peasant International. Political quarrels discredited parliamentary systems which became the targets of nationalist attacks. Conservatives identified the defence of their own sectional interests with the maintenance of national ones and rallied around the armed forces. Even in Czechoslovakia Gayda, a leader of the anti-Bolshevik Czechoslovak forces in Siberia in 1919, posed a threat, successfully countered. Elsewhere the military took over. From May 1926 government in Poland was in the hands of Marshal Pilsudski and a team of military men, known collectively as the colonels. On his death in 1935 his military colleagues succeeded him. In Bulgaria a bloody military *coup* against the Agrarian Union Government of Stamboliski was successfully carried out in June 1923. Hungary had passed under the control of Admiral Horthy by April 1921. The same processes led King Alexander of Yugoslavia to declare a royalist dictatorship in January 1929, while the Romanian King Carol followed in December 1933. Thereafter only Czechoslovakia remained a democracy, given cohesion and authority first by Masaryk, President from 1919 until his death in 1937, and then by his disciple and former Foreign Minister Benes. Even Czechoslovakia, however, was not immune from the nationalist and sectional animosities. A strong sense of political realism prevented breakdown, though successive crises sapped the vitality and confidence of the government. The increasing agitation of the Sudeten Germans under Henlein posed after 1933 a serious threat of internal subversion fuelled by external encouragement, fulfilled finally in October 1938.

Most governments claimed that the USSR posed the greatest threat. Apart from Czechoslovakia, the internal economic and social structure of the region was very similar to that of tsarist Russia. Between peasants, the overwhelming majority of the population whose ambitions and poverty posed a major if latent threat, and the governing classes yawned a considerable cultural as well as economic and social gulf. Power was in the hands of a small governing elite from the landowning and established professional and commercial classes. Such industrial proletariat as existed was heavily concentrated in a few production centres and was a cause of acute concern. Socialists, though few in number, were a continual reminder of the possibility of revolution, fear of which was confirmed by the recollection of the communist Kun regime. During 1919 eastern European socialist parties had followed the example of many of their western European exemplars and had split into socialist and communist parties. The only substantial socialist party in the region in 1918 had been in Czechoslovakia, and its position was confirmed as the largest party in Parliament by the 1920 election. In the same year it too split and the larger group formed a separate communist party, the last to be set up in the area. Throughout the life of the Czechoslovak Republic the two parties played a significant part in national life, though as elsewhere their mutual antipathy precluded effective combined action. Over all, the possibilities of socialist or communist regimes coming to power were remote, but their political organisations allowed inter-war governments to stress the danger. It also served as a convenient explanation for internal unrest, given periodic substance by Moscow's rhetorical support for local communists and by the occasional striking demonstration, such as the explosion at Sofia cathedral in 1925. Governments were able to declare communist organisations illegal, infiltrate, break them up, arrest their leaders and harass their members. As authoritarian regimes came to power the process was stepped up until by the early 1930s the communist movement was on the defensive. Only in Czechoslovakia did it remain a legal and substantial force until December 1938. Leaders of other communist parties were arrested and imprisoned, or fled to the USSR where many of them disappeared in Stalin's purges.

Despite this, unrest did not end. There were more than enough social and economic problems to ensure almost continual tension. The economic and social disruption of the First World War was severe. After 1919 it took time for agricultural output to recover and actual war damage to buildings and livestock to be made good. Where there was industrial capacity, as in Czechoslovakia, western Poland, in Saxony and Upper Silesia, and around Budapest, it was often cut off from supplies of raw materials, located in foreign countries after the break-up of the former empires. Its markets too were suddenly drastically reduced and protectionist economic policies exacerbated problems. Railway and communications systems had been devised to meet the needs of defunct economic and political units and frequently after 1919 ran in the wrong directions, while in the new states crucial internal links were non-existent and had to be established. Currencies had collapsed and new ones had to be created in Germany no less than in Poland or Hungary. Inflation soared, gold and silver were hoarded and bartering was commonplace. In the immediate post-war years there were widespread strikes and violent demonstrations as people encouraged to believe that national freedom would bring a better world were disappointed. By the mid-1920s immediate practical problems had been resolved and the easing of strains and increasing agricultural yields quieted internal discontents. The process was greatly assisted by the general international economic improvement. High unemployment rates fell and industrial production slowly revived as internal markets expanded and new ones were found abroad. There was, however, little industrial development and the prosperity of the region remained precariously based, though by 1928 economic performance generally exceeded that of 1913.

After 1929 the international economic storm of the Great Depression destroyed what modest improvement had been achieved. Exporters of raw materials, mainly agricultural, were hit by the precipitous decline in value which lasted throughout the 1930s. Prussian agricultural producers were as hard hit as those in Hungary or Romania. Industrial exports from Czechoslovakia fell victim to the great extension in protective tariffs which excluded its goods from industrialised countries. The balance of payments swung adversely and the eastern European states, following classic economic theory, launched deflationary policies and took measures to stabilise currency values. Economic self-sufficiency and the retreat into protectionism produced high unemployment, lowered living standards and destroyed the limited trading relationships slowly forged during the 1920s. Labour unrest and strikes increased and rural poverty intensified. In Poland the worst labour troubles of the inter-war years occurred in 1936 and 1937, problems were endemic in Romania after 1933 and even in overwhelmingly agrarian Bulgaria there were strikes and demonstrations. In desperation Hungary, Bulgaria, Romania and to a lesser extent Yugoslavia established close economic relationships with Nazi Germany after 1936. Bilateral trading agreements gave better prices for raw material exports to the Third Reich, but as these were paid for in non-convertible marks only exchangeable for German goods the advantage was questionable. In fact Germany never made available adequate quantities of industrial products to meet the demands of its captive suppliers who built up substantial credit balances of unexpendable marks.

By 1938 the outlook was gloomy. Eastern Europe was riven with internal tensions, the democratic process was discredited and authoritarian regimes were everywhere in the ascendant except for Czechoslovakia, while omnipresent nationalist animosities poisoned the political atmosphere. Nazi propaganda and political ambition found a ready response. It was particularly depressing that Czechoslovakia should be among the first victims. Its economy was better founded and its prosperity greater than those of other states, the democratic system functioned tolerably well and it had the most advanced social system in the region. It also had the most modern and best regarded armed forces in the area. Yet in October 1938 Czechoslovakia did not fight. Nazi occupation of Austria in March 1938 had outflanked its defence-works and Czechoslovakia's allies Britain and France, anxious to appease Germany at another's expense, deserted it. Resistance was deemed useless. The German-populated districts of Bohemia were taken into the Reich and the remainder of the state divided into three autonomous units. Finally in March 1939 the remnants were divided up. Hungary took the opportunity to occupy Ruthenia while Poland took the disputed district of Teschen, leaving the Czech and Slovak lands as German protectorates. To the last, national rivalries and animosities had asserted themselves. While Hungarian claims to Czechoslovak territory confirmed commitment to Germany, Polish behaviour was striking and cautionary. At the moment when Poland was profiting from German destruction of the eastern European state system, this same country was receiving a British and French guarantee of its own territorial integrity. Once more events in eastern Europe were moving inexorably towards a war with international ramifications.

Further reading

Macartney, C.A., and Palmer, A.W., *Independent Eastern Europe* (Macmillan, 1962).

Polonsky, A., *The Little Dictators: The History of Eastern Europe Since 1918* (Routledge & Kegan Paul, 1975).

Rothschild, J., *East Central Europe Between the Two World Wars* (University of Washington Press, 1974).

Seton-Watson, G.H.N., *Eastern Europe Between the Wars, 1918–1941*, 3rd edn (Harper & Row, 1968).

Warriner, D., *Eastern Europe After Hitler*, Fabian Research Series no. 50 (1940).

2

THE ESTABLISHMENT OF
COMMUNIST POWER

The Second World War began in eastern Europe, was largely fought there, and had its most dramatic consequences there. The conflict begun in October 1938 with the Munich settlement was not concluded until February 1948, when Czechoslovakia acquired a communist regime, or even 1949 when the German Democratic Republic (the DDR) was set up. The decade began with Hitler's attempts to reshape the map of eastern Europe and found a thousand-year Reich, and ended with the victory of that communism of which he was the sworn foe.

The successive steps in the process were readily identifiable. The map changed almost overnight. The Munich settlement followed by the complete annexation and division of the rump Czechoslovak state in March 1939 led to the Ribbentrop–Molotov pact in August, which in its turn paved the way for a new partition of Poland between the USSR and Germany while the former absorbed Estonia, Latvia and Lithuania. In October 1940 German troops entered Romania and the pro-German military dictatorship of General Antonescu became an active friend. On 1 March 1941 Bulgaria too became allied to Germany. Nazi troops passed through its territory *en route* for Greece and Yugoslavia in the same way as they had passed through Hungary in April. The governments of all three grew steadily closer to Germany. Their communications systems served German military needs, their economies were enmeshed into that of Germany and when the USSR was invaded in June 1941 both Hungary and Romania provided troops. Bulgaria remained formally neutral. The USSR thus found itself allied to Czechoslovakia and Yugoslavia, on the same side as Poland which it had recently despoiled, the enemy of both Hungary and Romania, and enjoying a curious, warily neutral relationship with Bulgaria.

The war was a disaster for eastern European governments. After September 1939 Polish and Czechoslovak governments in exile were cut off from home, as was the Yugoslav government in exile after 1941.

Despite Herculean efforts and miracles of ingenuity it was inevitably difficult to maintain close contact with supporters at home. The full rigours of German repression identified and eliminated many early leaders of the underground organisations. New groups appeared, semi-independent of exiled political leaders. German occupation – and especially German racial policies – bred either hopeless resignation or fierce hatred or both. Few Czechs and even fewer Poles collaborated. However, the majority of the population had to eke out a bare survival, which demanded daily acts of implicit acceptance of occupation, the cumulative effects of which were degrading. Contact with the underground served to reassure, and helped restore self-respect to populations deliberately brutalised and debased. The position of political leaders of the old pre-war days was especially difficult. If they emigrated they lost contact with their followers and their influence declined but if they stayed their prominence ensured their arrest and imprisonment or required their collaboration. In either event their influence and authority suffered. Property became a liability. Acquiescence in German demands inevitably identified its owners with the Nazis, while refusal to co-operate led to expropriation and imprisonment. Social, economic and political obscurity was a definite advantage. The war gave enormous opportunities to new men, ambitious for power.

The political upheaval was the tip of the iceberg of the economic and social revolutions that shook Poland and Czechoslovakia to their foundations. Jews were massacred and Slavs declared *untermenschen*, sub-humans, inferior beings to be exploited and dispossessed. The educated classes were decimated by arrest and deportation for forced labour and capitalists' assets were confiscated or forced-purchased at derisory prices. Plant needed for the war effort was Germanised and unneeded industrial capacity atrophied. In Poland land was taken from its owners and designated for redistribution among German colonists. Above all, the war ushered in massive population movements. Forced labour for industry and demands for auxiliary military works and whole-sale deportation and imprisonment in concentration camps produced a social upheaval of unimaginable dimensions. This was total war, and its results were socially and economically atomising.

The position in Yugoslavia was as bad. April 1941 saw speedy collapse before the German invader and total dismemberment. Border territories were incorporated into Bulgaria, Albania and Hungary as well as Italy and the Reich, while a rump Serbia passed under German administration. The remnants were constituted into a puppet state of Croatia, only half of whose population was Croat. There followed three and a half years of nationalist passions, as the Croat government of Pavelic mobilised squads of *ustasa* whose terror attacks on Serbs provoked a response from the remnants of the Royal Yugoslav Army under Mihailovic who had gone underground and organised the *cetniks*. This vicious civil war accounted for the bulk of Yugoslav casualties and produced internal faction fighting of great ferocity. Despite their ostensibly resistance character, the *cetniks* like the *ustasa* came to have close links with the Italian occupying forces, which both regarded more favourably than they did each other. The seeds of animosity present before 1941 were encouraged by war into luxuriant growth. In contrast, the underground resistance movement led by Josip Broz, known as Tito, was non-nationalist. A revolutionary communist, Tito determined to create a social and economic revolution. Fighting the invader was an integral part of this strategy. Using its experiences of underground organisation in pre-war Yugoslavia, Tito's partisan movement fought a long, bitter war against the invaders. It was willing to court reprisals against the civil population, believing these would win popular support for its revolutionary cause by mobilising the masses. As it freed local areas from Fascist control it declared them People's Republics where revolutionising policies were applied to social and economic life. The war became a classic guerrilla war, arguably the first in the history of liberation movements. By contrast, Mihailovic, made Minister of War in the exiled Yugoslav government in 1942, and his *cetniks* seemed increasingly preoccupied with the sterile faction-fighting which had marred Yugoslavia's history and offered no programme for the future. Though Tito's forces enjoyed wildly fluctuating fortunes they made steady progress. When he finally secured allied recognition in November 1943, he and his movement were marked out as the future government of Yugoslavia.

The disruption in Germany's three allies was less thoroughgoing, but had similar far-reaching consequences. The governments of all three became satellites of Germany, with serious effects on their prestige and authority. As the demands of war tightened, German insistence became greater. General Antonescu, King Boris of Bulgaria and Admiral Horthy were seen by many as German puppets. When Horthy's government sought in October 1944 to throw over the Germans, he was arrested and deported and Germany installed the Fascist Szalasi regime. As the war went increasingly badly for Germany its three allies became restless to make peace, yet this proved elusive, for Germany's enemies demanded its unconditional surrender. Only King Michael of Romania succeeded in overthrowing the pro-German Antonescu government in August 1944 and Romanian troops switched sides and fought with the USSR against Germany, but even he was unable to secure his position in the long term.

The economies and societies of Germany's allies were subordinated to the Reich war effort. Raw materials and especially foodstuffs were purchased cheaply but the deliveries of manufactured goods promised in return did not materialise and by 1945 each had large German debts outstanding. In addition, the industrial capacities of all three countries had been extensively Germanised. German interests bought British and

French-owned assets at a fraction of their value and local German minorities often purchased sequestered Jewish property. Over all, the economies of the three were tied even more tightly to that of the Reich. Whatever way the war ended, the transition to peace and the reoganisation of national life would be neither easy nor straightforward. Above all, there was no consensus on the future shape of society, economy or government.

After the Nazi invasion, the Soviet government decided to reorganise and re-establish the communist parties of eastern Europe as war brought a fundamental reappraisal of their potential value. Stalin, hitherto the advocate of 'socialism in one country', a programme for separate Soviet development, had denounced Trotsky, the proponent of international revolution, as an enemy of the proletariat and had had him murdered by a Soviet agent in Mexico in 1940. The USSR had joined the League of Nations in 1934, since when it has been a conventional member of the international community. Though the Communist International, or Comintern, founded in 1919 as the vehicle for assisting the spread of revolution, continued to mouth the rhetoric of Marxism, the reality was very different, as many refugee foreign communists had found. Having fled persecution at home or after fighting in the Spanish Civil War, they reached the USSR expecting security, safety and recognition. Instead they had been even more violently purged during the 1930s than Soviet citizens. The Polish Communist Party had been dissolved by Comintern in 1938, while Tito was the only senior Yugoslav communist to survive. Foreign communist leaders in Moscow in 1941 had learned by experience to survive under Stalin. Like their Soviet counterparts, they were 150 percenters whose superloyalty to the Stalinist system was beyond dispute. They were, however, cut off from their homes and had little prospect of returning. Local communist parties were weak and isolated. Only in Bulgaria, Czechoslovakia and the Serbian and Montenegrin territories of Yugoslavia was there a strong popular sentiment of friendship for the USSR. In Romania, Hungary and Poland national feeling was powerfully anti-Soviet. The evolution of communism in the USSR had caused deep misgivings. Not surprisingly such feelings were common among middle-class property-owners, but they were equally deep among the peasantry. Stalin's forced collectivisation of Soviet agriculture evoked deep anxieties among peasant farmers while the militant atheism of his regime affronted religious instincts, especially among the Catholic populations of Poland, Hungary, Croatia and Slovakia.

Stalin and Stalinism had two indisputable qualities. One was determination and single-mindedness; a course of action once decided, the full resources of resolution and iron discipline were brought to bear. The second was organising skill of the highest order. Remarkable and abrupt reversals of position had become a hallmark of the Soviet system, and the war produced another. The German invasion demanded the total gearing of all Soviet resources, one of the most potentially valuable of which was communists from occupied or enemy eastern Europe. Suspicion and reserve lifted and they were mobilised. In 1941 it was unlikely that Stalin foresaw the creation of communist governments throughout the area. The views attributed to him by the Yugoslav communist Djilas, which foreshadowed the imposition of a military victor's social system on the territory under his control, dated from April 1945 when the world looked very different. In 1941 communists everywhere were activated. In western Europe after two years of resolute opposition they became overnight the most ardent advocates of all-out opposition to the Nazis and supporters of an enhanced war effort. In eastern Europe they became an auxiliary to Soviet armed forces, and foreign communists in the USSR were identified and prepared. By spring 1942 a major educational and training operation had been launched to shape the cadres of eastern European parties. The instruction, closely modelled on Leninist teachings, was extremely successful as subsequent events showed. Developments in eastern Europe after 1944 can only be fully appreciated in the light of the instruction experienced by the leaders of the future communist governments. It reflected the deeply ingrained suspicion of spontaneous and unpredictable mass action so highly characteristic of Soviet communism and which it had inherited from Lenin. The war severely tested it. While the USSR called publicly for popular resistance to the Nazis, urging sabotage, non-co-operation and partisan attack, it did not intend such activities to be carried out without organisation. The problem was to control resistance and weld it to a re-created party network. Like the London-based exiled governments, Moscow-based communists found it difficult to ensure obedience and docility from their followers at home, where underground movements threw up their own leaders – such as Gomulka in Poland, Husak in Slovakia, Kostov in Bulgaria and Tito in Yugoslavia. These had their own views on future policy. Activities in Hungary, Romania and Bulgaria were inevitably more circumscribed, but in Bulgaria a powerful partisan force fought against its own government as well as against the Germans. Although therefore by 1944 an underground movement headed by communists and linked to Moscow came into existence, two rather different tendencies had developed: a 'Muscovite' orientation among communists educated at Comintern schools and closely linked to the Soviet leadership, and a 'nationalist' tendency among those working in the underground, more parochial in outlook. By 1944 both groups were united in their determination to establish communist control in the aftermath of war, but the inherent divergencies between them surfaced after that control had been established.

Two wars were fought between 1941 and 1944, one against the Germans and their allies, the other for people's minds, to undermine the older order and win support for communism. The enemies were the old governing classes and the old political parties, regardless of their role in the war or their attitudes to Nazism. The Hungarian communist Mathias Rakosi subsequently dubbed the tactics used 'salami tactics'. The opposition was divided by winning over some key figures, branding others as collaborators – that most emotive of charges, almost impossible to disprove – and non-communist organisations were split and the pro-communist sections portrayed as the true representative of the interests involved. In the underground communists and non-communists were thrown together. If some rivalries were intensified, others lessened, as a sense of shared purpose was created with some leading non-communists diminishing their suspicions and hatreds and establishing valuable connections. Until 1943 the position of the USSR was too weak for Stalin to risk alienating his Western allies, and prudence dictated communists work with non-communists. Communists served in the exiled government of President Benes, recognised by the USSR as the legitimate government of Czechoslovakia. Relations with the Polish government-in-exile in London were never good. The problem of the eastern frontier of Poland and the Soviet occupation of September 1939 were compounded by the crisis arising from the Katyn massacre, revealed when the bodies of captured Polish officers murdered by Soviet forces in 1939 were discovered. Relations were broken off and the USSR organised its own Polish National Council in Moscow in competition with the London Poles. A number of prominent non-communists were included. As for Romania and Bulgaria, the *coup* of King Michael in the former in August 1944 led to the acceptance of his new government's help against the Germans. In Bulgaria, despite official neutrality, the USSR assisted the partisan movement by landing weapons and men. The new underground formed the broad-based Fatherland Front, comprising agrarians, social democrats and radical independents as well as communists. In September 1944 it seized power in Sofia by a *coup* when Soviet troops entered the capital.

The Fatherland Front was a good example of the Popular Fronts that resulted from communist tactics. They all included non-communists and attracted a wide circle of sympathisers. Leading positions were often held by non-communists, drawn from the opponents of the previous regimes. Such figures were fellow-travellers, sympathetic to the communists. Particular attention was given to drawing in representatives of the powerful peasant parties, examples being the Romanian Groza, the Hungarian Erdei and the Pole Witos, brother of the leader of the Polish People's Party. Socialist leaders were also sought out, such as the Czech Fierlinger, the Hungarian Szakasits and the Pole Osobka-Morawski. As organisers of the small industrial proletariats of the region socialists were significant opponents and exact competitors for the support of organised labour. War glossed over some of the bitter animosities dividing socialists from communists in the pre-war years, as for rank and file Party members common anti-German feeling and war-weariness overshadowed their mutual suspicions and reservations. Communists emphasised their commitment to economic and social improvement and stressed their separation from the USSR. It appeared that separate ways to socialism were emerging, developed in accordance with individual conditions in each country and although admitting a regard and respect for the USSR, not slavishly imitative of it. Such aspirations were to prove illusory, but at the time they seemed sincere.

The remnants of the Nazi forces surrendered in May 1945. During the following three years communists took control of eastern Europe. It was surprising that it took so long, as many impatient Party members complained at the time. The crucial period came not after the end of hostilities but before. As Soviet armies advanced and crossed the frontiers of Poland, Romania, Czechoslovakia, Hungary, Bulgaria – and, briefly, of Yugoslavia – the next phase began. It had been reached in Poland in July 1944 when Soviet troops entered territory that all concerned acknowledged as indisputably Polish. A similar position had been reached in Romania in August 1944. After an intitial incursion into Czechoslovak territory in April the Soviet liberation began in October 1944. In early September Soviet troops reached the borders of Bulgaria and the USSR declared war on 5 September. The country surrendered five and a half hours later and was peacefully occupied. In October northern Yugoslavia was entered and Tito's partisans joined hands with Soviet soldiers. The latter rapidly moved on into Austria leaving Yugoslavia without a Soviet military presence. Soviet troops entered Hungary from Romania in late September 1944, though the occupation was not finally completed until April 1945 after the longest and bloodiest Nazi resistance in eastern Europe.

Administrative systems to run the liberated areas had to be set up. Only in Romania was the existing regime able to maintain a foothold, thanks to King Michael's timely dismissal of Antonescu. Elsewhere new systems had to be created. Soviet commanders needed to secure their communications, to feed and house their men and to round up pockets of resistance. In addition, German occupation had opened a Pandora's box of vendettas and vengeance. There were scores to be settled among the liberated peoples, yet disorder could not be tolerated. All the allies were faced with the same problems, and Soviet, British and US forces solved them in the same way. They appointed local men to operate and oversee the administration of the civilian population, chose those they regarded as reliable and kept a close eye on them. In eastern Europe, however, the liberating forces did not restore former officials and members of the established governing elites, as happened in the West. Soviet aims had developed beyond the simple defensive attitudes of 1941, for with victory all eastern Europe fell into the Soviet sphere of influence. Soviet troops held the key to every aspect of national life, as events in Poland showed. On 1 August 1944 the Poles of the London-controlled National Army staged an uprising in Warsaw, the outskirts of which Soviet troops had reached. For two months they fought desperately against superior Nazi forces before surrendering on 2 October. Soviet troops remained inactive and the Soviet government refused to allow the use of Soviet airfields by British and US aircraft flying relief from Italy. The crisis in allied relations was deep and prolonged yet it made no difference to their continued collaboration. Stalin apparently drew the conclusion that his allies would protest at Soviet activities but they could not break the alliance nor exact reprisals. This impression was confirmed by Churchill's willingness to agree a division of influence in eastern Europe, hammered out at his meeting with Stalin in Moscow in October 1944. All the signs pointed in the same direction. The USSR's allies were ready to recognise reality. They could not interfere directly in eastern Europe where the presence of the Red Army ensured the domination of Soviet interests. They tried to help their local protégés by diplomatic means. Stalin met them part way. At the tripartite conference at Yalta in February 1945 the Soviet leader agreed to a package of arrangements concerning Germany and Poland that devised face-saving formulas for his Western allies. Soviet interests, however, prevailed. Much suffering would have been avoided had this basic reality been publicly acknowledged in Britain and the USA.

Much was made of the role of the Red Army in spreading communism and in the emergence of communist governments in eastern Europe. Its role, however, was often misunderstood. Soviet troops played only a small direct part. Units in Poland rounded up members of the National Army and deported them to the USSR, in Romania Soviet troops occupied the General Staff buildings and disarmed Romanian soldiers and gendarmes in Bucharest in February 1945, and on 25 February 1947 Soviet troops arrested Kovacs, the Secretary-General of the Hungarian Smallholders' Party. But such instances were rather exceptional. Soviet forces had been withdrawn from Bulgaria and Czechoslovakia before communist regimes finally assumed power, and in Yugoslavia their presence had been transient. Certainly the moral and psychological importance of the Red Army ought not to be underestimated, for it demoralised opponents and encouraged friends. Even when withdrawn, Soviet troops were all too near. However, to ascribe communist successes solely to its presence was misleading.

The emerging communist regimes had their own muscle-power. In Poland and Czechoslovakia considerable armed forces recruited and trained in the USSR joined the Red Army in liberating their homeland, much as de Gaulle's Free French forces operated with the British and US armies. The Polish forces commanded by General Rola-Zymierski numbered approximately 280,000 by early 1945. Czechoslovak forces commanded by General Svoboda formed two armies substantially larger than the Czech forces that fought with the British. They contained about 20,000 Party members organised in secret cells. In Romania the Tudor Vladimirescu division had been recruited in the USSR by Anna Pauker, while Tito's partisans formed the strongest eastern European force under communist control. In addition there were various paramilitary organisations that mushroomed during 1944 and 1945 and provided the street-fighters who intimidated non-communists. The partisan forces of the Bulgarian Fatherland Front were well established by September 1944. They numbered about 15,000, had been equipped and organised with Soviet assistance, and were particularly strong in the industrial centres. They later became the nucleus of the workers' militia. After August 1944 the Red Army in Romania aided the recruitment of the Apararea Patriotica, composed of armed workers, to defend factories against native Fascist members of the Iron Guard and remnants of the German armies. Its claimed membership of 100,000 was probably an exaggeration but it was undoubtedly large. Similar militia-style organisations recruited heavily from the small industrial proletariat and armed and assisted by Soviet forces were established elsewhere. The obvious similarities between them and the Red Guards in Russia in 1917 must have been clear to all.

More important probably were the orthodox police forces responsible to the ministries of the interior. Communists in 1944 and 1945 were not in opposition but formed the leading groups in government. Under Soviet auspices and with some judicious coercion every state was provided with a Front government, though the precise title varied. In Czechoslovakia an agreement reached with Benes in December 1943 and March 1945 led to the establishment at Kosice in Slovakia of a National Front government of six anti-Fascist parties. Negotiations for the establishment of a similar government for Poland were more protracted. After breaking with the London Polish government-in-exile the purely communist Polish National Council had been expanded to include other Poles in the USSR and had evolved into the Committee of National Liberation under the socialist Osobka-Morawski. At the end of July 1944 this formed the basis of the Lublin Committee. Only after a year of difficult negotiations was it possible to arrange the introduction of some London-based Poles and of representatives of the old Polish People's Party into the Lublin Committee, thus forming in June 1945 the government of National Unity. It was highly fragile and formed the least successful national government from the communist point of view, containing as it did avowed and irreconcilable enemies fully aware of each other's intentions. In Bulgaria, the Fatherland Front government set up in September 1944 comprised representatives of the four parties that had combined in the underground. At first the initiative in Romania remained with the Royal government, but by October 1944 a National Democratic Front had come into being and demanded an increased role.

An initial reorganisation under General Radescu was an uneasy compromise, and communist-inspired pressures and demonstrations finally succeeded in forcing it from office in March 1945, when it was replaced by an exclusively National Democratic Front government. In Hungary, partial elections held in December 1944 in liberated areas of the country led to a National Assembly at Debrecen. This elected a provisional coalition government, confirmed in November 1945 after the freest election in Hungarian history produced a communist vote of nearly 17 per cent. As for Yugoslavia, as early as 1942 an avowedly coalition organisation had been created representing non-communist and non-political groups. Known as AVNOJ, the communists occupied its leading positions and it adopted an avowedly communist programme. As a gesture, the post-war provisional government and assembly set up at the end of 1944 contained small minorities representative of the pre-war political parties and of the Royal Yugoslav government. Despite Stalin's attempts to persuade the Yugoslavs to move slowly, a formal People's Front was created in the summer of 1945 and presented a single list of candidates at the November elections. In January 1946 the new Assembly proclaimed Yugoslavia a Republic and adopted a constitution modelled on the 1936 Soviet one. Yugoslavia thus became the first People's Republic.'

The key post of Minister of the Interior was always occupied by a communist or reliable fellow-traveller such as Georgescu in Romania, Erdei in Hungary, Nosek in Czechoslovakia and Yugov in Bulgaria. In Poland, the ministry was divided, and the less important Ministry of Public Administration held by Kiernik of the People's Party while the veteran communist Radkiewicz took the Security section. The Interior Ministry controlled the police and gave opportunities for maintaining surveillance over opponents. To a greater or lesser degree police forces were purged and reliable communists or fellow-travellers appointed to key posts. As important was the secret police, reorganised and strengthened as a reliable support for communists. Many former officers were employed for professional skills were in short supply and their compromised past made them malleable. The ministries of the interior also prepared and ran elections. Both functions aroused the concern of non-communists. The crisis in February 1948 in Czechoslovakia resulted from attempts to stop communist appointments in the police, and Mikolajczyk, the leader of the Polish People's Party, gave interesting examples of the massaging of ballots. Useful too was the capacity of the ministries to organise trials of alleged collaborators or enemies of the new order. These judicial controls were used to destroy the influence and authority of non-communists, especially prominent anti-Nazis whose war record and prestige was dangerous. Plots against the state were unearthed in a blaze of publicity and show trials 'unmasked' the accused. The earliest were held in Yugoslavia. In June 1946 Mihailovic was tried, along with an assortment of political leaders including Nedic, Ljotic and the leaders of the old

Serbian parties. In the autumn it was the turn of Archbishop Stepinac. In August 1947 Petkov, leader of the Bulgarian Independent Agrarian Party, was sentenced to death. A little earlier Pastuhov, a leader of Bulgaria's independent Social Democratic Party, had been sentenced to five years' imprisonment. In a series of trials in Romania during autumn 1947 Maniu, Mihalache, Bratianu and sixteen other leaders of the National Peasant Party were tried and condemned, the first two receiving sentences of solitary confinement for life. In 1947 the leaders of the Hungarian Smallholders' Party, including the Prime Minister Nagy, were implicated in an alleged conspiracy following the arrest of the Party's Secretary-General, Kovacs. In Czechoslovakia the target was the Slovak Democratic Party. The strongest anti-communist party in the country and dominant in Slovakia, its leadership was destroyed by a combination of allegation and trials during the autumn and winter of 1947. In Poland, so long as the Ministry of Justice was held by a People's Party minister, it refused to allow similar trials.

In addition to police powers and control of the judicial process, ministries of the interior and of information controlled the Press and broadcasting. Though the precise degree varied, at the very least opponents were obstructed while the work of communists and their allies was facilitated. The allocation of newsprint, issuance of permits, speedy or tardy processing of accreditations for journalists, arrangements for travelling and a host of other matters were manipulated to supplement more direct controls. As a final check there was censorship. Broadcasting was a state service whose facilities were under the direct control of government and staff were governmental employees. Determined communist ministers disposed of a wide range of powers. In many respects it was surprising that non-communists were able to mount such strong resistance during these years.

The spread of support was not merely the product of coercion and violence, for communists benefited from their commitment to change. War had greatly radicalised public opinion throughout Europe. The horrors of total warfare brought a conviction that the social, political and economic order that had produced them was morally wrong. A better world would arise out of the ruins of the old. Private greed and individual self-interest and self-obsession would be replaced by communal action and joint endeavour to ensure that the interests of all were safeguarded. The experience of wartime co-operation seemed to show that this was no pipe-dream. By taking power into their own hands the people could shape a world in which poverty and deprivation were things of the past and war would cease to be an ever-present threat. A new moral consciousness would create different social and personal values. The ending of privilege and elite status, the democratisation of decision-making and the ending of individual selfishness and possessive greed entailed restrictions on private property ownership and the destruction of the vested interest groups that had hitherto wielded power. Idealism and ambition to create a morally better world slipped easily into hostility towards the erstwhile powerful and influential and it became difficult to disentangle idealism from envy. The mood was apparent everywhere. Elections in Britain, France and Italy produced a swing to the left. Communists served in the governments of France and Italy, where a plebiscite declared in favour of the abolition of the monarchy and the country became a Republic. In eastern Europe too this deeply felt and widespread sentiment in favour of radical change influenced communists and non-communists alike. The Front governments were able to set the pace. By the time war formally ended they were well on the way to associating themselves with popular sentiment and had identified the Communist Party with the bestowing of material advantages. Key issues affecting the great majority of the population were land reform, the redistribution of sequestered property, the provision of relief from hunger, the stabilisation of currencies and the re-establishment of industry to provide employment. Any government would have used the situation to establish the political and economic order it wanted, but communists were distinguished by their anticipation of the possibilities and single-mindedness. A major item was land reform. Eastern European communists emulated Lenin who, appreciative of the revolutionary potential of peasants, had placed great emphasis on the alliance between peasantry and proletariat and in 1917 had adopted the demand that land be redistributed. Similar factors operated in eastern Europe as had operated in Russia. Poland, Hungary, Romania and much of Prussia were dominated by large estates, and although after the 1923 land reform Bulgaria had no large landowners similar legislation in Czechoslovakia in 1919 had only gone part way to following its example. The small peasant farmer with a plot too small to support his family was economically dependent on the great estates. The relationship bred resentment and class bitterness, which produced the peasant political parties. These had at times been more revolutionary than the communists, as had the Stamboliski government in Bulgaria. Communists seized on the potential of land reform as a means of mobilising support. In Poland the reforms began in liberated areas in September 1944 and were progressively extended to newly liberated districts. In both Romania and Hungary Front governments began the process in March 1945 while in Czechoslovakia revision committees were active during the same year. The intention was to create a large number of private peasant holdings, of rather small average size. The upper limit for private holdings was about 50 hectares (120 acres), while the average amount of land redistributed generally did not exceed 5 hectares (12½ acres).

Further opportunities arose from the redistribution of property formerly owned by Germans. Not surprisingly, war and Nazi occupation brought a thirst for vengeance while the disruptive behaviour of German minorities persuaded many of the need to expel all Germans and create homogeneous national states. The government-in-exile of Benes declared that the Sudenten Germans would be expelled, and the 3,250,000 German inhabitants of pre-war Czechoslovakia had been reduced to less than a quarter of a million by mid-1945. The westward shift in Poland's frontiers to the Rivers Oder and Neisse brought the incorporation of the western provinces, long occupied by Germans, over two million of whom were expelled. The expulsion of the German minority in Hungary was decreed in December 1945, though only about half of them in fact left. The German population of Yugoslavia fled. These developments – in addition to the pressures on Germans in Romania and on Hungarians in Czechoslovakia, the flight of German civilians before the onslaught of the Red Army in the closing days of the war and the Nazi extermination of Jews – brought a major change in the population patterns of the areas (see Table 2.1). Jews and particularly Germans everywhere had occupied important economic positions, and Germans tended to be wealthier than their non-German neighbours, an imbalance accentuated by the favour shown to them by Nazi occupation forces. They left, but their property remained.

It was a rich haul, and included more than land. Four and a half million Poles had been resettled in the new western provinces by mid-1948 and the programme continued. The expulsion of Germans from Czechoslovakia freed about 2,713,500 hectares (6,700,000 acres) of farmland for redistribution and vacated jobs in industry. Houses were also available for reallocation, together with the bulk of the household goods of the departing Germans. Very many gained materially. One of the advantages of control over the Ministry of the Interior was that communists dominated the machinery for reallocation of former German property. Recipients appreciated that Party membership enhanced their prospects, while communists successfully portrayed themselves as the unique defenders of the new order. Close links developed between communists and re-settled populations.

It was generally agreed that extensive state ownership of industry would be necessary, for the confiscations and disruptions of war had left a legacy of confusion. It was impracticable to return industry to its previous owners. War had brought considerable state intervention. Conversion to peacetime conditions would be prolonged and difficult, and there was a strong argument for a substantial degree of state control, which communists were not alone in supporting. It was an agreed item in the programmes of Front governments, yet communists more or less successfully depicted themselves as the sole proponents of state control and economic planning. Simultaneously they launched a drive to dominate trade unions, also assisted by the legacy of war. Pre-war unions had been destroyed, banned outright in Bulgaria in 1934 and in

Table 2.1   Ethnic composition of eastern European countries: post Second World War (selected countries)

1. *Yugoslavia* – 1953 census:			
Serbs	7,064,000	41.7%	
Croats	3,970,000	23.5%	
Slovenes	1,492,000	8.8%	
Total Yugoslavs		14,891,000	88.0%
Hungarians	507,000	3.0%	
Albanians	752,000	4.4%	
Turks	254,000	1.5%	
Total	16,927,000		
2. *Romania* – 1956 census:			
Romanians	14,996,114	85.7%	
Hungarians	1,587,675	9.0%	
Germans	384,708	2.2%	
Jews	146,264	0.8%	
Gypsies	104,216	0.6%	
Total	17,489,450		
3. *Bulgaria* – 1956 census:			
Bulgarians	6,506,541	85.5%	
Turks	656,025	8.6%	
Gypsies	197,865	2.6%	
Macedonians	187,789	2.5%	
Total	7,613,709		
4. *Czechoslovakia* – 1970 census:			
Czechs	9,318,018	65.0%	
Slovaks	4,199,892	29.3%	
Total Czechoslovaks		13,517,910	94.2%
Hungarians	570,478	4.0%	
Germans	85,662	0.6%	
Total	14,344,986		

Romania in 1938. Elsewhere centrally organised and state-controlled bodies had been set up, such as the Labour Front in Nazi Germany or in Czechoslovakia, where the Nazis had created two unions, one for white-collar the other for blue-collar workers. After 1944 unions were revived, but under strict communist or fellow-traveller control. This was more easily achieved as Soviet occupation authorities played a leading role in the resuscitation. Unions mobilised workers for demonstrations in support of state control of industry and of planned economies, and did so under communist leaders.

Nationalisation, land reform, the redistribution of confiscated German possessions and planning promoted communist parties as vehicles of revolutionary reordering of economic and social life. Given the strong political base they had created in the final months of the war they were able persuasively to identify themselves with popular sentiment for change. Moreover, they claimed that as the political allies of the USSR they could make more favourable arrangements with Soviet occupying forces than could their political opponents. The claim was very important, for Soviet economic pressure was a fact of life. The expenses of liberation were considerable. Until satisfactory peace terms were negotiated the Red Army remained as a drain on the resources of impoverished countries. This was especially true of the former enemy states, but it was true also in Poland and Czechoslovakia. It was therefore of immediate and pressing importance to re-establish normal conditions to lift the burden of maintaining Soviet forces. Former enemy states had a further inducement, for there were reparations to be settled. Soviet claims on Romania and Hungary for damage done by their soldiers during the war were less than those made on defeated Germany, but they were considerable relative to size and general economic conditions. They were not finally regularised until after the conclusion of treaties with the USSR, in the case of Hungary in September 1947 and with Romania in June 1948. Although the reparations burdens were reduced from the sums envisaged in the armistices, when added to the expenses of maintaining Soviet occupation forces they were very considerable. In Hungary, for example, the payments made during 1947 for reparations accounted for approximately 18 per cent of its total expenditure, while Romania was estimated to have paid well over half its national income to the USSR in reparations and maintenance costs between the armistice on 12 September 1944 and 1 June 1948. The argument that communists would be able to modify Soviet demands had considerable practical force.

Another economic necessity turned to advantage was currency reform. The runaway inflation was attacked in such a way as to destroy the position of private capital. The war had spawned financial expedients. The huge inflation of paper currencies and the shortage of goods had been compounded by the simultaneous circulation of several different currencies, official and unofficial, comprising pre-war official governmental bank-notes, Nazi bank-notes, occupation paper and private tokens. There were no stable currencies in the area and reform was essential as the conservation of scarce foreign convertible currencies was crucial for the slow task of recovery. All existing currencies were frozen, bank accounts blocked, and private citizens permitted to exchange no more than a bare minimum of old currencies for new ones. In Czechoslovakia, for example, the reform of December 1945 restricted each private person to 500 crowns, about £2.10s. at then exchanges rates, and in Poland each adult over the age of 18 was permitted 500 zloties, the official exchange rate being 406 to the pound sterling. At the time the average weekly earnings in British industry amounted to £4.16s. Similar reforms were carried out in Hungary in August 1946 and Romania in August 1947.

Native capitalists were virtually eliminated. Heavy, steeply graded direct taxation, currency reform, land reform, nationalisation of industry and the heavy drain on resources for maintaining the Soviet forces and meeting reparations had destroyed the foundations of the old economic order before the establishment of communist regimes. The process was in effect supported by non-communists, who remained members of the Front governments under whom the economic foundations essential for the new communist regimes were laid.

Between 1945 and 1947 there were more or less free elections, contested however only by member parties of the Fronts. They gave some indication of the state of political opinion in eastern Europe. The results showed a significant but not overwhelming degree of support for communists. In Czechoslovakia the communists took 38 per cent of the vote and seats in Parliament. Elsewhere results were less convincing. In both Bulgaria and Romania Fronts swept to success, taking 86 per cent of the votes in the former, where the opposition abstained, and 348 seats from 414 in the latter, where communists held 73. No government in the history of independent Bulgaria or Romania had ever lost an election. In Romania there was widespread violence and intimidation, as there was in Poland where at elections in January 1947 the government bloc won 80 per cent of the vote and 392 seats out of 444. In every instance communist members formed a minority within the Front, but they were the solid core of their respective blocs.

The next stage in the political evolution of the area was the creation of single, united parties formed by amalgamating communists with socialists. The pace accelerated during 1947, almost certainly as a result of the deteriorating relations between the USSR and the USA. The continued involvement of non-communist parties in government in states firmly within the Soviet sphere of influence must have seemed potentially dangerous. Matters were brought to a head by the launching of the Marshall Aid Plan in 1947, an essential feature of which was that recipients should join the Organisation for European Economic Co-operation to administer the aid on an international basis. It was a major challenge. The USSR, its economy seriously impaired by war, was in no position to match – let alone outbid – the US offer. When the governments of Hungary, Poland and Czechoslovakia began to show interest, the Soviet reaction was immediate and decisive. Czechoslovak ministers were summoned to Moscow and there rejected the invitation, and pressure on Poland and Hungary led to the same result. The political consequences were probably inescapable. The introduction of single-party government and the ending of the Front phase of post-war history was speeded up.

Although there was no neat symmetry to the pattern of events, communist and socialist parties were amalgamated into single organisations and then declared the effective governing party. Socialist parties were first purged of those opposed to fusion and party conferences dominated by its advocates voted for union. Opponents were arrested and tried or merely quietly relegated to obscurity. More direct pressures were used such as the invasion of party offices and destruction of newspaper plant where this was necessary. Suitably named coalition parties were created that could claim to represent all workers in each state. In Romania the United Workers' Party was created in October 1947, and during 1948 the example was followed elsewhere. The process was concluded by the establishment of the Socialist Unity Party, the SED, in the Soviet zone of Germany in January 1949. Workers' Parties and United Workers' Parties symbolised the establishment of *de facto* communist states. Other parties were outlawed or left as token oppositions fully appreciative of the limits beyond which they would not be allowed to stray.

Power was given institutional shape by new constitutions. Modelled closely on the 1936 Soviet constitution, they established People's Democracies. Last to be introduced was the Polish Constitution, which did not appear until July 1952. Elsewhere the process had been achieved first in Yugoslavia in 1946, then in Bulgaria in December 1947 and in the other states by 1949. In fact these constitutions were of minimal importance, for they could be ignored at will as no organisation existed to enforce obedience of governments to them. Their role was symbolic, the formal statement of the new order, the legal enshrining of the transfer of power. Single-list elections, on the Soviet model, were held at approximately the same time though they were not crucial to the exercise of power. In Poland, for example, they were not held in until October 1952, the Sejm elected in 1947 continuing until then though purged of many opposition deputies.

The new regimes' grasp on power was still insecure. The delay in formulating the Polish constitution and holding elections there was the most striking example. But there was also indications elsewhere that many remained unconvinced. In the single-list Czechoslovak elections in May 1948 over one and a half million blank or spoilt ballots were cast, while in Hungary the government after June 1948 made little secret of its reliance on the police.

Further reading

Betts, R.R., *Central and South-East Europe, 1945–8* (Oxford University Press, 1950).
Clemens, D.S., *Yalta* (Oxford University Press, 1970).
Leonhard, W., *Child of the Revolution* (Collins, 1957).
McCauley, M. (ed.), *Communist Power in Europe 1944–9* (Macmillan, 1977).
Mikolajczyk, S., *The Pattern of Soviet Domination* (S. Low, 1948).
Polonsky, A., and Drukier, B., *The Beginnings of Communist Rule in Poland* (Routledge & Kegan Paul, 1980).
Seton-Watson, G.H.N., *The East European Revolution*, 3rd edn (Methuen, 1956).

3

THE COMMUNIST POLITICAL SYSTEM

The new communist governments may have established themselves, but
they appreciated that they were surrounded by enemies. Though they
saw themselves as representing the forces of progress and as standard-
bearers of a new world, they were under no illusions that the old,
class-based society and capitalist ways of thinking still existed, even if
communists had destroyed its organisational vitality and independence.
The Socialist Unity Party in the DDR, the Polish United Workers'
Party, the Romanian Workers' Party and the Hungarian Working
People's Party were apparently coalitions. In fact they were Leninist
parties functioning on democratic centralist lines and built on the Soviet
model. They differed in no essential characteristic from the
Czechoslovak and Yugoslav parties, which unashamedly called
themselves communist. In one important respect, however, these parties
did differ in 1948 from their Soviet exemplar. Almost in defiance of
Leninist precepts they had deliberately set out to attract substantial
mass membership. Miniscule in 1944 and 1945 they had launched
recruiting drives, without asking too many questions. If they were to take
power it could only be on the basis of an adequate membership. In some
parties, such as the Romanian, the accusation was made that former
Fascists had been recruited in substantial numbers. Elsewhere party
leaders such as Eric Honecker, the first head of the Free German Youth
organisation, made it clear that former Nazi Youth activists were
acceptable provided that they repented and disclaimed their past. In a
continent torn by war and in which active membership of right-wing
Fascist and semi-Fascist movements had formerly been essential for
promotion and social prominence, this acceptance of members with
dubious backgrounds was probably inevitable. Moreover, such
members were unlikely to be too critical of their new leaders whose
knowledge gave them valuable leverage. It contrasted strongly,
however, with the established Soviet practice of careful screening of
potential members, coupled with more or less lengthy periods of

Map 2   Eastern European frontiers.

candidate membership of the party during which the neophyte was required to study and master the basic works of Marxism–Leninism and attest familiarity by success in examination. Moreover, it cast a dubious light on the claim that party members were the best elements from among the working class. All too often they were nothing of the sort. One of the causes of the striking internal conflicts characteristic of the years between 1948 and 1954 may well have been the quality of the membership recruited in those heady first days.

Purges, show trials and the breach with Yugoslavia, 1948–54

The achievement of power did not usher in a period of united endeavour. Far from settling to a purposeful drive to build socialism there was everywhere internal discord and convulsion. Contemporaries saw in these a struggle for power, with the Soviet party and especially Stalin behind a universal drive to reduce the new governments to blind obedience. Undoubtedly personal ambition played its part as did the rupture in relations with Yugoslavia. Yet one of the striking features was the mass shake-out of ordinary party members. Once power had been achieved the mass memberships enrolled after 1944 became less necessary and the indiscriminate recruitment a positive handicap. The well-established technique of recall of party membership books and the screening of their holders to ensure adequate knowledge of and dedication to the ideals of Marxism–Leninism thinned out at least some of the time-servers. The other established technique of self-criticism and admission of failings before audiences of party members helped discipline individual members. It was an elaborate and time-consuming process. In the German case some 6,000 examining commissions were set up yet the SED was one of the smaller parties in the area. There emerged more homogeneous and reliable, if smaller, parties. In Czechoslovakia a party of about two and a half million members was reduced by about 900,000 between 1948 and 1951 while membership of the Hungarian party fell from about 1,400,000 in 1949 to approximately 830,000 in 1950. A similar purge halved the Romanian party, while the SED membership was reduced by about 360,000. Over all, it has been calculated that one in four members were purged.

Contemporaneous with this there was a major upheaval among the leadership of the various parties. Unlike the mass membership the stakes were higher, for in many cases the deposed leaders were disgraced and executed. There seems little doubt that the impetus did come from the evolving Cold War between the USSR and the Western powers and from the unexpected clash between the Yugoslav and Soviet parties. Despite the deluge of rhetoric to explain the breach, there were no obvious differences on policy questions between the two parties prior to 1948. If anything, the Yugoslav was the most hard-line and emulative of the new regimes. Even after 1948 it followed the orthodox Leninist–Stalinist pattern set in the USSR, and it was not until 1949 that the Yugoslav party's chief theoretician Mosa Pijade began the often painful re-examination that led to the elaboration of a specifically Yugoslav road to socialism. The immediate cause of the breach between Moscow and Belgrade almost certainly stemmed from the caution that typified Stalinist policy. In contradistinction, the new Yugoslav regime seemed almost recklessly adventurist. A long-running dispute with Italy over the frontier of the two states in the vicinity of Trieste led to steadily worsening relations. Yugoslavia displayed a willingness to challenge the

USA and shot down two US planes in 1946. Yugoslav support for the communist guerrillas in Greece also threatened relations between the communist and Western blocs, while plans announced in 1947 for an economic union between Yugoslavia and Bulgaria produced heavy Soviet pressure that led the Bulgarians to withdraw hastily. While the USSR was willing to challenge the Western powers it was clear that it had to be on the grounds of Soviet choosing, as with the Berlin blockade. It was also clear that the military capacity of the Western powers that still enjoyed a monopoly of the atomic bomb could not be challenged recklessly. Interests of state and power politics alike required that Soviet leadership of the new communist bloc's overall foreign policy be not disputed, and that was exactly what the Tito government was doing. Whatever the later evolutions of Yugoslav internal and external policy and the compromises and co-operation with the capitalist West that Yugoslavia accepted, in 1947 it was Tito and his followers who were the radicals of the communist world. This pattern of an active foreign policy in which Yugoslavia played a role far exceeding its intrinsic weight and world influence was closely associated with Tito personally and remained a feature of his government until his death in 1980. He had then become the apostle of unaligned countries and a leading exponent of Third World politics, but he started as the supporter of active international communism and the apostle of the spread of Marxism. The Soviet denunciation in 1948 of Tito as a Trotskyite had a basis in logic. Trotsky too had been a supporter of world revolution and of the spread of Marxism beyond the frontiers of the USSR. Stalin had fought him on the basis of the policy of building socialism in one country first. It was perfectly reasonable that he should oppose Tito in the name of building socialism in eastern Europe before challenging the power and military strength of the capitalist world.

The aftermath of the Tito crisis was a thoroughgoing purge of potential Titoists in other eastern European parties. There were striking similarities with the USSR during the 1930s. Extravagant charges of treachery, espionage and sabotage were made and admitted in the established traditions of public self-criticism elaborated in the USSR since the 1920s. Dramatic show trials were held and lurid accounts of the crimes of the accused and of the proceedings were published. It was quite clear that many of the distinguished Party leaders dismissed after 1948 were as guiltless of the charges made against them as those condemned during the 1930s had been. The general atmosphere of suspicion and barely suppressed fear was not unique to the communist world, as the activities of US Senator McCarthy showed. However, they provided an ideal cover for the settling of personal scores and for the imposition of the same disciplined and unthinking obedience to orders that had been imposed on the Soviet party by Stalin. It is a moot point whether the Soviet leader personally directed the campaign. The dictates of

democratic centralism, Stalinist style, may well have required that the
international movement be constructed on the same pyramid structure
as the Soviet party and that it required a single directing centre. The
party Stalin forged in the USSR may have been unconsciously accepted
as a model by communists who lived in the USSR during the 1930s and
returned after the war. Once in power they proceeded to act as Stalin had
and sought to construct in their own countries the same party system
Stalin had created in the USSR. Emulation of the USSR's achievements
was, after all, the principal guide for their political activities. In either
case, whether Soviet-inspired or the outcome of unqualified acceptance
of Soviet practice, throughout eastern Europe there took place power
struggles within the leadership of the local parties. In each case
accusations of Titoism played a major part and Jews were a particular
target. Stripped of its emotional implications, the nub of the charge
related to a suspicion that the offender would not subscribe to the
conception of a party whose blueprint for action was derived wholly from
Soviet experience and whose evolutions were guided by advice from
Moscow. In some cases the offence was overt and, by communist
standards, flagrant. Gomulka, for example, the First Secretary of the
Polish United Workers' Party, was identified with the programme of a
specifically Polish road to socialism and was unenthusiastic about the
programme of the Communist Information Bureau, set up in 1947.
This and his distinctly stated opposition to the forced collectivisation of
agriculture marked him out as a candidate for purging. Demoted
during summer 1948, he was expelled from the Party late in 1949 and
secretly arrested in 1951. Unlike many of his contemporaries elsewhere
he was not executed or subjected to public trial, and re-emerged to lead
the Polish Party in October 1956. Elsewhere, among others, the
Bulgarian Kostov, Slansky and Clementis in Czechoslovakia, the
Hungarian Rajk and the Romanian Patrascanu were executed after
trials at which they were accused of Titoism and of contacts with
Western intelligence services. The removal of Patrascanu in 1954
marked the end of the process. It left bitterness and suspicion and tainted
some communist leaders with a legacy of duplicitous behaviour. Janos
Kadar's part in securing the confession of his friend Rajk to charges
subsequently the basis for the death penalty was never forgotten.

After 1954 the system lost much of this ferocity and surrealistic
accusation of ill-defined crimes. With the passage of time the various
ruling parties strengthened their monopoly of power which was thereafter challenged only intermittently. The regimes in Bulgaria, Romania
and Yugoslavia never suffered from serious outbreaks of popular
discontent. There was no serious trouble in the DDR after 1953, nor in
Hungary after 1956. The crisis of 1968 shook the Czechoslovak regime to
its foundations but under Gustav Husak a combination of purges,
substantial increases in the supply of consumer goods, presence of Soviet

and other Warsaw Pact troops and massive application of censorship enabled the communist system to re-establish itself. Only in Poland was there a more or less continuous series of crises that suggested that there the system had not succeeded in securing a degree of popular acceptance – let alone positive approval. Indeed outbreaks of violence by industrial workers in 1956, 1970, 1976 and most recently in 1980 showed it to be the most volatile and least well-founded communist state in eastern Europe. As it was also the largest in area and population and occupied a key strategic position astride the communications lines between the DDR and the USSR, its persistent internal troubles remained a cause of continuing concern to both, and its example was watched with alarm elsewhere in the bloc.

Party membership and organisation after 1954

Times of crisis apart, after 1954 membership of the Communist Party did not involve a high risk. While admission was restricted and the procedures prolonged, from the early 1950s the parties sought out suitable potential members and encouraged them to join. They once more became parties with substantial mass memberships. They recruited relatively more heavily among white-collar than among blue-collar workers, and least of all from the peasantry. There were proportionately few women in eastern European parties and only a small number of these rose to senior positions. With the spread of educational opportunities, the overall educational standards of Party members improved after the late 1960s. Increasingly the effect was to create parties composed of officials and administrators and its penetration of industrial workers somewhat diminished. This was enhanced by steady erosion as members drawn from the latter moved out of industrial work as they acquired Party seniority. The outcome was a pronounced tendency for the Party to be proportionately overrepresented in the ranks of management and administration and underrepresented on the factory floor, where skilled rather than unskilled workers formed the backbone of the membership. Communist parties become organisations of the educated and socially upwardly mobile and vehicles for advancement. By 1980 they were no longer composed of the under-privileged. They had become parties of governors and office-holders.

This development of the mature eastern European political system was a mark of its success. In the early years east European parties were concerned to secure the occupation of positions of power and influence by those whom they could trust. Hasty programmes were launched to provide crash training courses for new judges, teachers, police, army officers and administrators of all types. Party members were sought from ideologically acceptable social backgrounds, especially from poor peasant families, from the landless or those with miniscule holdings, as well as from workers or those from proletarian families. The resulting upheaval as these groups replaced the former ruling- and middle-class professional office-holders amounted to a social and political revolution of profound importance. It was this that created the new political map of the region. The process was probably most thoroughly carried through in the Soviet zone of Germany where under the aegis of the Soviet occupation forces it was possible systematically to provide a network of night schools and crash training courses for the new elites. Elsewhere it was a more haphazard process. Yet its dimensions were enormous. In Hungary, for example, approximately 100,000 such newcomers were trained and placed in office between 1949 and 1951. In the DDR a key role was played by the Free German Youth organisation from whose ranks many of the leaders of the new state came. Throughout the region a stratum of office-holders was installed in power. These office-holders were the products of the Party, owed their positions to it and also controlled it and the machinery of promotion. Not surprisingly they became a major conservative force. Frequently of limited educational background, they sometimes displayed an inadequate grasp of the demands of their posts and reacted with ill-concealed animosity to intellectuals who disputed their judgements. The Czechoslovak and Romanian parties had particularly bad records in this respect. With the passage of time and the emergence of new generations of communist-educated specialists during the 1960s the challenge to the position of the founding generation was to become more acute. Many of the latter had achieved their positions at a young age and were unready for retirement. After a long period spent in the service of the regime they possessed considerable skill as operators of the Party and state bureaucracy and had built up impressive networks of political allegiances and patronage contacts. They also possessed great power systematised in the machinery and operational procedures of the Communist Party itself. The mechanism for recruiting, screening, regulating, monitoring, placing and overseeing the activities of members and its regular promotional structure had given the Party many of the characteristic features of a governmental bureaucracy. As with all formal structured organisations those who operated it were in positions of quite exceptional power which they were able to wield largely unseen and unsubjected to the scrutiny of a critical public. Such organisations acquire an identity and interests of their own, and the communist parties of eastern Europe were no exception.

By the late 1960s the problem of reconciling the pressures of the newly skilled and technologically trained generations that had grown up under the communist system with the power monopoly of the older Party managers reached a climax. In Czechoslovakia and Poland the transition was only achieved with great difficulty as the reformist groups in the former and the technocrats in the latter sought to replace the dominant Party groupings associated with respectively President

Novotny, ousted in 1968, and First Secretary Gomulka, persuaded into retirement in 1970. Things were better managed in the DDR. In 1971 the long-serving Ulbricht who preferred the politically sound to the technically skilled was replaced in a smooth transition by Honecker, his recognised deputy.

Membership of the Party was attractive for the concrete privileges it offered. In the early post-war years of austerity and shortage the special rations, housing rights, access to special stores and availability of such scarce commodities as travel and superior clothing to Party members aroused much resentment and ill-will among the population at large. These were progressively de-emphasised in Yugoslavia in a process that began in autumn 1950. Elsewhere too as material conditions for the populace at large improved the material privileges of Party members, though still significant, declined in relative attraction. The appeal of power and authority however remained. The elaboration of a full-fledged totalitarian system, with power firmly in the hands of the Party, ensured that the ambitious and able came to accept membership as the essential prerequisite for career advancement in all walks of life. This remained true even in Yugoslavia where the role of the Party was most de-emphasised. In return the Party demanded that its members accept considerable obligations. Not only were they available for nomination and appointment to posts allocated to them, they had also to steep themselves in Marxist–Leninist thought and to become thoroughly imbued with the Party's interpretation of history, economics, culture, philosophy and society. Members of the Party were committed to a lifetime's educational programme, requiring active and wholehearted participation in Party-run courses held during the evenings, at weekends and in annual holidays.

The importance attached by the Party to this intensive educational process to equip its members with appropriate ideological orientations can be seen from the speed with which the new regimes began to elaborate the mechanisms after 1945. From 1946 onwards, Party schools were being held in the Soviet zone of Germany and by the early 1950s the fully elaborated system of Party educational institutions was created. In Romania the first courses, lasting eight weeks, were provided in 1945. By the 1950s communists everywhere were required to participate in the annual programme of study prescribed by the Party. Part-time classes concentrated on a theme of especial topicality and relevance, under guidance provided by specially trained Party propagandists. At the end of the course there was an examination. At each level of Party activity an appropriate Party institution offered short, intensive courses to selected Party members. Participation was a considerable privilege and selection marked out members for future advancement. At the top of this hierarchy of Party Schools stood the national Party Colleges, or Higher Political Schools, offering full-time courses in subjects considered appropriate for those destined for the higher reaches of the Party apparatus. Outstanding candidates for the topmost posts were frequently sent to the Soviet Higher Party School in Moscow which brought together future top office-holders from the entire eastern bloc, with the exception of Yugoslavia and, since the 1960s, of Romania. This intensive and continuous training programme lay at the basis of the capacity of eastern European parties to guide and control public opinion. Party members were equipped to provide appropriate explanations and advance arguments in favour of governmental policy. The extent to which individual parties succeeded in providing convincing and sophisticated analyses of contemporary problems for their members, and through them for the population at large, always varied. By the later 1970s it seems to have been most successful in the DDR, Bulgaria and perhaps Romania, and manifestly least successful in Poland. The crises in Hungary in 1956 and Czechoslovakia in 1968 revealed the lack of success of the Party's educational processes. In both, majŏr overhaul of the Party structure was followed by redoubled efforts in the field of cadre education.

At the basis of the organisational structure of the east European parties was a network of Party units. These primary organisations could be established in production units, such as collective farms, enterprises, schools, university faculties, or on a territorial basis, or on a mixture of both. Despite Soviet preferences manifested since 1962 for an organisation based on production units, the most common form of basic Party unit was the territorial one, which predominated in the DDR and Hungary. Only in Czechoslovakia was the production-based unit, or cell, the more common. Throughout the region in fact the mixed principle applied. The total number of units varied. In the early 1970s there were about 54,000 in the DDR, a number that increased to some 70,000 by 1981. Elsewhere there were some 24,000 units in Hungary in the mid-1970s, and about 70,000 in Romania at the end of the decade. These basic units had from as few as three to a maximum of about twenty members. Each had a voluntary secretary directly subordinate to the secretary of the next tier in the Party at county or district level. Secretaries of these bodies were full-time, paid officials appointed to their posts by the national Party organisation. They serviced committees composed of delegates elected by the basic cells. In their turn these county delegates chose their own representatives to the Party Congresses held every four or five years. Between meetings of Congresses a Central Committee acted as caretaker and overseer of the Party's well-being. Meeting for short periods four times a year the Central Committee monitored the implementation of Congress resolutions and received reports from the key committees which, in permanent session, were the real wielders of power. The most important of these bodies was the Political Bureau, composed of between ten and fifteen members. This body was the effective head of the Party. Even when formally abolished, as in Romania in 1974, it always re-emerged with a different name but fulfilling the same functions. It usually included the First Secretary of the Party, the Prime Minister, the Head of State, the First Secretary of the Youth League, the leader of the trade union movement and the top figure in the National Front. It thus brought together the leaders of Party and government, and also of the mass organisations to which virtually every citizen belonged. On the nomination of the Political Bureau the Central Committee elected the various members of other key party committees and appointed the full-time paid officials who manned the Party's own organisational structure – the secretaries and heads of the departments into which the Party secretariat was divided. Membership of these various bodies could be and frequently was combined with membership of other bodies, especially in the trade unions, governmental system and Front organisation. In both Czechoslovakia and Yugoslavia there was a federal Party structure. National susceptibilities required a specifically Slovak as well as a Czechoslovak Communist Party, while in Yugoslavia the realities of national antipathies led to the reorganisation of the Party in 1952 into the League of Communists, with six separate organisations each based on one of the six republics into which the country was divided. At the top a co-ordinating structure was created, membership of which was proportionate to the size of the component republics.

The *nomenklatura* system

Crucial to the cohesion and discipline imposed by the Party was the professional Party apparatus. Members of this may have been termed *apparatchiks*, a term of semi-contempt, but they were powerful and feared figures who rarely came before the public eye. They maintained the Party records and identified and monitored the performance of members. Given the emphasis on obedience and discipline inherent in Party membership, selection and appointment to posts in Party, government and society at large were based on nomination by the Party organisation. The system whereby all influential and significant posts were reserved for Party members and appointment to them was on the nomination of Party officials was known as the *nomenklatura* system. At every level certain key positions were filled on the nomination of the appropriate Party organisation. Details were rarely forthcoming. However, at the Fourteenth Congress of the Czechoslovak Communist Party, held in 1968, information was given of nearly 9,000 such posts overseen by the Central Committee and its Political Bureau and secretarial heads. It was subsequently estimated that after the re-imposition of close Party control under Husak, approximately 100,000 posts at all levels in Czechoslovakia were controlled by the system. No aspect of national life was immune: journalists and editors, economists, administrators of enterprises, scientists, artists, professors, trade union leaders, as well as Party officials, policemen and officers in the armed forces came under it. It was at the heart of the controlling mechanism that oversaw national life. The objective was to ensure that key posts were in the hands of loyal Party members who could also be depended upon to support those currently in control of the Party. It was also the mechanism whereby the ambitious constructed for themselves a web of supporters and clients within the system. The creation of such personal empires, and the infiltration, disruption and finally demolition of the personal empires of rivals was crucial to personal advancement and took the place of the public political manoeuvring more familiar in the West. Political power in eastern Europe was closely geared to the size and ubiquity of aspirants' entourages and led to wholesale personnel changes whenever a new leader emerged. This policy of saturation ensured that the more power and influence an office possessed, the greater the likelihood that its holder would be a Party member in good standing with the leadership. Communists enjoyed a monopoly of the posts that really mattered. The principle was explained clearly by Rankovic at the sixth Congress of the Yugoslav Party in 1952 when he emphasised that the significant element in Party control was not the number of members but their influence over the public through their activity and continual involvement in Party work ensuring the maximum penetration of the Party through society at large.

Political crises within parties

This cadre structure placed enormous power in the hands of the Party leaders who were able to mobilise and direct it, and it was tempting to assume that united, monolithic parties buttressed politically sophisticated leaders well versed in Marxism–Leninism. Parties liked to depict the system marching confidently onward to the goal of the creation of a socialist society whose principles were clearly perceived. The realities, however, were different. The unity and overall efficiency of the parties in the region could be overestimated. There was a constant debate within the leadership over policy matters and objectives and goals were not as clearly perceived as was claimed. Within the closed ranks of communist parties such contentions were rarely publicised and surfaced only in times of extreme tension. It was long a matter of controversy whether or not the totalitarian system established in eastern Europe and its progenitor in the USSR required a single leader to control it. Certainly the Party that Lenin built after 1902 was designed to reflect his own political perceptions and was structured to respond to his leadership. Yet even during his lifetime there were outstanding examples of controversy among the Bolshevik leadership and occasions when Lenin's colleagues publicly disowned him. After his death internal struggle and manoeuvring preceded Stalin's emergence as undisputed Party leader, but it was not until the 1930s that he stamped his ruthless elimination of opponents and all-pervasive terrorism on the system. After his death neither Khrushchev or Brezhnev was an undisputed leader in the Stalinist sense. Khrushchev indeed was removed from power in 1964 as the result of a Party rebellion against him, while under Brezhnev there was a collective leadership with many examples of disagreements over policy within its ranks. The relative positions of Party leaders and the overt trappings of political power understandably attracted onlookers. It was easy to interpret eastern European politics as the personal political manoeuvrings of ambitious men seeking absolute power. It was almost certainly wrong to do so. At the root of political struggles in eastern Europe as elsewhere there were major policy issues. Leaders may have been ambitious but they were also men, though rarely women, with clear ideas. Personality clashes melded with profound disagreements over policy matters. True in the Bolshevik Party under Lenin, it was equally true between 1924 and 1929. The Stalinist system emerged from the decision to impose radical economic and social change on the USSR, which could only be achieved by a politically totalitarian system. After the death of Stalin Khrushchev encountered considerable opposition to his adventuristic economic policies, which eventually led to his downfall. Political struggles in eastern Europe were caused by similar policy disagreements. So long as one viewpoint prevailed and commanded a majority, internal divisions remained a matter for debate within the small closed circle of Party leaders and their entourages. Democratic centralism, by which a policy once determined was supported by all members of the Party, ensured that the debate was not revealed to a wider public. Censorship of Press and broadcasting supported this. When the protagonists were equally balanced and there was a stalemate within the Party leadership its control was weakened and it became impossible for a 'correct Party line' to be laid down. Propagandists and censors lacked instructions and guidance and the resulting paralysis of purpose removed the firm leadership that the system required in order to function properly. Groups formed seeking to establish their own predominance over the Party machine and there ensued a more or less prolonged political crisis that was not resolved until one group or other was able to secure its control of the Party and then use its position to regularise matters.

Public debate and media discussion of policy matters as opposed to the explanation of broad policy objectives and purposes was therefore an indication of internal Party division. It almost invariably had wider repercussions that could not be localised and which passed beyond the limits that the Party set and that it found tolerable. Managed public debate in a political system unaccustomed to controversy passed quickly beyond Party control, and throughout eastern Europe the reconciliation of it with public criticism and debate proved highly elusive. It came closest in Yugoslavia: but even there in 1971 and 1972 Tito decided that such discussion had developed beyond the limits of the tolerable and intervened. An uneasy *modus vivendi* emerged after 1972. Uncertainty and dispute within the Party and public debate led easily to criticism of Party members, as in the *Two Thousand Words* statement in Czechoslovakia in June 1968. Accusations of graft, corruption, nepotism and the misuse of position sapped the prestige of the Party and the morale of its members and functionaries. It was easy to construe such criticisms into attacks on the Party and its monopoly of power and to see in them manifestations of 'counter-revolution'. When coupled with an emerging debate over choice in elections, the merits of some real alternative Party that might contest the communist monopoly of power or even the relaxation of the controls on public criticism, the unease turned to outright hostility and the other bloc parties evinced alarm.

Crises: DDR in 1953, Hungary in 1956, Czechoslovakia in 1968

The first example of this occurred in the DDR. Internal Party debate over economic policy and the relaxation of the rigidity of Party control over national life began in June 1953. Absorbed in this the attention of the leadership was distracted from growing unrest among the labour force in Berlin which had been adversely affected by increased workloads. Strikes and demonstrations evoked no response from the SED leadership and escalated into major rioting. Confronted with a breakdown in control the Soviet military commander declared martial law and Soviet troops put down the demonstrations. Short though the interlude was, it demonstrated the potential dangers arising should internal dissension paralyse the ruling party. A much more serious example occurred in Hungary.

The policy debate over the pace and nature of economic policy and an end to repressive internal measures begun in 1954 turned into a struggle between the Secretary of the Hungarian Working People's Party, Rakosi, and reformist groups that coalesced around Nagy. The replacement of Rakosi by Gero in 1956 was a change of personality not of policy and the pressures continued. The ensuing public debate and the paralysis within the leading ranks of the Party led to a progressive breakdown in internal authority and to the panic acceptance of Nagy by a reluctant Party. By then, however, the process of disintegration had progressed too far for him to control and the Party's monopoly of power and Hungarian membership of the Warsaw Pact were alike denounced. Both led to Soviet military intervention in November 1956. A similar process of internal policy disagreement occurred in Czechoslovakia, where stalemate within the Party spread first to Party members and subsequently to the public at large. Here too there resulted a widening of the debate beyond the original economic issues. Internal Party disagreements over correct economic policy and the problems of rejuvenating a decaying industrial capacity acquired a political dimension. By 1967 the

Party leadership was locked into a fierce struggle at the centre of which was the figure of Novotny, Party Secretary since 1953. The internal battle was not resolved until January 1968. By then the debate could no longer be contained and it became public. As the gravity of the country's economic crisis was explained, notably by the new Minister for Economics, Professor Sik, in a series of television addresses during June and July, criticism of the system and demands for change grew. In particular, long-standing Slovak grievances against what were seen as governmental preferences for the Czech regions of the country led to renewed demands for a federal structure with extensive powers for the Slovak component. This acquired added force since Novotny's successor, Dubcek, was a Slovak. Like Nagy before and like the Pole Kania who was to succeed Gierek in 1980, Dubcek was a loyal communist dedicated to the system. He found himself being pushed farther and farther, as Nagy had been and as Kania was to be. Adverse criticism of the communist power monopoly coupled with the novel spectacle of a ruling party accepting the need to justify itself to the public merged with an increasing call for a more pluralistic form of government and for a real choice between candidates at elections. This challenge to the ruling party's monopoly of power and the triumph of what were subsequently branded 'anti-Party elements' aroused the fears of Czechoslovakia's neighbours, and led to the Warsaw Pact invasion in August 1968 and the installation in April 1969 of Husak as First Secretary of the Czechoslovak Communist Party. As with Hungary's Kadar, Husak was to re-establish the Party's authority and restore unity and cohesion to its ranks.

The Polish problem
Poland had the least effective eastern European party. The remarkable failure of the Polish United Workers' Party to secure a respectable level of popular support led to a defensive and beleaguered attitude. It had a bad history of internal division and faction fighting in a tradition that dated back to the end of the First World War. The uniquely Polish blend of nationalism, as anti-Russian as it was anti-German, Roman Catholicism, central to a sense of national identity, and a well-entrenched peasantry prepared to fight for its land as it showed after 1945 combined to make the task of impregnating the country with communist values particularly difficult. The Party was unable to present itself as the sole repository of political, social and economic verities. Its relations with the Soviet party were coloured by memories of executions of Polish communist *émigrés* in the USSR during the 1930s and of the forced disbanding of the Polish party on Stalin's orders. Successive leaders since 1945 were unable to achieve the same personal authority within Poland as others achieved elsewhere in the region. Gomulka came closer than others to securing a degree of popular support. This was due in no small measure to his role in 1956 when he was seen by Poles as

defying the USSR and as the champion of a flexible, overtly Polish brand of socialism. Personal asceticism and genuine distaste for the privileges of Party members reinforced his popularity. This was, however, progressively reduced by continuing economic troubles and an increasingly unimaginative authoritarianism during the 1960s. Repressiveness coupled with anti-semitism in the aftermath of the crisis of 1968 culminated in the brutal suppression of demonstrations by shipyard workers in 1970 and completed the alienation of the public from Gomulka. His replacement in 1970 by Gierek produced a temporary improvement in the Party's standing but continuing economic troubles vitiated by heavy borrowings in the West demanded the regularisation of the economic structure, a key element in which was the reform of the price system and especially of the price of foodstuffs. As in 1970, increases in prices led to riots in 1976 and 1980.

As in Hungary and Czechoslovakia, economic problems and the inability of the Party to formulate and stick to an agreed policy led to vacillation and to increasing public debate and argument. Groups emerged that acquired an increasingly political dimension. These included KOR (Workers' Defence Committee), originally created to provide legal advice to those arrested after the 1976 riots and assistance to the families of those imprisoned. Another development was the demand for the establishment of independent trade unions to defend the interests of workers against both managements and state authorities. In Poland as elsewhere in eastern Europe authorised unions had their leaders appointed through the *nomenklatura* system and their activities were carefully monitored. The demand for independent unions was quite incompatible with the communist political monopoly and, as the events of 1980 and 1981 showed, if conceded would remove an important element in the Party's control mechanism. Such demands influenced the country's neighbours. Even before the creation of Solidarity, rumblings of support for independent unions were heard in Romania, and after it there was evidence of sympathy in both the DDR and Czechoslovakia, while the official Hungarian unions offered discussions with Solidarity. The crisis of irresolution in Poland was deeper and longer lasting than in Hungary prior to 1956. It was similar in intensity to that in Czechoslovakia where internal debate began in earnest in 1961 and did not reach its climax until 1968. In the Polish case it was accompanied by a major Party crisis. The Hungarian party collapsed in 1956 and was replaced by the Hungarian Socialist Workers' Party. In Czechoslovakia the party was reconstructed after 1969. In Poland the chronic weakness characteristic of the Party showed little sign of coming to an end.

After periods of prolonged and damaging internal dissension within eastern European parties new controlling groups appeared. These proceeded to ensure the dominance of their political line by the removal of those of contrary persuasion from positions of influence and power. The most eye-catching examples of purges in such circumstances followed the troubles in Hungary in 1956 and Czechoslovakia in 1968. After the former, from a membership of about 850,000 in January 1956 it sank to about 37,000 at the end of the year when the Party was reconstructed. In Czechoslovakia about 600,000 members were purged from a total membership of 1,600,000, and over half of all army officers under the age of 30, about one-half of all school supervisors and 40 per cent of journalists were removed. Purges followed changes of regimes elsewhere. After Gomulka's return to power in Poland a determined drive during 1957 and 1958 removed about 15 per cent of Party members on charges of dogmatism and revisionism. An even more extensive purge followed General Jaruzelski's advent in 1981. Purging was fairly frequent in Bulgaria, where there was an especially significant one in 1965 after an internal crisis apparently arising from discontent in the army. Similar purges were also reported in Romania, where an especially notable one accompanied President Ceausescu's tightening of the reins in winter 1972 and a further full-scale one was launched in spring 1982 when serious economic problems required a political escape valve. Similar developments also occurred in Yugoslavia in 1971 and 1973. Purges marked the end of a period of faction-fighting and the emergence of a new consensus within the Party.

The testing, guiding and controlling of public opinion

By itself an effective and cohesive Party system was insufficient to ensure regular control over the entire population. There was a continuing process of persuasion and education to persuade the public that the policies pursued by the Party were historically correct and well conceived in the interests of the individual state. This educational process was intended to extirpate dissenting views, disparaged as the last remnants of 'bourgeois thinking'. The sustained programme of exhortation and moral argument created an atmosphere of earnest intensity reflected in the quasi-military terminology mingled with metaphor of war in which eastern European leaders addressed their public. Having assumed total responsibility for everything in society, it was not enough to issue orders and compel obedience. The Party sought to govern by securing the wholehearted consent of the public and by the example of Party members' behaviour. A range of mechanisms for sampling public opinion and involving individual non-Party citizens in the day-to-day life of society was elaborated, albeit at a technical level rather than at the level of policy-making. Force may have been the instrument of last resort, but consent and popular participation channelled by the Party into constructive activities were by far the norm. It was a process that gathered momentum after about 1960.

A good example of the attempts made to guide public attitudes was the care governments took to promote the USSR. Far more than political and diplomatic matters were involved. With the overall objective of fostering 'positive' attitudes towards the USSR and combating traditional reserve towards it, communist governments engaged in an unremitting campaign that extended to every aspect of national life. A corner-stone was the incessant repetition of the argument that the USSR was the guardian of peace. Soviet forces were everywhere described as the liberators of eastern Europe from Fascist tyranny and defenders against its renewal. Soviet war memorials and cemeteries were the object of official solicitude. Annual demonstrations of remembrance of Soviet war dead, laudatory passages in official speeches and publications on every suitable occasion, the organised visits of schoolchildren and youth organisations to memorials were a conspicuous feature of national life. Anniversaries of the outbreak of war and the making of peace were kept with a solemnity and given a degree of publicity now virtually unknown in western Europe. Visits by Soviet dignatories were prominently reported, and invariably depicted as leading to the deepening and strengthening of mutual friendship and assistance. Close links existed between eastern European organisations and their Soviet counterparts and featured fraternal exchanges, visits of delegations, frequent messages of mutual regard and the exchange of news and information. Such contacts were subsumed under the overall description of peaceful comradely emulation and penetrated every aspect of national life, from places of education and work to trade unions, from youth organisations to sporting associations and from music and theatrical companies to recreational bodies of all types. Eastern European governments were careful to make available in large quantities the products of Russian as well as Soviet culture. The classics of Russian literature were translated and published in large editions, and the music of Russian and Soviet composers provided a large component in the standard repertory. Formal ties were the province of cultural organisations which linked each state with the USSR through bilateral bodies. They were responsible for arranging exchanges of artists, tours by orchestras, visits by amateur ensembles to festivals, the import and screening of films and lectures and demonstrations, all of which were designed to heighten awareness) of the USSR and its people and cultivate a taste for Soviet culture. Russian became a compulsory subject in all schools, except in Yugoslavia and, after the mid-1960s, Romania. It was an impressive example of the determination of eastern European states to guide their public into attitudes deemed satisfactory. That it was necessary suggested consumer resistance.

Fundamental to any effective governmental action was the need to be acquainted with popular feeling on issues of the moment. Eastern European governments, to varying degrees, instituted mass sampling techniques to gauge this. Examples have been published of public opinion poll results in Czechoslovakia dating from the years 1967–9, while by the 1960s Poland had a well-established reputation for sophisticated sociological surveying techniques. By the early 1970s Romania too was making extensive use of polls and surveys to establish popular feeling. Probably the best-documented studies have been made of the system as it operated in the DDR. In the early post-war years sampling techniques were used in the Soviet zone at the instigation of the Soviet Control Commission. Teams of interviewers operated in carefully delimited areas to survey the mood of the population using techniques pioneered in the USSR. From these origins the system evolved and became formalised in the Institute of Public Opinion of the Central Committee of the Socialist Unity Party, founded in 1964. These information-gathering mechanisms supplemented the normal channels of Party work. A major duty of local Party organisations was to survey and report the popular mood so that the Party's agitational work could be directed to appropriate objectives. In addition, public participation through approved organisations was invited in the drafting of projected legislation and in the working out of directives at factory or district level. For example, the draft legislation for the 1965 Family Law Code, the 1968 law on the equality of men and women and the 1973 third Youth Law were all extensively discussed in the DDR and amended in the light of public suggestions and scrutiny. Elsewhere it was specifically recognised in Hungary that something more was required for popular identification with the regime than the occasional casting of a ballot, and that workers should examine the extent to which they could take part in the implementation of policies. In Poland after the 1960s it was regular practice to consult widely on projected legislation. The process went farthest in Yugoslavia with the establishment of works' councils and the deliberate attempt to devolve decision-making to plant and district level. This took the attempt at direct democracy one step beyond that obtaining elsewhere, though the overall framework of decisions and guiding principles was established by Party and government. Though popular participation was at the level of application of such measures, it was a considerable advance on the cardboard stereotype authoritarianism sometimes assumed to exist in eastern Europe.

Wherever the Party leadership came into serious dispute with its communist neighbours the attempt to court and win mass popular support and approval was strengthened. One consequence of the rupture between Yugoslavia and the other bloc governments in 1948 was the almost flamboyant manner in which President Tito courted popular appreciation in a style more typical of the USA than communist eastern Europe. His example was followed by President Ceausescu who, as disputes with the USSR grew, came to embody highly personal exposure to popular approval. Dubcek too during his brief period as First

Secretary adopted a far more public and populist style than either his predecessor or successor.

Other channels existed for popular involvement in the life of the state. They offered a limited opportunity for public participation. There were various legal organisations and associations that required a permit from the Ministry of the Interior to operate. Any grouping of more than minimal size required such authorisation. If refused, it was *ipso facto* declared illegal and open to repression. Permission once given could as easily be rescinded and many transient bodies first authorised were subsequently disbanded. Good examples were the Petofi circles established in Hungary in 1955 and 1956, the Club of Non-Party Activists (KAN) and the Club 231, comprising former political prisoners, both permitted in Dubcek's Czechoslovakia and subsequently banned under Husak, and the Solidarity Union in Poland, authorised in 1980 and declared illegal in 1982. Once licensed, associations were eligible for the allocation of premises by local authorities and the provision of printing equipment, could own property as legal entities and could be eligible for allocation of state funds as well as being permitted to collect donations and open bank accounts. Non-authorisation and illegality involved more than the threat of police action. It was tantamount to elimination as no large-scale organisation can exist without premises, finance and rudimentary equipment. All authorised organisations of a political or quasi-political nature were incorporated into an overall, umbrella body. In Czechoslovakia and the DDR it was called the National Front, in Poland what was originally the National Front became the National Unity Front. In Bulgaria it was the Fatherland Front, in Hungary the People's Independent Front was by 1981 the Patriotic People's Front, while the Romanian body was twice retitled as the People's Democratic Front became first the Front of National Unity and latterly the Front of Socialist Unity. A similar body in Yugoslavia, the Patriotic Front of Yugoslavia, was subsequently renamed the Socialist Alliance of Working People. Such organisations could have individual membership as well as group membership, as was the case for example in both Yugoslavia and Bulgaria.

Youth organisations and trade unions

The most important independent bodies were the various youth organisations and the trade unions. In both cases the structures evolved in the USSR were more or less closely followed. All competing youth organisations such as the scouts and guides or Church youth bodies were disbanded after 1948 and in their place two new bodies were generally established. The first catered for younger children aged from 5 to about 15, while the second covered young people from 15 until approximately 30 years of age. Romania was unique in having three organisations covering the age range. When membership was compulsory, as was the case in Czechoslovakia until 1968, it was rarely enforced. The real attractions of membership to youth and parents alike lay in the opportunities for social intercourse and entertainment, sporting facilities and holidays. Membership was also virtually obligatory for anyone wishing to enter higher education, access to which was normally – and in the DDR specifically – restricted to members in good standing of the appropriate body. The role of trade unions underwent a fundamental alteration after the establishment of communist governments. Once the means of production, distribution and exchange were in the hands of a party representing the leading elements of the working class, there was no place for organisations of workers devoted to the protection of specifically working-class interests. The latter were held to have disappeared and to have become the interests of the government and society at large. The former adversarial and defensive function of unions accordingly also disappeared. They became instead auxiliary bodies whose function was to ensure the interests of the working class, now embodied in the directives and policy decisions of Party and government, were explained to individual workers whose enthusiastic and committed support would be mobilised behind the decisions taken. They became one of the various 'transmission belts' linking society at large with its leaders and assisted in the development of the workers' state. Unions were not established for rural workers, deemed to be members of their co-operatives, nor for small-scale property-owners, independent self-employed craftsmen or handicraft workers. Membership was made compulsory for all industrial workers and for white-collar workers, and unions played a key role in the provision of health insurance and operated medical facilities at sanitoria and cures at spas and health resorts. They were also an integral part of the pensions structure and distributed such fringe benefits as subsidised holidays. As it was in the interests of communist union leaders to demonstrate their own success in securing a contented labour force, successful union officials had to be sensitive of and responsive to their members' moods. Although conceived as organising agencies to control workers, they could and did become representative in limited respects, acting for example to secure improved facilities or provide cultural amenities at places of work. They acted too as mediators with enterprise managements or civil or Party authorities. However, it was not part of their function to negotiate rates of pay or working conditions and official strikes were unknown. The largest memberships were to be found in the most industrialised countries: the DDR, Czechoslovakia and Poland, but everywhere trade unions were the most numerous mass organisations. The top posts in both them and youth organisations were subject to Party nomination and were firmly in Party hands.

Yugoslavia and the DDR after 1960

If the major objective was the mobilisation of the enthusiastic support of the population for the objectives set out by the Party and the sustaining of a high level of commitment, the overall level of success was patchy. Enthusiasm, transient by nature, was difficult to sustain over several decades. The two countries in which such commitment was probably highest were the two standing in greatest distinction to each other, the DDR and Yugoslavia. Since 1950 they hád followed diametrically opposite paths within the communist orbit yet seemed to have succeeded in arousing positive support and some degree of real involvement among their citizens. Elsewhere, enthusiastic mass involvement was rarer. In Czechoslovakia, during the Prague spring in 1967 and 1968, and in Poland in 1956, 1968, 1970, 1976 and 1980 it was enthusiasm outside the Party's control and hostile to it.

Both Yugoslavia and the DDR were proud of their success in securing acceptance of the communist system and of the process that had established its legitimacy in the public mind. In the case of Yugoslavia this was achieved by a steady if uneven progression to wider popular participation in decision-making and by overtly reducing the part played by the Party in national life. Divided into regional units, each part was given a high degree of regional autonomy as the democratic centralism inherited from the Soviet model was gradually circumscribed. This was possible because the enormous personal prestige and influence of President Tito could in times of crisis be thrown into the scales, as was shown most graphically in the crisis that began in 1971 at a time when similar signs of strain were visible in other countries of the bloc. The growing receptivity of the Party leadership in Zagreb to an upswelling of Croat nationalism under the impact of economic policies designed to redistribute wealth from the economically advanced regions, such as Croatia, to the backward ones such as Macedonia and the Kosovo district, caused tensions. Underlying this was a recrudescence of the traditional rivalries between Croats and Serbs symbolised by the allegedly overcentralised financial system with its headquarters in Belgrade, simultaneously the state capital and capital of Serbia. A purge launched in autumn 1971 removed the Zagreb leaders and many Party members. There was a clampdown on Croat cultural organisations. During 1972 certain of the Serbian leaders were accused of pseudo-liberalism and lack of determination in using the mechanisms of planning and central control and a too slavish obedience to capitalist-style economic indicators. The outcome was to make clear the limits beyond which the Party in Yugoslavia was not prepared to withdraw and to establish the parameters of action of participatory public bodies, It seemed as if the Yugoslav party was moving closer to the mainstream of bloc Party activity. More probably after twenty years the relationships between Party and non-Party bodies and the inner requirements of Party discipline had to be restated. Since the early 1950s the elaboration of a network of workers' councils and a steady devolution of powers of decision-taking to them had progressively reduced the power of the state bureaucracy. After 1960 the process was compounded by the search for a viable relationship between federal and republican governments in the field of economic planning. The overall effect was to reduce the range of intervention of the federal planning apparatus and to restrict its role to broad outline planning. Inevitably decentralisation widened the possibilities of effective popular involvement in the construction of economic policy and workers' councils acquired a real degree of power to make local, though important, decisions at enterprise level. During the early 1960s the process was reinforced by a steady reduction in the power and influence of the Party. Restrictions unparalleled elsewhere were introduced. Limits were imposed on the length of time that one individual could hold an office, Party officials were barred from filling posts in local government, the functioning of the *nomenklatura* system was rigorously curtailed and the principle of the rotation of offices among a collective leadership was established. This was applied even to the presidency of the Yugoslav Republic, though it was waived uniquely for Tito. The dismissal in 1966 of Tito's close associate Rankovic symbolised the new course. The revelation that Tito and other leading figures had been subjected to close and continuing surveillance and had had their mail and telephones monitored led to a massive investigation into the activities of the secret police. Rankovic, its head, was dismissed and the decision taken to bring the network under effective political control. The combined effect was to limit the role and powers of the Party, remove something of the coercive threat underlying the exercise of political power and to throw open a widening area of decision-making in day-to-day matters to non-Party organisations whose membership was drawn from the citizenry at large. The events of 1971–3, the distinct hardening of Tito's public pronouncements and his promptings of the need to ensure a properly socialist, and somewhat puritanical, tone to public affairs marked the end of this phase of development but did not mark the return to the original centralist system and Party domination. Popular acceptance of the regime was based on the integrating of a monopoly of power in the hands of the Party with a relatively partici-patory system of councils and local non-Party organisations, and a reasonable level of political openness.

Developments in the DDR were a mirror image of Yugoslav ones. The post-war leadership headed by Ulbricht was as hard-line as the Yugoslav one in the early years, but its evolution took an entirely different path. As the pressures of the post-1948 split led the Yugoslavs to relax the Party grip to win over popular support, in the DDR the massive Soviet military presence and geopolitical realities of Cold War pressures forbade relaxation. The DDR was unavoidably compared with the evolving Federal Republic of Germany. The latter was a showpiece for capitalism in action, and the DDR was the exemplar of communism. The continued possibilities for flight to the West permitted over two and a half million Germans to leave between 1949 and 1972, the overwhelming majority of them before the construction of the Berlin Wall in August 1961. Until then flight and the claims of the Federal Republic to constitute the sole legitimate German state hindered the emergence of a sense of identity for the communist German state.

After 1961 it was possible for the full weight of orthodoxy to be brought to bear and the transformation of the DDR to be truly launched. The history of the new state fell into two phases. Before 1961 the objective proclaimed by it and by the USSR was the reunification of Germany. After 1961 the government of the DDR acknowledged it was creating a communist German state. Its goal was the identification of its citizens with the DDR specifically rather than with the wider conception of Germany. It heightened the differences between itself and the Federal Republic and emphasised its Marxist legacy. The realities of the relationship with the USSR prevented any possibility of following the Yugoslav path, though there was no evidence that the East German party wished to do so. Close Party control over all apects of national life was more systematically elaborated in the DDR than in any other eastern European state, and all the resources of a modern centralised state unremittingly utilised to create a distinctly East German identity. It secured international recognition with the signature of the four-power agreement on Berlin in September 1971. The spectacular sporting successes of the DDR national teams during the 1970s and the widening range of the country's international economic and cultural contacts, especially with the Third World, attested its maturation. A major element in legitimising popular acceptance of communist rule in Yugoslavia was the conflict with the USSR and its Warsaw Pact allies, and a similar role was played in the DDR by a sense of pride in shared achievements. Economic performance under extremely adverse conditions since 1945 was as remarkable in its way as anything achieved by the Federal Republic. The Communist Party was able to secure the credit. It was aided by the willingness of many of its subjects to accept a high degree of state direction and control. The core of the DDR was formerly part of the kingdom of Prussia whose tradition of state control and total direction of national resources was markedly at variance with traditions elsewhere in Europe. As in Yugoslavia, major efforts were made in the DDR to involve its citizens in active executive and deliberative functions. There was, however, no downplaying of the role of the Party. The work of mobilising popular activity was firmly under Party control. Nevertheless the DDR showed a solicitous and successful concern to draw its citizens into social as distinct from political activity. By 1980 it was estimated that one in four adult citizens of the DDR was engaged in some form of voluntary, spare-time social activity which gave those involved a sense of real participatory activity, be it in local lay courts to deal with minor misdemeanours, in self-help groups to improve the environment, or in other forms of socially useful work.

Each country acted as an example to its neighbours. For traditional communists the success of the DDR was proof that centralised planning and a total monopoly of political power was consistent with securing popular support and participation consonant with oversight and direction. This was confirmed by economic success. By 1980 the DDR had the best economic performance in eastern Europe, enjoyed the highest living standards and showed few signs of serious internal strains. Yugoslavia proved attractive to those critical of the centralising and supervisory brand of communism who argued that socialism required the population to be trusted with responsibilities and be delegated powers. Workers' councils in Yugoslavia were an inspiration for similar bodies set up in Poland in 1956 and 1957 which, although after 1958 progressively stripped of their powers and reduced to obedience to Party control, remained a central plank in worker demands at subsequent periods of crisis. The Yugoslavs were also an inspiration to the Czechoslovak reformers during the 1960s. Tito was rapturously received in Prague in August 1968 and the Yugoslav system of federalism was a model for devolution in Czechoslovakia as enshrined in the 1969 constitution. Elsewhere the shedding of power over decisions at local level to local, non-Party organisations went farthest in Hungary. A crucial element in the Hungarian economic reform was the acceptance of a relatively large degree of local decision-making within an overall national centralised framework. After 1961 it became accepted that whosoever was not opposed to the communist system was an ally, indicating a significant widening of the conception of the political community. It led to a marked reduction in tension and a much freer and more relaxed atmosphere, far closer to that in Yugoslavia than to any other eastern bloc state.

Nationalism in communist eastern Europe

Along with the appeal of idealism and altruism, based on the claim to be creating a new society without exploitation or economic deprivation, the other key element in attempts to secure acceptance was the traditional one of nationalism. This did not assume the historically familiar guise but a more subtle form. Traditional nationalism was fuelled by hatred for other national groupings, and especially for Jews. Few eastern European communist leaders were overtly nationalists in this sense. Generally nationalism took the new shape of arousing positive pride in national achievement, identified with the success of communism in constructing a new national economic and social order. At its simplest it vaunted industrial production indices, lauded increases in output of coal, steel, textiles and motor vehicles and paraded the statistics of birth and death rates. By virtue of the campaigns of socialist emulation, by which such performances were compared with those of neighbouring countries, it was possible to play on nationalisms without arousing the hatreds and bellicosity that typified the area before 1939. Governments were not, however, totally guiltless of arousing traditional national territorial grievances, taken over from their capitalist predecessors. The Romanian government periodically commented on its claims to Bessarabia, incorporated in the USSR, while the Hungarian government reminded the world that Transylvania with its substantial minority of Hungarians had traditionally been part of Hungary, lost to Romania in 1919. Bulgaria intermittently renewed its claims to those areas of Macedonia now part of Yugoslavia. This reaffirmation of long-standing claims against communist neighbours could help consolidate domestic sentiment and rally support to communist governments. Similarly an important role was allotted to national themes in the culture of the area. Its importance in helping consolidate support behind communist governments by representing them as defenders of national tradition should not be underestimated. In the case of Yugoslavia and Romania, both governments were able to utilise an ostentatiously independent foreign policy as an indirect appeal to nationalist sentiment. Elsewhere governments were able to establish themselves as the custodians of national identity or, as in the case of the DDR, as its creators. Only in Poland was this impossible. Nationalist sentiment there based on both anti-German and anti-Soviet feeling was closely associated with the Catholic faith. It was extraordinarily difficult for communists to accommodate all three elements. Gomulka's persistent and undisguised anti-German sentiment and accommodation with the Catholic Church may have been in part designed to neutralise national anti-Soviet feeling. After his departure his successors did not try to do so. The situation was made more complicated by the election in 1978 of a Polish Pope, thus symbolising one of the irreconcilable components of Polish nationalism.

The governmental and constitutional structure

The relative importance of the Party, compared to the state, apparatus was attested by the assiduity with which powerful political figures held on to their Party posts. In the first years of communist governments, the posts of Party First Secretary and of Prime Minister were usually combined. In Hungary Rakosi held them until 1953 while in Bulgaria Dimitrov held both until his death in 1949 and was succeeded by Chervenkov who took both offices until 1954. In Czechoslovakia Gottwald was President and Party head, as was Bierut in Poland. When the post of Polish President was abolished, Bierut became Prime Minister. In the DDR and Romania the pattern was different. Ulbricht was General-Secretary of the SED while Grotewohl, a former socialist, became Premier and Pieck became President. In Romania the two posts were combined in 1952 by Gheorgiu-Dej. After Stalin's death the new Soviet model of collective leadership began to be applied in eastern Europe. The combination of the top posts in both Party and government in the hands of one man was condemned as a manifestation of the cult of personality. Thus offices were separated. Almost without exception the leading figures held on to their Party posts. Bierut's eventual successor, Gomulka, took the Party secretaryship, relinquishing the premiership to the former socialist Cyrankiewicz. On Gottwald's death in 1953 Zapotocky succeeded him as President while Novotny took the Party post. When compelled by Soviet pressure to choose, Rakosi opted for the Party secretaryship and left the premiership to the reinstated Nagy. Only in Romania did Gheorgiu-Dej choose the governmental post, and significantly eighteen months later in October 1955 he swopped offices, resuming the Party secretaryship. Only in Bulgaria did a First Secretary choose the governmental post. In 1954 Chervenkov handed over the secretaryship to Zhivkov, the first step along a road that led to eventual eclipse. Power lay with the Party and its professional administrators. Ambitious men made their careers in the Party though they might also try to combine posts in government with their Party duties. The men who controlled their respective parties after 1953 came out on top.

There were some limited advantages in combining a top governmental position with the Party secretaryship, most notably in connection with the conduct of foreign affairs, and there were subsequent examples of Party Secretaries resuming important governmental posts. Gomulka never did, and Rakosi's successor Kadar only took both posts between 1956 and 1958 and between 1961 and 1965. In November 1957 Novotny became President of Czechoslovakia on Zapotocky's death and held both posts until 1968. In Bulgaria Zhivkov assumed the premiership in 1962 while Husak became President of Czechoslovakia in 1975. As for the DDR, though Grotewohl was succeeded as Premier in 1964 by Stoph, Ulbricht as chairman of the Council of State was effective head of state. In Romania the post of President was invented for Ceausescu.

It was a fundamental proposition of Marxism that political parties were the expression of the interests of particular classes. As the abolition of all classes was the ultimate objective, parties would necessarily disappear. In the meantime socialism was the transition phase during which the conditions necessary for the abolition would be created, and it was the task of the government and state structure to administer and protect the spread of socialism. The constitution and administrative structure of the state reflected the extent to which the transition had been accomplished and the frequent changes in the constitutions of eastern Europe were presented as the formal expression of steady evolution along the road indicated. Neither constitutions nor state organisation represented eternal verities. In Yugoslavia, for example, the original constitution of 1946 was amended in 1953, replaced in 1963, amended on several occasions thereafter and finally replaced again in 1974. Subsequent to its inception in October 1949 the DDR had three constitutions, the most recent being in October 1974, and there were also three constitutions in Czechoslovakia. The essential continuity and legitimacy was provided by the Party and not by the institutions of state. A similar situation pertained in the state bureaucracy. There were frequent reorganisations of the administrative systems, and especially of those branches dealing with the economy, economic planning and day-to-day control over its implementation. In Yugoslavia there were also major changes resulting from the transfer of responsibilities from the federal government in Belgrade to local republican governments in regional capitals. Without the steadying ballast of Party control such changes could have led to administrative paralysis, and would certainly have been indicative of major crisis. Eastern European communist governments and administrations had a considerable degree of organisational flexibility. It was possible for constitutional changes to be debated quite widely and for administrative reorganisation to be readily instituted to meet specific *ad hoc* requirements. Government was only infrequently concerned with contentious policy issues or with the real exercise of power. For the most part its function was administrative and formal.

The intensely bureaucratic nature of communist rule, with its emphasis on due administrative procedure and central control, spawned substantial bureaucracies. They grew steadily more numerous, intensifying a tendency already present before the Second World War. In pre-war eastern Europe state employment was socially prestigious, economically relatively secure and much sought. Although communists invested the bureaucracy with new values and gave it new significance, they were able to build on already existing attitudes of mind to produce a structurally impermanent bureaucracy liable to be reorganised regularly. It was of pervasive function. The process created a substantial interest group of supporters of the system which provided them with jobs, incomes and social standing. Its size ought not to be underestimated. In Czechoslovakia, for example, over 11 per cent of the whole labour force was employed in the state administration in the mid-1960s, and by 1970 it was estimated that there was one administrative employee for every three workers in Czechoslovak industry.

Parliaments

Although eastern European states were not parliamentary democracies, all had elected parliamentary bodies. These assemblies were not totally dominated by members of the Communist Party, in form at least. Their relative unimportance was shown by the acceptance of remnants of non-communist parties which, emasculated prior to the establishment of the people's democracies, still maintained a shadowy independent identity and were ideologically explained as rumps representing the decaying remains of older social classes not yet finally eradicated. Only in Romania did the Communist Party hold every single seat in the National Assembly. Elsewhere a proportion was allocated in advance to each organisation contesting the elections, the medium for negotiation and for approving candidates being the appropriate state Front organisation. Such sharing produced a further mechanism for the drawing together of Party and people by creating broadly representative bodies with which all sections of society could identify. After the initial period of repression that lasted until about 1954 there was some tendency to permit contested elections within the confines of a single slate. All candidates were carefully screened in advance to ensure their suitability. Nevertheless some candidates were always preferred by the official ruling group. In contested elections the results could sometimes be surprising. In 1967, for example, there were several notable examples in Yugoslavia of the election of traditional rather than of preferred reformist candidates who supported the then-dominant decentralising and liberalising tendency in the Yugoslav League of Communists. Not all hard-line communists were necessarily unpopular with eastern European electorates.

The smallest percentage of communist members in a national assembly was to be found in the DDR, where one-quarter of deputies were Party members, and each of the other four rump parties had just over 10 per cent. The balance was made up of representatives of mass organisations such as the youth bodies, women's organisations and trade unions. Elsewhere communists comprised over half the total number of deputies. However, in Bulgaria one-quarter of the deputies were from the Agrarian Union, the rump of the formerly powerful Peasants' Party. In the case of Poland there was a numerically very small group of deputies representing various Catholic bodies, who enjoyed considerable prestige. Such assemblies were little more than discussion bodies whose real powers were very restricted. However, in times of crisis even the most docile and hand-picked of assemblies could become surprisingly lively. During successive crises in Poland in 1956, 1968 and again in 1980 assemblies comprising carefully screened deputies became extremely critical of government and witnessed surprisingly vocal and sweeping condemnations by hitherto tame parliamentarians. The same phenomenon occurred in Czechoslovakia in 1968 while the robust behaviour of the Yugoslav Parliament between 1967 and 1971 helped set the scene for the purges and restrictions on criticism then introduced. Furthermore, crises generally brought demands from rump non-communist parties for a degree of independence, for permission to resume recruiting and for a role in Parliament closer to the function of a loyal opposition. The existing leadership of such parties, chose for acceptability to communists, were forced into resignation and new ones emerged. Such demands sometimes bore fruit. This was especially true in Poland, where at each period of internal difficulty the remnants of the old peasant and democratic parties were able to press their claims. Such parties were also identified as possible nuclei for the formalised representation of alternative views. Such, for example, was the proposal that seemed to be emerging under Dubcek before the 1968 invasion.

A major element in the reluctance to accept that rump parties had any function other than a purely symbolic one lay in the ideological perception of the permissibility of differences within a socialist society. This caused much heart-searching for eastern European communists. Ideologically it was difficult to accept that under a classless Marxist state sectional differences could exist, and it was only under the intensive pressures of the 1960s that it came to be accepted that while class differences could not exist, group differences could and did. The pioneering work in elaborating such conceptions came from Poland and Czechoslovakia, and by 1973 it had come to be widely accepted in eastern Europe and in the USSR that clashes of interest were an understandable feature of socialist society, as specific personal and group concerns were not always reconcilable. This acceptance eased the recognition that governmental supervision, guidance and suppression and the omnipresent power of communist parties had not stopped discontent. The right to grumble was formalised through official acceptance of humorous magazines critical of bureaucratic folly which defused popular indignation by permitting criticism while at the same time spurring on officials to improve their performance. Substantive criticism of the system, policy or underlying values remained taboo. That did not, however, mean that such criticism did not exist.

Popular discontent and control of opponents

To avoid major trouble or movements of popular discontent the tactics devised to weaken and divide non-communists in the immediate postwar years were adapted and applied. Potential opponents were fragmented and isolated from one another and from society at large, thus avoiding the coalescence of interest groups into broad movements of opposition. Possible centres of disaffection were identified and prevented from influencing other groups or from propagating their grievances. They were decapitated by the harassment and arrest of spokesmen and potential leaders. Human rights movements, the signatories of *Charter '77* in Czechoslovakia, critics of official Romanian trade unions, the leaders of Solidarity in Poland were all subjected to such treatment. Especial care was taken to avoid any link between industrial workers and intellectuals. Both had their own preoccupations and demands. Whenever the two groups came together in a common manifestation of discontent it was difficult to contain them. The various opposition groups were well aware of this policy and appreciated the difficulty of constructing bridges linking different social groups and different demands under a system of total state control. Only in Poland was something of the sort achieved. After 1976 a conscious and determined effort was made to link industrial workers and intellectuals. The machinery was the organisation known as KOR, a body of intellectuals including lawyers, teachers, journalists and other professional workers. From it grew a greater sense of shared interest and common purpose, and an appreciation that the success of the objectives of both could only be achieved by a united thrust. The troubles that erupted in 1980 were fuelled by that analysis. Many of those most active in KOR had close links with those who founded Solidarity, and it was disbanded and its leaders interned in 1982.

However carefully devised the policies of the various communist regimes in the area were, it was impossible to prevent discontent. The great demonstrations in June 1953 in the DDR, in 1956 in both Hungary and Poland, in 1968 in Czechoslovakia and since 1980 in Poland were merely the most eye-catching and dramatic. There was a more or less constant undercurrent. It was difficult to identify or quantify such movements because of censorship of news of domestic strife. Although strikes were illegal, they were far from uncommon. Poland had the best-known history of these. The well-known work stoppages in 1956, 1970, 1976 and 1980 were supplemented by many more restricted, local troubles such as that involving tram drivers in Lodz in 1957 or the various local disturbances arising from religious questions during the early 1960s. These were not unique. Long after, it was admitted officially that between 1958 and 1969 there were over 2,000 strikes in Yugoslavia. During the 1970s there was a succession of industrial troubles in Romania, with especially serious outbreaks in the Jiu Valley coal-mines and in August 1980 at Tirgoviste. Even in relatively peaceful Bulgaria there were strikes among, for example, the tobacco workers at Plovdiv.

Such outbreaks had specific, local causes that could be met by prompt conciliation. They were important reminders, however, that whatever the official view of the relationship between workers and the communist state, of the inapplicability of the strike weapon, of socialist societies without the conflicts or troubles of their capitalist counterparts eastern Europe was not free of the phenomenon of industrial action. Because of the economic monopoly of the communist state, all such action was inevitably directed against the government and the system. It thus acquired political significance and could develop into a major political challenge. All governments were extraordinarily sensitive to the threat of industrial action and moved swiftly to meet it. As the Polish examples showed, their response customarily took the form of physical repression by the security police.

Worker dissatisfaction did not inevitably attract support from other social groups. Indeed, as intellectuals took over many of the functions performed elsewhere by capitalists their sympathy for worker demands eroded. Those whose occupations required qualifications and were technical, creative or intellectual showed no signs of wishing to return to free-enterprise capitalism or of being attracted by the Western economic or political system. By no means all were critical of the communist system but those who were offered a serious challenge, for at the root of the criticisms lay an acceptance of the basic tenets of Marxist socialism coupled with a rejection of the claim that the system that had developed in eastern Europe embodied them. Some of these critics concluded that the system did not provide the society Marx had envisaged and desired, or discerned the development of a socialist class system, based not on ownership of the means of production but on control over them and on power to dispose of the profits of the economy. Others complained of the rigidity of the system and lamented its inability to respond to challenges and adjust flexibly to innovation by making the changes clearly essential in both the economy and social policy. Others objected that the concentration on the means by which socialism and communism were to be attained neglected the purpose and ultimate objective, the creation of conditions permitting all men to develop and fulfil their capacities freely. Creative artists found the requirements of conformity to censorship stultifying. Philosophers objected to the formalisation of Marxism into a quasi-science bereft of challenge or new application. Such critics were not numerous and the opportunities for the dissemination of their ideas were limited. Yet in times of crisis they could rally others whose dissatisfaction arose from material considerations. They also cast doubts on the scientific certainty underpinning the whole theoretical basis of communist ideology. Such criticisms challenged the fundamental assumptions upon which the Party's monopoly of power was based.

The theoretical critique

After 1953 such critics emerged throughout the area. At first they operated within their respective parties forming a 'loyal opposition' from within. The example best known in western Europe was Djilas in Yugoslavia. The earliest substantial critic of the emerging communism of the People's Democracies, he took up themes first elaborated in the USSR during the 1920s by the so-called 'Left Opposition' and 'Workers' Opposition' and subsequently developed in exile by Trotsky. Djilas's criticism began in the Party paper *Borba* in October 1953 earning him first expulsion from the League of Communists and subsequently imprisonment. The criticisms voiced in his work *The New Class* remained consistent and infused his 1981 biography of Tito. Critical of the corrupting effects of power on his colleagues he denounced their privileges and ambitions, the outward symbols of a new hierarchy and governing class of bureaucrats who fulfilled in eastern Europe the functions of entrepreneurs in capitalist systems. Having carried through the industrialisation of the region not formerly achieved by capitalism, they had begun to behave like ruling groups elsewhere, and were betraying the humanist values inherent in Marxism. The blame, however, lay with Stalin. Discussion, debate and toleration had been eradicated from the Soviet party whose ideological line was fundamentally at variance with the true Marxist inheritance. It was buttressed by the machinery of Party monopoly control over all aspects of national life. Control over economy and government gave Party officials great power. They formed a class, based not on ownership but control. Worker control, it was stated, must be extended and power diffused away from the Party. Such arguments were shared to some extent by other Yugoslav leaders. Successively since 1953 attempts were made to institute a system of workers' councils in individual enterprises, to decentralise power and to reduce or remove the privileges afforded to members of the League of Communists. The adaptation of this name replacing 'Communist Party of Yugoslavia' symbolised a commitment to a changed conception of the relationship between Party and people. As critics of the system elsewhere in eastern Europe acknowledged, the process of reform and change still had far to go in Yugoslavia, but it had started there.

These arguments had a wide circulation. Central to them was the issue of power and responsibility. However disguised and whatever the philosophic premise, the heart of the debate was the issue of control over those who took decisions and the mechanism by which they were made. Especially crucial was the exercise of real control by workers, which became a major demand of dissidents throughout eastern Europe and was symbolised in the call for workers' councils. These were popular with workers, for whom they had immediate, practical functions associated with work rates, production targets, wage rates, piece-work and working conditions rather than the broader, more philosophical and political objectives of dissident intellectuals. Communist parties were intensely aware of the danger of a fusion of worker and intelligentsia opposition based on the call for industrial democracy. Such fusion occurred in 1956, 1968 and 1980. To avoid the recurrence of such a challenge, communist parties emphasised the differences in the arguments of the two separate oppositional currents and tried to alienate workers from intelligentsia by arguing that the latter sought to use the mechanisms of workers' councils to worsen living conditions and intensify the demands placed on labour. As proof it argued that the intelligentsia had operated the existing system of centralised planning and control. If that had deficiencies they were responsible and their espousal of change must therefore be suspect. The decline in economic performance accompanying internal upheaval in eastern Europe did indeed lead to falling living standards for workers. Governments in Hungary and Poland after 1956 and Czechoslovakia after 1969 successfully broke up the alliance of workers and intellectuals by playing off one against the other. In the DDR such an alliance did not emerge, largely as a result of the superior economic performance, while in Bulgaria and Romania a lower level of social development had not as yet produced the same dangers. In Poland the combination of a dismal economic performance and the lesser degree of penetration achieved by the Party made the danger of such a combination more acute than elsewhere.

Like Djilas, many other critics initially joined their respective parties and sought to propagate reform from within. Between 1956 and 1968 some degree of latitude was allowed within eastern European parties for the recruitment of exponents of varying opinions. This was also true of the Soviet party under Khrushchev, and may reflect the more relaxed and disputative style of party characteristic of his leadership. A considerable degree of debate was permitted in Party publications and heterodox ideas were developed by writers such as Havemann and Christa Wolf in the DDR, Markus and Hegedus in Hungary, and Brus, Lange and Kalecki in Poland. Similar evolutions occurred in Bulgaria, Romania and Yugoslavia. The process went farthest in Czechoslovakia where by 1967 the reformers were on the point of taking over the Party apparatus. In 1968 this phase of internal pressure for change ended, and not only in Czechoslovakia. The ensuing purge was of course greatest there, but a similar tightening of freedom of criticism within the Party occurred everywhere else between 1969 and 1972. Thereafter opposition was no longer possible from within. It moved outside, and during the 1970s was expressed at considerable personal risk. The enormous difficulties in securing publication of critical ideas within eastern Europe were mitigated to some extent by the possibilities of preparing and circulating duplicated or photocopied materials, or by sending manuscripts abroad for publication in the West. As Western wireless and in some places television broadcasts were also accessible in eastern Europe these too gave opportunities for dissident criticism to circulate. While such publications as *Charter '77* in Czechoslovakia or the demands of Solidarity in Poland were significant, the more or less steady trickle of criticism based on Marxist and socialist precepts was probably more important in encouraging the discontented and prompting critical reassessment among an increasingly well-educated public. A substantial group of former Party members purged and removed from their original occupations existed. Frequently sent to work at manual occupations for purposes of 'rehabilitation', they came into contact with ordinary citizens. Contact with former Party members deeply critical of their colleagues' motives must have influenced ordinary citizens' perceptions of the ruling parties. The more wholesale the purges the greater were the numbers to be accommodated. In the most recent case the number involved in the post-1981 purge by Jaruzelski was considerable. The whole process attested the increasing sophistication required of governments in their guidance and control of modern, educated, industrial societies.

The police and the military

In the final eventuality, opposition was controlled by coercion, the mechanisms of which played a significant role since the early post-war days. The elaborate police network then established was crucial. It was based in part on the system inherited from previous regimes, often none-too-squeamish in their willingness to use repression against opponents. To this was grafted Soviet experience of application of police control techniques. Once the communist regimes were established the police were used as an arm of government to eliminate resistance to its policies. Coercion became an institutionalised executive mechanism. As resistance to policies was automatically equated with 'bourgeois anti-communism', an enemy to be extirpated with the utmost ruthlessness, all who opposed the new governments and many whose enthusiasm was lukewarm were stigmatised as enemies and plotters. It was the function of the police to identify and liquidate them. This repression and assumption of premeditated sedition continued to characterise official attitudes in eastern Europe. To varying degrees the tendency since the mid-1950s was for governments to become less heavy-handed, yet the temptation to relapse into police measures, euphemistically called administrative measures, and the assumption of hidden enemies whose malevolence tainted the entire populace, was close to the surface and re-emerged in times of crisis or strain.

Symptomatic of the importance of the secret police were the early steps taken to establish it. In Yugoslavia one of Tito's closest colleagues, the Serb Rankovic, established in 1944 the OZNa (Department for the Protection of the People), later renamed the UDBa (State Security Administration), which rapidly won the reputation of the most ruthless and unsavoury eastern European secret police. In Czechoslovakia a similar result was secured by converting the pre-communist force into a loyally communist one, while in Hungary in 1945 the AVO (State Security Department) grew out of the merger of the security section of the Communist Party with the regular police force. These organisations operated outside the usual mechanisms of civilian control. The Yugoslav police were under military control until 1946 and from then until 1951 there were no limits placed on their power. After 1980 the secret police, again under military control, was widely used by Tito's successors to snuff out opposition, with the result that in 1981 there were reputedly more political prisoners there than anywhere else in the region. A similar evolution took place in Poland. There too secret police powers were largely uncontrolled until December 1954 when a process of steadily tighter civilian governmental control began. At the end of 1956 the Ministry of the Interior assumed responsibility, with the winding up of the Committee of Public Security, and in 1957 the Sejm began to conduct regular reviews of the activity of the security organs. With the gradual acceptance of communist power throughout the region it was possible for Party control over the secret police to be tightened. Reliance on it became less crucial and its activities less omnipresent. The process went farthest in Poland and Yugoslavia, and least far in Romania, Bulgaria and the DDR. There were no publicised scandals elsewhere to match the culling of the Polish security forces which took place between 1955 and 1957 or the spectacular dismissal of Rankovic in 1966.

Apart from the secret police, eastern Europe was well supplied with security organs. It was characteristic of communist states that a high priority was given to such bodies and that relative to their populations and resources they always maintained substantial military and para-military forces. This was already clear by 1950. Indeed, by the early 1950s paramilitary forces amounted to an additional element between one-quarter and one-third of the strength of the regular armed forces. The proportion did not change greatly thereafter. The variety of such forces was considerable. The DDR was not unrepresentative. Its regular armed forces were under the command not of the DDR government but of the Warsaw Pact. Initially comprised of all-volunteer units, conscription was introduced in 1962. In addition to these there were the civil and security police, border guards, a transport police, the riot police of the Ministry of the Interior, and an elite Guard Regiment of the Ministry of State Security. By the late 1970s these together constituted additional forces amounting to approximately 40 per cent of the regular ones and were under the direct control of the government of the DDR. Moreover, there was a paramilitary force of factory workers totalling in the mid-1970s about 400,000, more than double the size of the regular armed forces. This emphasis carried over into the educational system, where military training for schoolchildren and the elaboration of military-oriented spare-time activities was commonplace throughout the region. The most systematically developed programmes were to be found in the DDR, where by 1980 military training was part of the school curriculum for those aged 14 and older, but similar arrangements in both Romania and Yugoslavia were well publicised during the 1970s and were normal elsewhere.

This emphasis on the armed forces and military preparedness was evocative of the traditional role of the military in the pre-communist states of the region. Only in Czechoslovakia had the military not played a significant part in national life in general and political life in particular. Not surprisingly it was an especial object of concern to secure communist control over the armed forces. At first this was achieved in part by the substantial utilisation of Soviet advisers and officers. The most marked Soviet involvement was with the armed forces of the DDR and Poland. In the case of the latter, the Soviet Marshal Rokossovsky was commander-in-chief of the Polish army until November 1956 and many seconded Soviet officers served under him. Elsewhere the services of officers cashiered under the previous governments were utilised. This was the case in Hungary, for example, where such officers played a crucial part. In Czechoslovakia and Romania the nucleus of the army was drawn from the ranks of forces recruited in the USSR during the war and sent back as the vanguard of the liberating armies in 1944 and 1945. Former wartime partisans played a similar role in Yugoslavia while in the fledgling DDR the armed forces evolved out of units of border guards, riot police and security police which were set up in 1949 and formally reconstructed as the regular armed forces in January 1956. In all cases the officer corps was the subject of solicitous concern. In command of organisations able to challenge the Party they were selectively recruited and subjected to progressively tighter Party discipline. As Party members they were required to participate actively in Party work and were subjected to the ordinary controls of Party discipline as well as to military orders. By the late 1970s representatives of the military were regularly found in the Central Committees of the various parties and were increasingly members of Politbureaus. In a development widespread during the later 1970s the armed forces gained in status and acquired direct links with ruling party organisations. The outstanding example of this new role and influence was the part played in Poland by General Jaruzelski. Appointed Prime Minister in February 1981 he became First Secretary of the Party in October and in December imposed martial law. Other officers also began to play increasingly important roles elsewhere. There were persistent rumours of an abortive military-led *coup* in Bulgaria in 1965, and in Romania in 1982, while in 1967 and early 1968 some Czechoslovak army commanders tried to rally military support for Novotny and sought to pressurise the Central Committee during 1968. In 1971 and 1972 Tito on several occasions threatened to bring in the army to defend Yugoslav national unity against fissiparous tendencies in the Party. Such examples of direct intervention and of the cultivation and institutionalisation of military influence illustrated the potential political power of the region's armed forces.

Behind these stood Soviet armed forces. As with US and British forces in the Federal Republic, there was a substantial Soviet military presence in the DDR. Initially justified by military conquest, the position of these and other Soviet troops quartered in eastern Europe was regularised under the terms of the 1955 Warsaw Pact. The large staff that controlled the Pact's armed forces was drawn from the member states and located in Moscow, where it was attached to the Soviet Ministry of Defence. It was commanded by Soviet military personnel. In addition to the Soviet troops in the DDR, there were also substantial numbers in Poland, justified by the need to keep open lines of communication, in Hungary, where despite Stalin's promise of 1946 Soviet troops had remained ever since the end of the war and whose removal had been a central issue in the events of 1956, and in Czechoslovakia, whither they had returned in 1968. There were no Soviet troops stationed either in Bulgaria, withdrawn in December 1947, or since July 1958 in Romania. The presence of Soviet forces was a permanent reminder to Germans, Hungarians and Czechoslovaks of the role played by them in 1953, 1956 and 1968 respectively, while Poles were well aware of the possibilities of Soviet action should the Polish party lose control over events. Moreover, joint Warsaw Pact manoeuvres were a standard weapon used by the USSR to influence events, as was shown with regard to developments in Poland in 1981, and to pressurise the Romanian government whenever its foreign policy seemed too provocative. Behind such operations lay the memory that in 1968 the prelude to the invasion of Czechoslovakia had been joint manoeuvres held there and on the country's borders.

Communists and organised religion

A partial exception to the elimination or absorption of traditional institutions was provided by organised religion which remained one of the few forces challenging Party dominance. The record was patchy and varied from state to state. In some countries an historical identity between Church and government was maintained under the new atheistic communist regimes. Elsewhere, as in Poland and to a lesser extent Hungary and Slovakia, the Catholic Church succeeded in maintaining a distinct link between itself and national identity. Whatever *modus vivendi* was established, religion everywhere confronted Marxists with a challenge. In some cases the close identification between religious and national identification had been a major cause of traditional tensions, as was the case in Yugoslavia. Governments determined to end such divisions inevitably found themselves involved in confrontations. Beneath these, however, lay a far deeper and more profound conflict. By offering a moral and philosophical justification for human existence based on non-materialistic foundations, religion was an ideological competitor. The close link between organised religion and non-communist economic and political systems led Marxists to perceive faith as the ideology of feudalism and capitalism. It was, in Marx's famous phrase, the 'opium of the masses' which distracted attention from worldly injustices by focusing on eternal rewards. It was a competitor, offering alternative values conflicting with the communist ones of materialism and economic determinism. By preaching submission the Church blunted the edge of class antagonisms and discouraged the activist mentality valued by Marxists. Finally, religion in eastern Europe was deeply rooted in the peasant world. The new communist regimes were determined upon rapid industrial development, and the destruction of the traditional peasant outlook was an essential part of the process.

Eastern European Marxists were aggressive atheists. After coming to power they tried to stamp out religious belief, conducting vigorous campaigns to propagate irreligious thought. Church property was attacked and Church lands treated as privately owned lands, subjected to seizure and redistribution in the great land reforms. This was especially serious in those countries where the Church had been a major landowner, and affected the Roman Catholic Church more than it did Protestant or Orthodox communities. Monasteries and convents were closed. The Church's rights to buildings used for religious purposes also came under attack. As with all private property they were nationalised and extreme difficulties put in the way of repossession. Religious communities were treated as organised groups, requiring state authorisation, and great pressure was brought to bear on individual members to persuade them to abjure religion. It was made difficult for the churches to reach young people. Religious education in schools was ended and the churches' organised youth movements closed down, while the teaching of religion was made into a private matter between priests and parents on an individual basis, impermissible in groups. Church schools were closed down and their properties confiscated. It was made very difficult for the churches to recruit and train priests; theological students were not exempted from military service and theological colleges were closed down. Theology indeed became part of the state educational apparatus taught by priests who had come to terms with the new communist regimes and were deemed reliable. Over all it was clearly anticipated that in time the pressures against and disincentives associated with belief would lead to its weakening and eventual disappearance. Organised religion was to be incorporated within the official Party-controlled framework of national life.

This first phase of the campaign was marked by considerable, though varied, resistance. Those churches with a tradition of close links with state power found themselves able to adapt to the new requirements. This was especially true of the Orthodox churches. Traditionally closely linked with secular authority, the autocephalous churches of Serbia, Bulgaria and Romania were able to adapt and adjust, as had the Orthodox Church in the USSR. More interested in piety than protest and with theologies closer to mysticism than to rationalism, the Orthodox communities had always stressed faith, suffering and redemption through inner religious conviction rather than works. They had traditionally been linked to national movements. The Serbian and Bulgarian churches in particular had played major roles in rallying their respective nations. It proved easier for the Bulgarian than for the Serbian Orthodox Church to adapt to the new conditions, but neither experienced the troubles encountered elsewhere.

The Bulgarian Church was soon closely linked with the secular, communist authority and the treatment it received contrasted strongly with the attacks on other churches in the country. Protestant Church leaders were imprisoned and fined in 1949 and their Roman Catholic counterparts imprisoned and sentenced to death in 1952. Orthodox priests were, however, co-operative and the hierarchy's cordiality was attested by the Bulgarian government's willingness to support and advance the Church's claims to independent status, symbolised in the establishment of the Bulgarian Patriarchate. This was achieved in 1953, at the time when elsewhere the struggle between Church and communist authorities was reaching its apogee. It was politically advantageous to emphasise the independent identity of the Bulgarian Church as distinct from those in Yugoslavia, Greece and at Istanbul yet it was also illustrative of the co-operation between secular and religious authorities in Bulgaria.

Protestant churches in eastern Europe had a tradition of close association with secular power dating to the Reformation and to the dependence of Protestantism on the patronage and protection of secular princes. This was especially true for the Lutheran Church in Germany, the established religion of Prussia and Saxony. In the DDR the population was overwhelmingly Protestant, and perhaps no more than 8 per cent were Roman Catholic. Elsewhere there were important Protestant communities in the Czech lands of Czechoslovakia and in Hungary. It had earlier been identified with the nationalist ambitions of Czechs as opposed to the Roman Catholicism of the Habsburg Empire. By emphasising their identity with nationalist ambitions the Protestant churches gained strength and influence but everywhere lacked inter-national organisation. They were accordingly particularly vulnerable when the new communist governments showed themselves hostile. Lacking moral support abroad, and all too often unable to arouse foreign interest in their fate, eastern European Protestant communities had little choice but to make the best of difficult conditions. Individual clerics resisted, but the overwhelming consensus was to come to terms with government. Within the DDR, for example, relations with the Synod of the Lutheran Church were strained throughout the 1950s and 1960s though there was no question as to its subordinate position. It was not until 1976 that a formal agreement was concluded enshrining a working relationship between the two. As with their Protestant brethren in Hungary and Czechoslovakia, those in the DDR settled for an accom-modation that recognised their existence as religious communities and permitted them to worship and celebrate Christian rites but isolated them from public life. Communicants active in Church matters and unwilling to accept the professed atheism required of members of youth movements of the Communist Party were excluded from influential positions in public life, from the universities and from the higher reaches of the economy. To be a practising Christian was to accept serious restrictions on career and social prospects as well as exclusion from political power.

The serious opposition came from the Roman Catholic Church. This was particularly strong in Poland, Hungary, among the Slovaks in Czechoslovakia and among Croats in Yugoslavia. Once more there was an historically close connection between nationalism and religion in all these areas, though it was less strong in Hungary than in the other three. Far more importantly, the Catholic Church in eastern Europe formed part of a great international community, whose head resided outside the area and was therefore unamenable to control. Deriving moral strength from this international dimension, eastern European Catholics were also able to mobilise world attention. The ensuing publicity at times seriously embarrassed communist governments while the evolution of normal relations with non-communist countries placed a premium on the regularisation of relations with local Catholic communities. From the start communist regimes recognised that the Catholic communities posed a particular problem. In both Poland and Hungary special arrangements were made to soften the impact of land redistribution measures. In Poland such measures, though introduced in 1944, were not applied to Church lands until 1950, while in Hungary specially favourable dispensations were applied that still left the Catholic Church a major land-holder after the redistribution had been carried out. The close identification of Roman Catholicism with conservative political parties and with peasant movements required, however, that its influence on rural society in particular be fought. The ensuing struggle had many features reminiscent of Bismarck's *Kulturkampf* against the Catholic Church in Imperial Germany. Direct persecution and harassment served however to strengthen the moral influence of Catholicism. Its communicants were resistant to efforts to apply salami tactics by sponsoring rival Catholic organisations under priests willing to support communism. The best known of these, the Polish Pax movement, established a flourishing Press and formed a virtual private publishing empire. Elsewhere similar groups appeared in the Peace Movement in Czechoslovakia and Hungary. Such bodies did not secure significant popular backing despite the substantial assistance provided by the state. Catholic laymen remained loyal to the official Church leaders who were violently attacked. In Poland, Hungary and Yugoslavia the Catholic primates were arrested. The Yugoslav Archbishop of Zagreb, Stepinac, was arrested, tried and sentenced in 1946 to sixteen years' imprisonment. Released in 1951 he lived until his death in 1960 in restricted residence. The two charges against him had been his resistance to the new communist government and his wartime record. A similar combination of charges, coupling the political crime of resistance to the communist authorities with a charge intended to destroy the moral authority of the head of the Church, was made against the Hungarian primate, Cardinal Mindszenty. Arrested in 1948 he was the subject of a show trial in 1949. In his case the Hungarian regime wished publicly to destroy a prominent non-communist as a warning to all other opponents that no one was able to resist. The Cardinal's public confession to charges admitted in 1956 to be false were the closest eastern European equivalent to the Stalinist show trials in the 1930s. Whereas the Lutheran Bishop Ordas who was also arrested and jailed in 1948 was released in May 1950, Mindszenty was sentenced to life imprisonment, for which house arrest was substituted in 1955. His successor Archbishop Grosz was sentenced to fifteen years' imprisonment in 1951. Elsewhere Catholic prelates in Romania, Czechoslovakia and Poland were also imprisoned. The Polish primate Cardinal Wyszynski was placed under house-arrest in 1953. Lower-ranking clergy also suffered. Over 6,000 monks and nuns served prison terms in excess of five years in a campaign of repression in Czechoslovakia at its peak between 1949 and 1951. Throughout the region Catholic priests and members of religious orders were imprisoned or driven to forced labour.

As in so many other fields, 1956 marked the beginning of a long, slow process of adjustment by both communist governments and the Catholic Church. Mindszenty, released during 1956, took refuge in the US embassy in Budapest where he remained until 1971 when he was permitted to leave and retire to Rome. Relations between Church and state were regularised in 1964, when it was agreed that bishops would be appointed in consultation with the government and would take an oath of allegiance to the state. In 1974 the Vatican removed Mindszenty from the primacy of Hungary and a steady improvement in relations culminated in Kadar's official reception by the Pope in June 1977. Religious observance in Hungary was, however, in decline, so that in 1982 Pope John Paul II felt compelled to call for a missionary effort to re-establish the vitality of Hungarian Catholicism. In Czechoslovakia the regularisation only began in 1968 with the release and reinstatement of imprisoned bishops and clergy. The respite proved short-lived, for by the mid-1970s the licences to preach of approximately one-eighth of the country's Catholic priests had been withdrawn and pressures on parents led to marked falls in attendances at religious instruction classes in Slovakia. In 1968 the Church and government in Romania opened a cautious dialogue. The Yugoslav government also opened links with Rome, in its case exchanging representatives with the Holy See and permitting the Church to re-establish youth organisations and organise pilgrimages. Most impressive of all was the recuperation of the Catholic Church in Poland. There Cardinal Wyszynski, released in 1956, established a working relationship with Gomulka by which the Church secured a considerable amelioration of its position. It continued to operate its own university at Lublin, two theological academies, seminaries and had more churches and priests than in 1939. Over half the clergy was under 40 years of age and 90 per cent of them were of peasant or industrial worker origin. It continued to maintain religious orders and operated a widely read Catholic Press. Relations between Church and state continued uneven, with periods of considerable tension. However by the mid-1970s the position of the Church was substantially strengthened by the willingness of the communist authorities under Gierek to seek a joint approach to political problems and, as events after 1980 showed, the Church was able to capitalise on this to establish a mediatory role between the Communist Party and its critics. With a small group of Catholic deputies in the Sejm and an outspoken hierarchy, its moral influence over the population was maintained. As a result it was able to establish for itself a role and influence unique in eastern Europe – and uncommon in western Europe. The election of the Polish Cardinal Woytila as Pope in October 1978 provided international confirmation of the vitality and standing of Polish Catholicism.

By 1980 the regimes in eastern Europe had come to terms with organised religion. Permitted to celebrate and to solemnise births, marriages and deaths, the churches did not interfere in political matters. The relationship was however uneasy, and religion remained an ideological and moral competitor with communism. The number of communicants grew, congregations increased and Christian belief among the young appeared to be strong. Moreover, on certain issues the borderline between belief and politics could be blurred. Most notable of all was the part played by the Catholic Church in Poland where during the crisis of martial law the government accepted the Church's freedom to make political pronouncements and criticisms of martial law and welcomed the appeals for calm made by the Polish primate. As interesting was the less spectacular but increasing part played by the Protestant Church in the neighbouring DDR. There the moral issue of nuclear disarmament was taken up in 1981 by the Church only to arouse a vigorous reaction by the state which condemned the Church for weakening the country's spirit of self-defence by campaigning for nuclear disarmament in both western and eastern central Europe.

Further reading

1. *General works:*
Brzezinski, Z.K., *The Soviet Bloc: Unity and Conflict* (Harvard University Press, 1967).
Fejto, F., *A History of the People's Democracies. Eastern Europe Since Stalin* (Penguin, 1974).
Fischer-Galati, S. (ed.), *The Communist Parties of Eastern Europe* (Columbia University Press, 1979).
Rakowska-Harmstone, T., and Gyorgy, A. (eds), *Communism in Eastern Europe* (Indiana. University Press, 1979).
Rubinstein, A.Z., *Communist Political Systems* (Prentice-Hall, 1966).
Sik, O., *The Communist Power System* (Praeger, 1981).

Silnitsky, F., and Silnitsky, L., and Reyman, K. (eds), *Communism and Eastern Europe* (Harvester Press, 1979).

2. *Crises:*
Ascherson, A., *The Polish August* (Penguin, 1981).
Baring, A., *Uprising in East Germany, June 17 1953* (Cornell University Press, 1972).
Golan, G., *The Czechoslovak Reform Movement 1962–8* (Cambridge University Press, 1971).
Kusin, V.V., *Political Grouping in the Czechoslovak Reform Movement* (Macmillan, 1972).
Ulc, O., *Politics in Czechoslovakia* (W.H. Freeman, 1975).
Zinner, P.E., *Revolution in Hungary* (Columbia University Press, 1962).

3. *Biographies:*
Auty, P., *Tito*, 2nd edn (Penguin, 1980).
Bethell, N., *Gomulka*, 2nd edn (Longman, 1972).
Catchlove, D., *Romania's Ceausescu*, (Abacus Press, 1972).
Djilas, M., *Tito* (Weidenfeld & Nicolson, 1981).
Lippmann, H., *Honecker and the New Politics of Europe* (Angus & Robertson, 1973).
Stern, C., *Ulbricht* (Pall Mall Press, 1965).

4. *Critical writings emanating from eastern Europe:*
Committee to Defend Czechoslovak Socialists, *Voices of Czechoslovak Socialists* (1976).
Djilas, M., *The New Class* (Allen & Unwin, 1957).
Konrad, G., and Szelenyi, I., *The Intellectuals on the Road to Class Power* (Harvester Press, 1979).
Rakovski, M. (pseud.), *Towards an Eastern European Marxism* (Allison & Busby, 1978).

4

THE COMMUNIST ECONOMIC SYSTEM

Map 3   Mineral resources in eastern Europe.

The elaboration of such an all-pervasive and sophisticated political system was closely intertwined with the transformation of the economic and social structure of the region. If political power came as the result of a revo-lution, it was to usher in a further upheaval. Whatever Marx envisaged when he wrote *Capital* and predicted that political change would follow a prior economic evolution, eastern European communists belonged to the tradition of Stalinist modification of Marxism–Leninism, then called Marxism–Leninism–Stalinism. Political power was to sponsor and control industrialisation. The trail blazed in the USSR was followed in eastern Europe, giving added confirmation to the thesis that communists were committed exponents of developmental economics. Totalitarian power permitted the mobilisation of all available resources for the objective of rapid economic growth (see Table 4.1). It was this that explained the fascination of many Third World countries with the communist system.

Future economic policy in eastern Europe was under discussion long before the end of the war. Representatives of the governments-in-exile, scholars and other interested parties shared a general agreement that structural reform of their economies required immediate attention. The heavy rural overpopulation had to be reduced to permit economic and social progress, for overpopulation led to rural poverty, as true in the most advanced states of the area – Czechoslovakia and the future Soviet occu-pation zone of Germany – as it was for the most backward – Romania, Bulgaria and Yugoslavia. The key was industrial development that would provide jobs, decant population from the land, stimulate the economy by providing a new consumer market for the products of industry and agriculture and permit the growth of a more balanced society. Further land reform was essential. Land had been partly redistributed after 1918, but only in Bulgaria, Bohemia and parts of Yugoslavia did small peasant farmers predominate. Only in Hungary had the pre-1914 system of large landed estates survived more or less intact, but such great land-holdings were also a feature of agriculture in Romania and Poland, despite land reform there. Land redistribution had not led to more efficient exploit-ation of the land, for yields on peasant farms were low. Their small size precluded adequate investment and the instinctive attitudes of peasants led them to shun the sale of farm products except to meet taxation demands or to provide money to buy the small number of essential products they were unable to make for themselves. Peasant attitudes changed slowly, and the impact of market relationships had been rela-tively small. The privations of war may even have confirmed traditional peasant self-sufficiency and suspicion of the commercial nexus. As opinion was agreed that the development of industry was a priority and that the reserve and isolation of peasant agriculture had to be broken down, post-war eastern Europe would have been subjected to a radical pro-gramme of economic and social change irrespective of the form of govern-ment that emerged.

Table 4.1   Annual percentage increases in net material product (for Yugoslavia in gross national product): averages for the periods indicated

	1949–54	1956–63	1950–67	1963–73	1966–70	1974	1971–5	1976	1978	1979	1976–80
Bulgaria	10.4		8.0		8.7		7.9				6.2
Czechoslovakia	8.0		5.2		6.9		5.7				3.7
DDR			6.1		5.2		5.4				4.1
Hungary	8.0		5.8		6.8		6.3				3.2
Poland	9.0		6.7		6.0		9.8				1.6
Romania	13.9		8.3		7.7		11.3				7.1
Yugoslavia		9.6		5.9		8.5		3.9	6.9	7.0	

Pre-communist governmental economic policies

There was general agreement that the key to success lay in planning and direct involvement of governments. It was assumed to be an easier process than proved to be the case. This view reflected many of the realities of eastern Europe. By 1939 governments had been extensively involved in economic matters. That was not merely true of Nazi Germany, where before 1939 government had been heavily involved in economic policy and had created an advanced engineering capacity in the eastern part of the country, much expanded during the war. There was everywhere a deep-rooted tradition of governmental involvement in economics, and state monopolies were commonplace before 1939. Among items of consumption the sale of salt, matches, tobacco and alcohol were often state monopolies while the import and export of various products were also controlled by the state. In Czechoslovakia there was state control of the grain trade, in Hungary grain, wool and dairy products were controlled, while in Poland, Romania and Yugoslavia trade in wheat was a state monopoly, as was that in plums in Yugoslavia. The government of the latter controlled the export of most other agricultural products. The monopolies on cereal exports had extended also to the internal marketing of grains. In addition the Polish government had fixed wholesale and retail prices for meat, milk, lard, and pork, while milk-marketing schemes operated in Czechoslovakia and Hungary. These examples were compounded by governmental involvement in industrial activity. Czechoslovakia and Germany apart, the region had little private, indigenous industry and few capitalist entrepreneurs. The role of native entrepreneur was played to a large extent by Jews and Germans; anti-Jewish feeling was characteristic of the area. Shortages of capital and skills had sucked in foreigners who dominated economic life. Over two-thirds of the share capital of Yugoslav mining companies and 40 per cent of that in railways was foreign-owned. The Romanian oil industry, one of the most important economic resources of the area, was controlled before 1939 by foreign capital, 40 per cent of which was Anglo-Dutch, 16½ per cent French and 12½ per cent American. It was not until 1938 that a Romanian-controlled company had been set up, and that was a state company. Indeed, concerned at the lack of industrial growth and alarmed by the domination of foreigners, the Romanian government decided in 1938 that a state planning system was essential. A similar decision had been reached by the Polish government which from 1936 had sponsored an ambitious state plan that sought to bring into existence a Central Industrial Region, regarded as a key factor in the complete reorganisation of the Polish economy. On the eve of war in 1939 the government was involved in planning a fifteen-year programme covering every aspect of national life. This network of market controls and traditions of governmental intervention had been expanded during the war under German occupation or intervention. Much of the industrial capacity of the area had been forcibly purchased by German companies and integrated into the Nazi war economy. The unscrambling of this would inevitably involve governments and would require of them a major role in future economic policy.

It was reasonably certain therefore that governments committed to industrial development and to the concept of state planning would come to power throughout the region. Economic issues would be at the heart of their preoccupations. But the advent to power of communist governments added another dimension to these economic issues. No other political movements were as committed to such a clearly economic conception of society as were the communists. The central role allotted to economic development in the writings of Marx had been given specific shape by the experiences of the USSR, and by 1945 there was a readily identifiable economic policy that was particularly communist and specifically Soviet in character. It was associated with Stalin. Soviet resistance to Nazi invasion and eventual victory gave the USSR an allure that attracted many all over the world. Not only committed communists believed victory to be the legitimising proof of the system. In the immediate post-war years Soviet experience with planning and the total devotion of resources to a centrally conceived and regularised development of the productive forces of society were attractive to many who rejected the failures of pre-war society and compared the record of the capitalist world with that of the communist USSR – to the latter's advantage. For many eastern Europeans the attractions were all the greater because of the comparisons that could be made between the backward, agrarian economy of Russia in 1918 and of eastern Europe in 1945. The Soviet programme had resulted in the creation of a powerful industrialised economy. It appealed to undeveloped states, to which category all except the future DDR and Czechoslovakia belonged. The example of the USSR's escape from economic backwardness was stressed by the new communist leaders. It was a theme that coupled nationalism with loyalty to the Soviet system: by following the path already charted by the USSR other states would emulate its example. and never again suffer occupation and exploitation. Reason of state was reinforced by the promise of higher living standards. The poverty of the pre-war years and the grinding deprivation of the war were rejected as avoidable by hard work and a government devoted to the common good of all citizens. Such aims were indeed specifically enshrined in the Soviet constitution of 1936. The new communist regimes promised government devoted to economic growth and egalitarian social policies, that is, to national development and future greatness.

Nationalisation, early communist planning and economic relations with the USSR to 1955

The first experiments in government-directed planning began once the fighting stopped and pre-dated the communist achievement of total power. Under the impact of immediate post-war problems and of the need for rapid recovery short-term economic plans were launched: in Yugoslavia in December 1945, in Poland in September 1946, in Bulgaria, Hungary and the Soviet zone of Germany in 1947. Longer-term plans came later, after the establishment of fully fledged communist governments. Once more Yugoslavia led the way with the introduction of a Five-year Plan in 1947. In Bulgaria and Czechoslovakia they came in 1949, in Hungary and Poland in 1950 and in Romania and the German Democratic Republic in 1951. The all-important prerequisite of a nationalised economy had been established beforehand. In Yugoslavia, for example, the process began *de facto* in November 1944 and was formally completed by April 1948. In Czechoslovakia it stretched from October 1945 until January 1949 while in Romania the nationalisation law was passed in June 1948. Interestingly, there remained a significant private sector in the economy of the DDR until the late 1950s, and even in 1971 900,000 workers and employees were recorded as working in the private and semi-nationalised sectors of the economy. The objective of full nationalisation was announced only in 1972. Apart from large-scale industry, small-scale handicraft production by skilled craftsmen in areas such as carpentry, plumbing and repair shops came under pressure. There were, however, significant differences between states. In Yugoslavia this sector of the economy was largely untouched and began modestly to grow after 1951. Elsewhere its turn came after the successful completion of nationalisation of large-scale industry: in Poland measures of control were introduced between 1949 and 1953, while in Bulgaria this sector was virtually destroyed by 1951 and pressure was increasing in Romania too. The case of Hungary was somewhat different. The attack on the handicraft sector was maintained until 1953, after which it eased and by 1955 the total number of those employed in this sector returned to the levels of 1948.

The new planning systems were modelled on their Soviet counterpart. The 'market' system of the capitalist world was rejected as unscientific, wasteful and geared to the gratification of private interest at public expense. In its place was substituted a planned, scientific approach to all aspects of the nation's economic life. The state sought to design an integrated plan to meet the goals specified by the political authorities. Government stipulated the objectives or 'targets', and the way in which they were to be achieved was the task of the planners. There was thus produced a command economy, designed to respond to instructions from the top and to obey the orders of those in political control. Power and authority were removed from the individual production unit, known as the 'enterprise'. This had a certain rationale in the first, uncertain days of the new regimes. With relatively small followings of reliable supporters and given the miniscule number of reliable specialists available, it made sense not to allow too much initiative to men drawn overwhelmingly from the ranks of supporters of the old system.

The implications of this approach for the whole structure of national economic life were profound. It required the complete re-casting of all the traditional mechanisms of economic control and the replacement of established ideas of assessing value and worth. Along with this went concomitant difficulties over the pricing of goods, assessment of wages, distribution policies both wholesale and retail, decisions as to the nature of the product mix, the mobilisation of capital and the creation of investable wealth by society, or 'accumulation'. To succeed, a totally controlled economy was required. This had evolved in the USSR while it had been hermetically sealed from the outside world. Its vast geographical area, replete with raw materials and embracing every type of agricultural product apart from the truly tropical, allowed the USSR to operate a closed, autarkic economy, independent of the world and largely free from outside influences and pressures. There were communists who recognised from the start that it was improbable that the countries of eastern Europe could follow the same path. During Stalin's lifetime it was dangerous to voice such suspicions. Those who did suffered for their temerity. Attempts at regional co-operation, such as that proposed between Yugoslavia and Bulgaria in 1947, were firmly squashed by the USSR. Each state was to follow the sole legitimate example of the path to socialism and to create a carbon copy of the Soviet autarkic model.

In fact, it is doubtful whether autarky in Poland or Hungary was ever much more than a myth, and the short period before the death of Stalin in 1953 hardly gave time for it to be fully elaborated anywhere. Moreover, given the massive Soviet penetration and exploitation of the economies of the area until 1953 it is debatable whether national autarky was the Soviet objective. For the USSR took full advantage of its position. Direct reparations payments from its former enemies were a heavy burden. They gave it a virtual mortgage on Romanian oil until 1955. Reparations payments by Hungary did not end until 1953. In addition there were the expenses of Soviet occupation troops. Such direct claims were supplemented by the establishment of joint companies, in which the Soviet share took the form of confiscated German assets. In this way strong Soviet influence was exerted, especially in the economy of Romania but also in those of Hungary and Bulgaria. Native raw materials such as Romanian oil, Hungarian bauxite and various Bulgarian minerals passed under indirect Soviet control, as did air transport and the navigation of the Danube. Not only former enemies were exploited. In 1947 joint companies were established with Yugoslavia for Danube shipping and civil air transport. They were liquidated in 1949. As for Poland, her major asset was coal resulting from the aquisition of Silesia from Germany. The USSR secured guaranteed quantities of this at specified prices far below those obtaining on the world markets in return for surrendering to Poland Soviet claims to erstwhile German assets. Uranium production in Czechoslovakia was brought under the auspices of another joint company. The worst plight of all was that of the Soviet-occupied zone of Germany which, as the principal former belligerent, suffered from extensive Soviet seizures and demands for foods and foodstuffs as reparations that continued until 1953. In addition there were the heavy costs of the occupation troops. Paradoxically it was the creation of a form of joint company that rescued the economy from the worst effects of Soviet occupation. *Sowjetische Aktiengesellschaften*, or SAG, were set up using German plant and techniques and these were instrumental in putting an end to the indiscriminate seizure and arbitrary and uncontrolled stripping and removal of plant by Soviet officials which characterised 1945 and early 1946. By the end of the year they covered about one-half of all industrial production in the Soviet zone.

These various direct and indirect economic pressures came gradually to an end in the mid-1950s. Apart from those engaged in mining uranium, joint companies, including SAG, were wound up after September 1954, though under terms that required the Soviet share be purchased. This arrangement was cancelled and the assets transferred free of charge after the troubles in Hungary and Poland in 1956. In November 1956 unrest in Poland led to the cancelling of the coal agreement and debts of 525 million dollars owed by Poland to the USSR were cancelled in partial recompense for the estimated 900-million-dollar profits made by the USSR from coal deliveries. Finally, the acceptance in 1959 of the principle of support costs for Soviet troops stationed in the DDR placed the relations between the various countries of the region and the USSR on a new footing and freed their internal economies from a considerable incubus of Soviet control.

The industrialisation drive

Despite these difficulties for governments that aimed at a rapid rate of industrial development, the first decade of state planning was distinctly encouraging. Throughout the area strong industrial sectors emerged. The state planning organisations subordinated every aspect of their national economies to the common, politically decided objective of industrial growth: investment, money supply, wages, employment policies, the provision of consumer goods, welfare expenditure were all linked to the overriding purpose. Most crucial of all were the twin components of investment and labour. The industrial advance was fuelled by heavy investment in plant and equipment and by the provision of a steady flow of labour displaced from the land. The sheer volume of the momentum was impressive. Under the Polish Six-year Plan between 1949 and 1955 average annual investment in industry amounted to 32.6 per cent of the national income and there was a 9.2 per cent yearly increase in employment in industry. In Romania between 1961 and 1965 annual investment amounted to 24.9 per cent of income, a figure that rose to between 30 and 32 per cent in the plan for 1971–5. These figures were not exceptional. The percentage of the economically active workforce engaged in industry rose steadily as did the contribution of the industrial sector to the total gross national product in each state. Particular attention was paid to the establishment of heavy metallurgical industries and the development of mining. Enormous steel-making complexes were built: at Stalinvaros, later renamed Dunaujvaros, in Hungary, Nowa Huta in Poland, Kremikowzi in Bulgaria and, somewhat later, at Galati in Romania. Steel manufacture and coal production were flaunted as acknowledged indicators of economic achievement. Alongside these went a massive expansion of electrical power production (see Table 4.2) and of engineering and machine manufacturing capacity. The east European countries, especially Czechoslovakia and the DDR, became major producers. States such as Romania and Bulgaria became significant manufacturers of products that they had imported before 1945. Romania indeed was to acquire the most diverse engineering capacity of any of the east European states and produced by the end of the 1970s a wider range of engineering products than any of its neighbours apart from the USSR. After 1960 the emphasis began slowly to change as new interest was shown in chemicals and electronics and the economy of the area moved away from the initial concentration on the extractive and smelting industries to newer, technologically based ones. During the 1970s attentions switched further and oil and gas production were given priority.

The dimensions of these developments may have been somewhat exaggerated by the statistical system adopted. Unlike that used in the West, the communist system omitted a large part of the activities of the service sector from its measurement of the national product. The overall effect was somewhat to inflate apparent output because of the tendency to take repeated account of the same items at different points of the production process. Yet after making allowance for this, a considerable rate of growth in industrial production was achieved. Moreover, the use of gross material product as the basis for statistical analysis reflected the technique of planning adopted. Modelled on the system that evolved in the USSR during the 1930s, it was known as the 'material-balance' system. It relied upon a series of calculations of the quantifiable material inputs required for a given volume of output. Such balances cover raw materials, labour, capital, working capital, energy supplies and all other necessary inputs. These demands were then reconciled with one another

Table 4.2 Industrial production of eastern European countries, excluding Yugoslavia: electricity (in MWh), coal and lignite (millions of tons), pig iron (millions of tons) (selected years)

	1937	1949	1954	1960	1965	1970	1974	1975	1978	1980
Electricity:										
Bulgaria	0.2	0.6	1.8	4.7	10.2	19.5		25.2		34.8
Czechoslovakia	4.0	7.5	13.5	24.5	34.2	45.2		59.3		74.1
DDR	1.0	14.5	24.2	40.3	53.6	67.8		84.5		98.8
Hungary		2.0	4.8	7.6	11.2	14.6		20.5		23.9
Poland	3.4*	7.5	15.4	29.3	43.8	64.5		97.2		121.9
Romania		1.5	3.7	7.6	17.2	35.1		53.7		67.5
UK	25.7†	50.6	74.2	121.4	178.2	228.9		252.0		281.5
Coal and lignite:										
Bulgaria	1.8	4.1	8.6	17.1	26.3	29.2		27.8		30.2
Czechoslovakia	35.0	41.3	57.6	84.6	101.0	105.7		114.4		123.1
DDR		112.9	181.9	225.5	251.3	260.6		247.2		258.0
Hungary	8.9	10.6	21.5	26.5	31.4	27.8		24.9		25.7
Poland	36.3*	75.3	97.5	104.4	141.6	172.9		211.5		230.0
Romania		2.4	5.5	8.2	12.1	20.5		27.1		35.2
UK	227.0†	215.2	224.1	194.7	188.6	149.5		130.8		123.6‡
Pig iron:										
Bulgaria					0.7	1.2	1.5		1.6	
Czechoslovakia	1.7	1.5	2.8	4.7	5.9	7.5	8.9		10.3	
DDR		1.6	1.3	2.0	2.3	2.0	2.3		3.0	
Hungary	0.4	0.2	0.7	1.2	1.6	1.8	2.3		2.4	
Poland	0.9*	1.2	2.7	4.6	5.8	7.3	8.2		11.6	
Romania		0.2	0.4	1.0	2.0	4.2			8.3	
UK	6.8†	9.5	11.9	15.8	17.5	17.7	13.9		11.8	

* 1937 frontiers.
† Figure for 1938.
‡ Figure for 1978.

and with the overall planning targets set by the political authorities so that an overall balance of all the resources available set against the targets required was achieved. The resulting national balance sheet constituted the national plan. Such plans were usually cast for a period of five years and broken down into annual plans, which enabled a more precise matching of resources to objectives on a running basis within the overall long-term conception. At first this method of planning was rather rough-and-ready, but with the passage of time and the acquisition of experience it was possible to devise elaborate tables of required inputs in all their diversity for every aspect of national economic life and to use these tables as the basis for assessment and decision.

Shortcomings of the communist planning system

Whatever the theoretical merits of this system of planning there were considerable practical problems. These were made worse by the excessive optimism of governments that continually demanded improved performance and higher rates of development. This resulted in a lack of elasticity in planning and in continual revisions of the targets within the Five-year Plans. The case of Poland during the 1950s and 1960s was not untypical. The Six-year Plan was revised upward in July 1950 and downward in March 1954; the Five-year Plan of 1956–60 was revised upward in October 1958; the Five-year Plan of 1961–5 was revised upward in June 1959, June 1960 and February 1963, and downward in November 1963; and the 1965–70 plan was revised upward in April 1969. The first Yugoslav Five-year Plan was never really completed and was followed after 1951 by *ad hoc* yearly plans until the 1957 Five-year Plan. That was completed in four years, but the following plan collapsed in 1962 after which the system was revised so that planning did little more than identify problem areas needing priority in investment. Such changes reflected the difficulties and aspirations of the planners. In the DDR, whose growth record and sustained levels of achievement were probably the best in eastern Europe, the planning process was even more chaotic and for considerable periods there were no long-term plans. Between 1951 and 1955 there were several revisions in the Five-year Plan. That due to come into operation in 1956 was one and a half years late and ended after six months, while the new Six-year Plan to run from 1959 to 1965 was admitted to be a failure in 1961 and was abandoned in 1962. There was a temporary transitional plan in 1963 in preparation for another Six-year Plan to run from 1964 to 1970. The latter was not presented until 1966.

The continual striving for the maximum degree of tautness and pressure for optimisation of development left little room for manoeuvre. There were few reserves of resources for the correction of miscalculations or to make inevitable adjustments. As a consequence, managers responsible for the achieving of the planned targets evolved their own techniques for supplementing the planning process, in ways that sometimes ran directly counter to the fundamentals of the system. Perhaps the best-known example of the lack of elasticity in the centralised planned economy was the frequency of 'bottlenecks' in the supply of inputs. Shortages were not merely a feature of the everyday life of the individual consumer: they were also apparent in all aspects of the industrial process. They led to the phenomenon of large-scale stockpiling as managers tried to build up and maintain a stock of precious raw materials. Since virtually everything might suddenly become hard to obtain, enterprises built up and kept far larger stocks than did their capitalist counterparts. Suspicious that the supply of inputs crucial in the expansion of the enterprise or its fulfilment of its quota might stop when most required, enterprises also maintained over-large supplies of labour on their payrolls. As expansion relied on the input of labour and capital, it made sense for the individual enterprise to seek to secure as large a share as possible of the one component that it could influence. The result was a heavily labour-intensive industrial sector with rather low productivity per head. Similarly the stock piling of material inputs led to a large proportion of working capital being tied up unproductively. In the first decade of communist planning the absence of any system of value assessment of economic performance rendered the assessment of economic potential wasted extremely difficult. The performance of the production unit was based on physical output, not on the unit cost of production. The individual enterprise was required to produce goods in accordance with the plan at the intervals therein specified. It was not required to take account of distribution, inputs or costs. It was a production unit, not a business concern.

Eastern European industry was notoriously extravagant in its use of materials such as steel or fuel. Products were physically heavier than their Western equivalents and consumed substantially more energy in their manufacture, reflecting the criteria in plan targets defined in terms of total materials used and the weight of ensuing output. Even the most efficient and productive economies in Czechoslovakia and the DDR compared unfavourably. In 1978, for example, per capita fuel consumption in the DDR was 40 per cent above the EEC average and as late as 1981, after strenuous efforts, it was still 15 per cent above the equivalent figure for the Federal Republic of Germany. In 1973 the Prague Academy of Sciences computed the steel consumption of Czechoslovak industry as nearly double that of Western industrialised economies. The classic Soviet model viewed investment capital and other 'producer goods' as investment, which was the responsibility of the state and was allocated without charge to the enterprise, whether agricultural, industrial or social, and there was consequently little or no incentive to economise. Continual exhortation by national leaders bore witness to the importance of the problem. Moreover, the recasting of the tables of balances used by the planners caused more problems. The more static the system the easier planning on the basis of material-balancing became. Innovation required the reassessment not only of the tables for the individual economic activity directly concerned, but for all those other products and activities indirectly affected. The sheer volume of recalculation was enormous, for overall planning involved total interdependence. No sooner had calculations been completed than innovation demanded reappraisal.

The tendency to hoard and to shun change was reinforced by the assumptions all too easily made by the political authorities that failure was the result of deliberate intent. At the core of Stalinist economic policy was the belief that a man is capable of any achievement provided he has the will to succeed. This 'can-do' philosophy was encapsulated in the view that man is the master of his own destiny and is actively constructing a new way of life. In this atmosphere failure to meet planned targets or demur from the aspirations of the planners was all too easily seen as lack of commitment or, worse, as deliberate sabotage, a familiar charge against Soviet management during the 1930s. The prudent sought to buttress their position by ensuring in advance an adequate supply of the necessary inputs and by representing their enterprise in as poor a light as was consonant with safety in order to secure modest output targets. These procedures were made doubly attractive since they offered the maximum opportunities to enhance the margin by which planned targets could be exceeded, with large bonuses to management and workers alike. For all, especially during the first decade of industrialisation, there was the spur of coercion.

The new communist governments followed the path already charted by the USSR. Actual or potential opponents of the new system were drawn into the drive to industrialise. During the 1950s they were enrolled as compulsory labour. In Poland, for example, prison labour was used in coal-mines until October 1956, while in Romania the short-lived Black Sea–Danube canal project was excavated by gangs of political prisoners and the development of the reed beds of the Danube delta as raw material for cellulose manufacture relied on a steady stream of forced labour. In Yugoslavia forced labour worked on the metalling of the Zagreb to Belgrade highway and built President Tito's summer villa on the island of Brioni. At times of economic difficulty the tendency to draft available manpower reasserted itself. Polish army recruits were reported drafted into coal-mines in September 1981. In both Poland and Czechoslovakia military labour units were permanently created to provide cheap manpower in mines, public works projects and for construction, and students were regularly recruited to help with the harvest in the DDR during the 1950s.

Collectivisation of agriculture and farm policy: the first phase
At the heart of the industrialisation process lay the total mobilisation of the nation's resources. Agriculture and private consumption bore the brunt. As in the USSR, rigid measures were taken against both as the resources for investment were diverted to industry. It is arguable that whatever form of government had been established major peasant opposition would have occurred. Changes of the dimensions necessary could not be accomplished without disruption of peasant life-styles or the inevitable transformation of the countryside. The lessons of the collectivisation drive in the USSR led communists to take this for granted. They possessed the necessary ideological determination and they perfectly appreciated that it was only by exploiting the agrarian sector that the resources necessary for industrial growth could be assembled. That there was an overriding commitment to the total recasting of traditional peasant society and the eradication of what was seen as backwardness, did not however mean that they were impervious to the lessons of Soviet experience. The relatively less disruptive impact of the collectivisation drive in eastern Europe when compared to the 1930s in the USSR was a tribute to this, even if there were significant regional diversities.

In the immediate aftermath of the war population exchanges and territorial redistributions in the region, coupled with the accepted political necessity to equalise land-holding, led to substantial expropriation and redistribution of land – especially in Czechoslovakia, Poland and Hungary. The total amount redistributed fell below the totals expropriated. In Hungary it amounted to 1,874,000 hectares (about 4,631,000 acres) out of 3,222,000 (about 8,000,000 acres), in Poland to 5,995,000 (about 14,814,000 acres) from 13,868,000 (about 34,268,000 acres) and in Czechoslovakia to 1,700,000 (about 4,201,000 acres) from 4,500,000 (about 11,120,000 acres). The record in Romania, Bulgaria and Yugoslavia was different. Far less land was expropriated in these countries relative to their size and most of it was redistributed: 73 per cent in Romania, 72 per cent in Bulgaria and 51 per cent in Yugoslavia. The balance was kept in state hands and formed the nucleus of state farms, state forests and model animal-breeding or experimental establishments. The overall effect was to create throughout the region a pattern of small-scale peasant agriculture. By 1949 the typical holding was of less than 2 hectares (about 5 acres) and the overwhelming majority were of less than 5 (about 12½ acres), and together accounted for over 70 per cent of all private farms. The worst example of miniscule holdings was Hungary, where over 68 per cent of all private holdings were less than 2 hectares in extent. Only in Poland, Bulgaria and Yugoslavia was there a significant sector of so-called 'middle' peasant holdings of between 5 and 10 hectares (about 25 acres). The land redistribution did not result in a real amelioration of the poverty of the peasant populations. That required major structural and organisational changes. The pressures on the agricultural sector to produce the capital and labour required for industry was therefore pressure applied to a stratum of society that already suffered from low living standards. Its effects in the short term could not but depress those living standards even more.

The pattern for collectivisation in the USSR was copied in eastern Europe. The first moves were made against the small minority of large private peasant proprietors. These were put under progressively greater financial pressures. Grain collection quotas and prices were steeply graded and loaded against larger holdings. For example, in Hungary from 1949 special exactions were laid on holdings over 10 hectares while in Czechoslovakia before 1948 three categories of prices had been fixed for grain, the lowest being paid to those peasants holding more than 50 hectares (about 124 acres). Land tax too was steeply graded and required the larger holdings to pay substantially more, as was the case in Czechoslovakia after 1948, in Poland after 1951 and in Yugoslavia until 1951. Credit was stringently restricted and the interest rates charged discriminated against larger holdings. The overall effect was to depress initiative and to induce lethargy among potentially the most productive sectors of agriculture, for the small holdings could not possibly hope to produce large surpluses for the market. Output of grain especially remained depressed below its pre-war level.

As in the USSR, the theoretical objective remained total state control of all land and the creation of state farms in which peasants would occupy the same position as workers in industry, that of salaried employees. It was however clear that the same sense of identity between peasant and holding and the same resistance to being reduced to the position of agricultural labourer which had existed in the USSR was present in eastern Europe. Accordingly, there too the effective unit of production became the collective farm, known usually as a co-operative farm. Theoretically composed of participating independent producers who had pooled their land, implements and livestock to work together, their members derived their incomes from their share in the work of the enterprise during the year. The income of the co-operative was divided in accordance with the total number of work-days performed by its members.

The process began in earnest in about 1950, though the pace varied from country to country. Even in Yugoslavia the drive to collectivise did not begin until 1949, that is, after the break with Cominform and at approximately the same time as elsewhere. It was pursued with greater vigour and ruthlessness in Bulgaria than in any other country, with consequences strikingly similar to those in the USSR during the 1930s. There were steep falls in output, no increase in productivity and an enormous fall in the livestock population. However, the process was completed earlier there than elsewhere. In Romania collectivisation only got underway in 1952 and it was not until 1957 that the pace really quickened. It was effectively completed in 1962. Armed force was used to break resistance, and some 80,000 peasants were sent for trial. Many were used as forced labour on industrial projects. As a concession, peasants joining collectives were permitted to retain their livestock. In Hungary the process was virtually stopped as a result of the events of 1956 and there was a drift away from the collectives already formed. However, in 1958 the process was begun again and was completed by spring 1961. During the second period much less reliance was placed on coercion and attempts at persuasion made. Peasants retained the theoretical ownership of the land they brought into the collective and a part of its income was paid out to members as a form of rent, varying in accordance with the amount of land originally brought into the collective. In the DDR the first collectives were set up in 1952. Progress was relatively slow, and by 1959 only about 45 per cent of agricultural land had been incorporated. It was stepped up between January and April 1960 when very heavy pressure was brought to bear on the remaining private farmers, many of whom fled to the Federal Republic. By May 1960 about 85 per cent of agricultural land was embodied in collectives. The two countries where collectivisation was not pursued were Poland and Yugoslavia. The effect was to create in both a distinctly different pattern of agriculture and national economy. In Yugoslavia, the collectivisation drive begun in 1949 was reversed in March 1953 when the withdrawal of peasants from collectives was legalised. The system promptly collapsed. In Poland collectivisation was always slow. By 1955 about 13½ per cent of arable land was in state farms and only just over 9 per cent in collectives. Here too the consequence of political upheaval was a major reversal of policy. The Gomulka government agreed to allow peasants to leave collectives and halted the extension of state farms. This led to the disappearance of collectivised agriculture. By 1967, although the area covered by state farms had not changed, that comprising collectives had fallen to 1 per cent of the total. However, there was little doubt that collectivisation remained the goal, and during the 1970s the amount of land in state hands steadily increased. An ageing peasant population was willing to surrender its holdings as the young left the land to work in the cities and the state offered pensions in return for title deeds. By 1980 about 31 per cent of the total arable land of the country was in state or collective farms, though they only accounted for 21½ per cent of total farm yields.

Whether agriculture was collectivised or remained in private hands the state still needed to devise means to exploit it to secure capital for industrial investment. This was at first achieved by demanding compulsory deliveries to state purchasing bodies at virtual give-away prices. These were then resold more expensively to consumers. They were phased out during the 1950s in most of the region. In Romania, for example, compulsory deliveries were ended in January 1957 for all foodstuffs except meat, and they began to disappear elsewhere. The system lasted longest in Poland, where quota deliveries of grain, meat and potatoes were not ended until 1972. The system was replaced by a more sophisticated manipulation of prices the purpose of which was to keep agricultural prices low and industrial ones high, thus creating an agrarian prices scissors. Agricultural produce was also a crucial element in eastern European exports. The imports of modern machinery and high technology and the interest payments on hard currency loans were financed in large part by agricultural exports. Bulgaria succeeded in building a close and profitable trade with the USSR, supplying by 1980 95 per cent of Soviet cigarette imports, half its tobacco requirements and half its vegetables. Specialising in market gardening and in growing tomatoes, peppers, apples, cherries and grapes, Bulgarian agriculture came to enjoy a considerable international renown. A similar part was played by the agricultural exports of Poland, Hungary and Romania. Only the DDR and Czechoslovakia have been free from a significant degree of dependence on such items.

Consumption and taxation policies

Control of private consumption in the interests of economic growth was a fundamental part of the system. By removing demand from the economy and by the introduction of a permanent prices and incomes policy it became possible to plan consumption. Instead of consumer preferences the scale of values of the bureaucracy governed the supply of consumer goods. Wages did not reflect the position, nor scarcity or abundance of labour. As the monopoly employer the state was able to determine wage rates in accordance with the overall objectives set by government. As for prices, these too were removed from the interplay of supply and demand and were fixed centrally, reflecting the priorities and desires of the planners. The key elements in the control mechanism were the transfer tax and turnover tax. The former, levied on goods as they left the producer, provided the state with part of its capital accumulation by adding a margin to the costs of production. It also created a spread between wages and the price of wholesale consumer goods. The second tax was the principal mechanism for balancing the centrally determined supply of consumer goods with the public's demand for them. It was accordingly highly differential in its incidence and varied, often in inverse proportion to actual consumer preference. Value and worth reflected decisions of the planners who then tried to adjust reality to their own conceptions by their control of the mechanisms of the economy. Apart from the obvious implications for the consumer, the system suffered from rigidity. There was an unwillingness to alter prices too frequently, reflecting the implications for the overall planning system of changes in the basic measures used. It reflected also the appreciation of the political implications of such changes. These were illustrated most graphically in Poland in the riots in Poznan in June 1956 and in Gdansk and elsewhere in December 1970, but similar public reactions to price increases occurred in Czechoslovakia, the DDR and elsewhere.

As a result of this caution, over the years prices increasingly lagged behind production and procurement costs. The price of foodstuffs in the shops remained static while prices paid to farmers increased, though insufficiently to match the rising costs of agricultural inputs; the charges made for public utilities fell increasingly behind the cost of providing the services. The system designed to squeeze consumption and release resources for investment seemed by 1970 to be evolving into one that subsidised a wide range of consumer goods whose prices were significantly depressed. Money wages rose quite sharply during the 1970s and retail prices frequently fell in real terms, with governments bearing a growing burden of subsidies. By the mid-1970s, for example, it was calculated that the prices in the DDR for gas, electricity, coal, bricks, wood, building stone and iron were being subsidised by the state at rates up to about 60 per cent of their cost to the consumer. The resultant pressures on supply were kept in check by deliberate restrictions, the visible sign of which were the long queues outside east European stores, and the acknowledged scarcity of many preferred items of consumption. These phenomena were the east European equivalent of inflation. Rocketing prices on the unrestricted or free markets, especially those where peasants traded the food products of their private plots, reflected the suppressed imbalance between supply and demand. So too did the burgeoning private savings bank accounts throughout the region. Between 1961 and 1969 such deposits in Romania increased elevenfold in value. In Poland per capita savings rose from 544 zloties in 1960 to 12,906 in 1979 when they amounted to a total of 456,632 million zloties, with a further 53,482 million tied up in housing deposits and 22,242 million in deposits on cars. The latter allowed their holders to secure allocation of a motor car by part payment of the purchase price, reflecting the concern of governments throughout the region to stimulate their subjects' appetite for the products of local manufacturing industry. Such efforts were necessary because of consumer resistance towards the often inferior quality of the goods on offer which were not attractive to an increasingly discriminating population. Within eastern Europe a distinct hierarchy developed. The best-quality goods were exported to the West for hard currencies, while the least saleable ones from the DDR and Czechoslovakia found a market in the USSR. The effect of wage increases without a price increase or a greater supply of consumer goods or quality control was to build up both personal savings accounts and stocks of sub-standard products, adding to the already high levels of unremunerative capital tied up in stockpiles.

Reforms in the system during the 1960s

By the later 1950s it was becoming apparent that the system had important deficiencies, as was recognised also in the USSR. By the early 1960s it was no longer possible to ignore the long time lags in building and commissioning new plant, the lack of concern by management for the economic use of raw materials and its hoarding of labour and resources, the steady diminution in the flow of labour from the countryside and actual shortages of skilled workers, felt most acutely in the DDR and Czechoslovakia. Each successive stage of economic and industrial development required equipment and processes of greater technical sophistication which ended the USSR's supply monopoly. Increasingly the states of eastern Europe looked west for their licences and equipment and east to the USSR for their raw materials – especially oil, natural gas and mineral ores. Their purchases on world markets required ever larger sums of convertible, or 'hard', foreign currencies. In eastern Europe as elsewhere the later stages of industrial growth demanded larger and larger capital investments and low labour productivity necessitated more and more investment to keep up the growth in output. As the demands for capital grew, the underfulfilment of investment projects, the long time lags and the over-ambitious spread of resources that tied up investment capital in unremunerative delay or waste or both was intolerable. The Polish Six-year Plan was a good example. At its conclusion in 1955 it had fallen far short of planned output capacity while absorbing the investment needed, and in every area there was a marked lag in the time required to bring new plant into operation as compared with that in western European states. Growth rates fell. In Czechoslovakia, for example, the average growth in national income fell from 9 per cent per annum between 1949 and 1953 to 2 per cent between 1961 and 1965, while in Poland erratic variations did not disguise a steady downward trend, which reached 2 per cent in 1962. Everywhere rates of growth in industrial production, construction and investment steadily declined. This sparked off a major debate throughout the region. It led to the partial reforms characteristic of the 1960s. Several broad strands of thought emerged. There were those who argued for major structural change in economic management and were increasingly critical of the performance of the command economy. Loebl, Selucky and Sik in Czechoslovakia, Kornai and Nyers in Hungary, Kunin and Milochevsky in Bulgaria argued for a recasting of the system, as did their Soviet contemporaries Nemchinov and Liberman. Best known and most influential of all were the members of the so-called 'Polish school' of economists who from the late 1950s mounted a sustained critique. Bobrowski, Brus, Kalecki, Lange and Lipinski influenced thinking throughout the region and their ideas played a major part in the restructuring of the command economy. Central to the process was the integration of elements of the traditional market economy into the new command system to ease the adjustment of national economic capacity to governmental targets and to permit a more satisfactory method of assessing performance. Many critics were supporters of the system, trained under it. Such technically skilled communist specialists were impatient of the earlier generation of planners who had learnt on the job, and believed that greater refinement and utilisation of modern computation and assessment would cure the system of its weaknesses. They were mathematically minded economists, computer specialists and constructors of economic models who argued that the application of modern technique was essential. By 1970 a third alternative had emerged, which sought to rejuvenate the economy by buying in Western expertise and technology. The investment capital necessary could be borrowed from capitalist states and paid back by exporting to the non-communist world the products of new, efficient industries. This approach avoided making many of the hard choices that the other two required, and was adopted by Poland and, to a lesser extent, Romania. However, it had its own dangers, as became apparent by 1981. The interplay of these groups whose aims and objectives differed but who were temporarily united in favour of change generated tensions and expectations during the second half of the 1960s.

Broadly speaking, the years between 1956 and 1972 fell into four periods. Weaknesses were acknowledged and analysed between 1956 and 1960. New ideas were cautiously introduced after the completion of full state control and lasted until about 1965. Between then and 1968 these experiments were expanded and applied on a wider scale, and from 1968 until about 1972 the experiments were either abandoned or incorporated into a new, improved centralisation. The Hungarian and Czechoslovak reform programmes favoured extensive and rapid change, those in the DDR, Poland, Romania and Bulgaria, as in the USSR, veered towards cautious evolution. But all changed, at varying speeds. Even in Czechoslovakia the tendencies to decentralisation, checked after 1968, re-emerged cautiously in 1978 and were extended to cover all industry in 1980.

Developments in Yugoslavia

Many of the new ideas characteristic of these reforms had first seen light in Yugoslavia, where adaptation of the communist economic system began and where it had a continuous history of evolution. Unlike the other eastern European states, Yugoslavia accepted the philosophy of reform and maintained the tempo of development throughout the 1970s. After the split with the USSR and the formal anathema of Cominform in 1948 the Yugoslavs became trail blazers in the search for a new style of socialist economy and society. This was a quite unexpected development. The Yugoslavs had previously been eager exponents of the Soviet-style economic structure, and had a model Stalinist economic organisation. The first state in the area to complete the nationalisation of industry, though not of handicrafts, its leaders were not initially shaken from their commitment. However, in 1950 major changes began. These modified the centralised command system by the encouragement of local enterprise initiative and by affording workers a wider degree of control by the establishment of workers' councils. In 1953 the principle of self-management was further developed when ownership of enterprises was transferred from the state to the employees, who were also made responsible for the means of production. Further changes in 1960–1 and 1966–7 added to the responsibilities of the councils and continued the progressive downgrading of the central planning apparatus. The dismantling of the command system of planning was accompanied by the growth of a system of indicative planning, whereby overall national objectives and major key developments were identified and the more backward regions given special encouragement in their economic expansion. Control over the national economy was maintained by economic and fiscal policies. The regional republics came to play an increasingly important role in economic matters. Under their auspices investment and banking organisations evolved, in which public and governmental bodies, enterprises, trade unions and other responsible organisations participated. In addition, during the 1960s there developed a system of chambers of the economy, to which all state-owned enterprises belong. These bodies at district, republic and federal level had the responsibility of helping to improve economic performance through better productivity rates, improved technology or better organisation. They also provided information of recent developments abroad and acted as co-ordinating and advisory bodies. They did not possess any powers of control or coercion, and their advice and help was accepted voluntarily by the member enterprises. The role and powers of the individual enterprises were greatly expanded and under the principles of self-management enshrined in the workers' councils by the end of the 1970s they played a major role in deciding development schemes and the appropriate investment, determining the product mix, and entering direct trading relationships with other enterprises and retailers as well as with foreign customers. Membership of the workers' councils was no sinecure. Real responsibility lay with them. They resolved problems of wage differentials and reconciled rates between different industries and areas. They decided wage rises and price increases and took account of the legitimate interest of society, the enterprise and workers as a group and as individuals.

The process of change and evolution that began in Yugoslavia was underway by the early 1960s but it did not reach its final shape until the later 1970s. It had however gone sufficiently far to exert an influence on events in eastern Europe in the 1960s. It foreshadowed similar developments elsewhere, though only in Hungary was a momentum like that in

Yugoslavia built up which carried the process through into the later 1970s, albeit with a period of consolidation between 1972 and 1978.

Reforms in the economic system elsewhere

Attention focused on the improved flow of data from enterprises, necessary to facilitate decision-taking and rational and effective planning. It was essential to detect and reallocate idle and scarce resources, to train managers in modern management techniques, to introduce modern stock control methods, and perhaps most important to devise satisfactory methods of assessing performance and plan fulfilment by individual enterprises. To question whether centralisation could ever hope to meet the challenges and to introduce measures of decentralisation, by which decision-taking would be devolved to a greater or lesser extent to enterprise management and local industry exposed to world conditions and required to conform itself to them, was the approach that lay behind many of the most dramatic developments in the region. It was the key to the economic thinking of the Czechoslovak reform movement between 1965 and 1968, whose chief architect, Sik, aimed, as he subsequently explained, gradually to dismantle the central command apparatus and gradually introduce market prices and competitive world pressures. It underlay too the quieter and more effective New Economic Mechanism in Hungary, and it has had a pervasive though indecisive influence in Poland. Similar principles had influence in the DDR, where the New Economic System operated between 1963 and 1967, and continued to affect the Economic System of Socialism between 1967 and 1970, paralleling almost exactly the Soviet pattern, for similar changes were implemented in the USSR between 1965 and 1970.

The basic feature of all these decentralising reforms was the steady reduction in specific economic dictates from above. Fewer 'commands' were issued and the directives with which enterprises were required to conform drastically reduced. There was a corresponding widening of the decision-making function of the enterprise. In addition, a greater role was allocated to market forces, to which enterprises were expected to respond. The responsibilities devolved to enterprises covered a wide range of hitherto centrally dictated objectives: enterprises were charged low rates of interest on capital borrowed for investment or as working capital, the rate varying in accordance with the profits and losses made. The introduction of the concept of profit and loss revolutionised the responsibilities of enterprise management, required for the first time to think of quality and sales of output rather than solely of quantity. Enterprises were made responsible for decisions on product mix, necessitating the studying of product demand; they were to enter direct relationships with each other and to arrange purchase and sale of producer goods direct rather than through the central government ministries. In some cases they were permitted to trade direct with foreign customers and suppliers without official sanction for every transaction, and if achieving exceptional performances they were allowed to keep a proportion of their foreign exchange earnings in foreign currencies, a precious commodity permitting its holder access to privileged supplies of scarce products. Investment policy was also substantially devolved, and enterprises were left to decide the extent to which investment was desirable and in which fields. Finally, the performance of management and workforce was to be judged by the profit earned on capital employed, and the bonuses paid assessed in its light.

The principles involved were the same throughout the area, but the manner of their application varied widely. At the heart of the difference was the degree to which the centralised system was dismantled and to which enterprises were left truly free to make their own decisions. It is not surprising that many communists saw the introduction of such changes as striking at the essence of the socialist system. Certainly there could be no doubt that there were potential clashes of interest between enterprises and central bureaucrats. There was great reluctance to press ahead too quickly, and infinite possibilities for opponents within the government to use the techniques of delay to hinder and discredit the changes. Only in Hungary were they introduced throughout the economy simultaneously, though arrangements to do so in Czechoslovakia were stopped by the invasion of 1968. Elsewhere the pattern was one of gradualism: of selective change and experiment with selected enterprises, as was the case in Poland and Romania, where small-scale experiments were carried out in 1965. Instead of direct devolution of power to enterprises, it was normal to replace the former ministries of the central government, hitherto responsible for the application of the plan to their own sectors of the economy, with enterprise associations, given the tasks of controlling and representing the collective interests of their branch of the economy. It was very easy for the erstwhile ministries and their personnel to re-form as associations, which thus continued to think and act in the old ways. The powers of enterprises to use their profits was restricted by the introduction of 'funds' into which such profits were paid. The proportions to be allocated to each were carefully defined and the purposes for which they might be used rigidly controlled. Many enterprise managers accustomed to the command economy and familiar with its requirements were clearly unhappy with the new responsibilities placed upon them. It was not surprising that they continued to operate in the old way and appealed to their association to defend them. In particular, it was the heavy industries that suffered most from the alteration in the method of assessing performance. The established system of gross material output gave disproportionate advantage to the output of industries such as coal, iron and steel manufacturing to which it was ideally suited. It reinforced the conservative thrust of communist development strategy. The new conceptions of profitability exposed these industries. They required large capital sums and the value of their output as assessed by the return on capital employed was low. Yet attempts to increase the price of steel or coal to the consumer – overwhelmingly other industrial enterprises – ran into heavy resistance. Conversely the return on capital in the consumer goods sector or in light industry was altogether more impressive. The alteration in criteria fitted in well with the expansion of such industries, then getting underway. The reforms were therefore to the disadvantage of hitherto favoured sectors of the economy upon which capital and effort had been lavished, and upgraded the former Cinderella industries. The consequences were predictable. The heavy industries lobby decried the new arrangements and many traditionally minded communists found new reason to deplore changes of which they were already deeply suspicious.

It was by no means obvious that the new system was to the advantage of the workers. Under the established planning arrangements overfulfilment of output targets had been rewarded with substantial bonuses for management and had been encouraged by a system of premium payments made to workers. Together they amounted to substantial sums and formed a vital part of the income of managers and workers alike: in the case of Romania they amounted to perhaps one-fifth or one-quarter of total income. These were abolished under the new system and new wage and salary scales introduced that took account of the previous bonuses within new, consolidated wage rates. The new, higher incomes were, however, balanced by new, higher output standards required of the whole workforce. Precise duties were allocated for the payment of the whole salary and a direct link established between basic salary and the output performance of the whole work unit. Reform of salary structure and work discipline went hand in hand and the overall effect was to require harder work of a higher standard. The new arrangements did not meet with universal enthusiasm.

Price fixing under the reformed system caused similar problems. For radical reformers a major role was to be played by the market mechanism. The Yugoslav model and the Hungarian New Economic Mechanism allotted a considerable part to the market, as did the abortive 1968 Czechoslovak reform. Elsewhere, however, changes were also introduced in the processes by which prices were determined. In every case a major difficulty lay in the manner by which profit was to be assessed, and in particular the components in production costs to which profit was to be related. One possibility was to link it direct to labour costs, with the disadvantage that the enterprise maximised its profits by using the most labour possible in the production process, thus exacerbating the labour shortage and obstructing technical progress which depended upon replacing labour by capital. Similar objections arose when profit was related to all costs and not merely to labour costs, for then too increased costs of production which automatically increased profit margins were in the interests of the individual enterprise. The third possibility, to relate profit to productive capital used for each unit of production, highlighted the problem of the role of capital as opposed to labour in the productive process and it was difficult to reconcile with Marx's labour theory of value, which ascribed the creation of value to the activities of labour and not to capital. It gave rise to a brisk debate among eastern European economists, notably in the DDR, before the idea could be accepted and applied. It too had practical disadvantages for labour-intensive branches of production which could not easily be improved technologically. Even when operating at maximum levels they could not be profitable by definition, and thus would in practice be deprived of the opportunity to earn the profits and capital required for future development. As a result, nowhere was the role of profits given absolute priority in determining prices, and governments maintained the role of the central planning bodies in deciding prices. Control over them remained an important instrument of state economic policy and the principles of fixing prices in accordance with criteria acceptable to government was reaffirmed, albeit in a more sophisticated form than before. This was reinforced by general popular suspicion that price reform meant in reality higher prices and lower standards of living. Ideological objections to freeing prices to find their own level coincided with political prudence.

The momentum for fundamental change in economic organisation was largely expended by 1971 except in Hungary and Yugoslavia. The reason was political. Change in the economic system seemed almost irresistibly intertwined with change in the political structure, which, as the invasion of Czechoslovakia showed, neither the USSR nor the other Warsaw Pact countries would accept. Only Romania declined to take part in the invasion. Its reasons for doing so were not a reflection of concern to protect and encourage economic and political reform, as was the case with Yugoslavia. The Romanian government remained as firmly wedded to the old ways as did the others. Alarmed conservative communists were reacting against economic reforms, long suspect to them, as much as against political challenge. After 1968 reform in the USSR petered out and the economy settled into an organisational structure new in shape but largely unchanged in attitude. In the DDR the Economic System of Socialism came to an end in 1970 when it threatened political consequences; in Poland the outburst that led to the ousting of Gomulka and to the installation of the Gierek government did not lead to a renewal of the drive for economic reform; in Romania Ceausescu's speech in 1971 heralded a return to orthodoxy. Even in Hungary the New Economic Mechanism reforms came under pressure and an increased degree of centralism and a return to central control became discernible after 1972.

Such steps did not, however, mean that the search for a reformed and improved centralised economic system was at an end. The pause that began in 1971 lasted until the end of the decade, when a further wave of decentralising reform in economic control, permitting the greater assumption of responsibilities at enterprise level, set in. Experiments in decentralisation in Czechoslovakia begun in 1978 were in 1980 extended to the whole of industry. In 1979 changes in Romania permitted enterprises to plan their own budgets and future developments. They were also permitted to retain one-quarter of their profits and to introduce profit-sharing schemes for their workforce. In Bulgaria too modest decentralising proposals and reforms in management structures began in 1978. The most striking example was that of Hungary, where the momentum of reform began to redevelop in 1979. Subsidies from government for essential services began to be phased out and moves were inaugurated to integrate the exchange rates of the florint with foreign currencies. This replaced the traditional system hitherto pertaining in Hungary, as elsewhere in eastern Europe, by which differential exchange rates were applied depending upon the purposes of the transaction in question. By 1981 the goal of a uniform exchange rate had been reached, and the government was predicting a fully and freely convertible currency early in 1982, and joined the IMF in May of that year.

Economic specialisation and co-operation

In 1972 the system of centrally prepared directive and detailed plans still operated in Poland, the DDR, Romania and Bulgaria. They were, however, much more sophisticated, and were the products of a scientific approach that tried to utilise the latest developments in cybernetics and mathematical techniques. There was an enhanced recognition of the importance of specialisation, rather than production in each country of a wide range of goods. This required a wide market, and reinforced attempts made since the late 1950s through the mechanism of Comecon to persuade member countries to accept a high degree of interdependence. Termed the 'international socialist division of labour' the object of this policy had been to achieve economies of scale. It had been espoused by the USSR and was closely associated with Khrushchev. It was his attempts to create a central Comecon planning organisation and to persuade the Romanian government not to proceed with the giant Galati steel complex which had led to the rift between Romania and the USSR, made public and explicit in 1964. The Romanian government declared this policy would favour the more advanced economies of the area at the expense of the more backward, and specifically the economies of the DDR and Czechoslovakia at the expense of that of Romania. The latter would be reduced to the rank of a producer of agricultural goods and of minerals, especially oil and gas. It is probably true that these objections influenced other states in the area, even if they were less forthright than the Romanians. Certainly the process of international division of labour never achieved the degree of interrelationship nor the supranational control feared by the Romanian government.

Stripped of the political implications, supranational specialisation made good sense, and there was steady progress in specific items. Components for the completion of Soviet motor cars were produced in Poland, Hungary, Yugoslavia and Bulgaria, with payment made in completed vehicles. By 1971 1,200 individual engineering products and a further 800 chemical ones were covered by Comecon-wide agreements, and joint production of computer and production control equipment was underway. In 1976 a ten- to fifteen-year programme of co-operation was launched, which tied in with the co-ordination of Five-year Plans among member countries, begun in 1971. There was however less result than might have been expected, and by 1980 the greatest progress had been made in freight transport, the standardisation of specifications, research co-operation and in energy, especially the integration of electricity supplies. The most effective forms of co-operation were bilateral, especially between the DDR and Poland and the DDR and the USSR. By the latter high-quality optical, electrical and engineering equipment from the DDR was traded against Soviet fuel, mineral ore, cotton and timber. Close Soviet–Bulgarian ties were symbolised by Bulgarian lumberjacks cutting timber in Siberia while 65 per cent of Bulgarian machinery and equipment exports went to the USSR. This government-to-government co-operation led to quite extensive provision of investment capital in the USSR by Comecon members for the development of Soviet raw materials, with payment made in the form of a percentage of the production. Such arrangements were first made between 1960 and 1964 for the building of the *druzhba* pipeline, which distributed Soviet oil to Poland, Hungary, the DDR and Czechoslovakia. A similar agreement in 1974 led to the construction of a gas pipeline linking Orenburg with Hungary, Poland, the DDR, Czechoslovakia and Bulgaria. The five latter countries in a series of bilateral agreements with the USSR met the costs of the project and were to be repaid in gas deliveries. Another example of joint co-operative ventures in the energy field was the *mir* electricity grid to permit the swopping of generating capacity to even out peaks and troughs in demand. Further examples of direct investment were provided by other raw materials, such as the Ust-Ilimsk cellulose combine and the Kiembaev asbestos plant. Other bilateral agreements were concluded outside Comecon. Joint enterprises between Hungary and Poland for processing coal dumps or between the DDR and Poland to set up cotton mills were typical, but the most spectacular example was the hydroelectric and navigational scheme at the Iron Gates on the Danube, the result of Romanian and Yugoslav co-operation. It came into operation in 1973 and its success encouraged the Romanian government to enter similar joint projects with Bulgaria at Turnu Magurele and Nikopol on the lower Danube and with the USSR at Stinca Costesti on the Pruth.

Comecon took the lead during the 1960s in seeking to harness statistical methods and the latest input–output tables to the planning process. Conferences were held in 1961, 1965, 1966 and 1967, and during 1966 and 1967 the Permanent Statistical Commission of Comecon put forward proposals for standard tables for all member countries. Such developments, permitting the analysis of structural growth and changes and offering the opportunity to improve the planning balances and allow inter-industry analysis were in their infancy in 1970. Another example of the introduction of new methods was the application of computers. The first such computing centre for a national planning body had been set up in the USSR as late as 1962. It was followed by similar centres first in the DDR, then in Czechoslovakia. The Polish centre was founded in 1967–8 and by 1972 such centres were established in all the eastern European countries. If computing techniques were in their infancy in 1970 it was none the less possible to argue that the application of them offered the hope of improving centralised planning, thus reinforcing the existing system without resorting to structural or institutional change which carried the threat of political repercussions. Other scientific refinements pointed in the same direction. Increasingly more sophisticated mathematical definitions were devised and applied to the collection of statistical data. The relationship between different variables in the economy as a whole as well as between individual enterprises were examined and appropriate algorithms devised. Enterprise production plans and the determining of optimum inputs and levels of production were subject to these new techniques, the overall purpose of which was to improve planning technique and shorten the time required for drawing up annual plans.

The import of foreign capital

At the same time as new techniques allowed governments to strengthen the centralised planning system without the risks attendant upon decentralisation, other new possibilities were also opening up to them. The growing problem of securing capital to finance the increasingly expensive investments on the wide scale desired, and the convertible currencies necessary to finance the import of Western technology, threatened to exacerbate the unrest caused by prolonged depression of living standards. Events in Czechoslovakia in 1968 and Poland in 1970 pointed the potential outcome.

Despite ideological constraints, the capitalist world offered opportunities to supplement domestic capital resources. The first to take advantage of the possibilities was Yugoslavia. In the immediate aftermath of the war Yugoslavia had been heavily dependent on UNRRA for food, clothing, medical supplies, seed and livestock and transportation equipment. Yugoslavia had been a founder member of the International Monetary Fund in 1945. After the break with Cominform in 1948 the first US credits for Yugoslav purchases in the USA were extended in November 1949 and the first loans from the International Bank for Resettlement and Development came in the same year. US food aid was crucial in permitting Yugoslav living standards to be maintained during industrialisation in the 1950s. The DDR too was an indirect recipient of Western economic aid, for inter-German links with the Federal Republic permitted the DDR access to the EEC avoiding the external tariffs. During the 1960s new opportunities began to emerge: foreign tourists; export of workers to countries short of labour and their remittances home; sums of money from families living in the USA or elsewhere in the capitalist world; joint agreements with foreign capitalist industry creating joint-venture partnerships in eastern Europe; and last, but not least, foreign bank loans and credits opened new prospects. Governments could hope to secure capital for investment and foreign currencies without threatening the internal political balance. Such opportunities allowed them to reinforce their domestic position by pacifying the more immediate and pressing complaints. It was possible to use the capitalist world to strengthen socialist, planned economies.

The boom in tourism affected certain states more than it did others. The trail was blazed by Yugoslavia, the first to encourage a mass influx of tourists. The process was underway by the mid-1960s and in 1968 well over 3¼ million tourists visited the country. This figure increased to over six million in 1973 and then settled back to approximately 5½ million annually until the end of the decade. In 1980 it rose to exceed six million once more. The lure of sandy beaches, sunshine, beautiful countryside and historic sites attracted affluent western Europeans and Americans with leisure time. The Yugoslav example was followed by both Bulgaria (see Table 4.3) and Romania, and to a lesser extent by Hungary. The benefit to the economies of the area was considerable. It was estimated, for example, that tourism was worth over 840 million US dollars to the Yugoslav economy in 1977, while the official United Nations estimate for 1980 valued the contribution of tourism to the economies of eastern Europe exclusive of Yugoslavia at 700 million US dollars.

Another significant source of foreign exchange has been the export of labour both within and outside the region. The migration of Yugoslav workers to western Europe and especially to the German Federal Republic increased steadily. From 250,000 in 1965 it grew to 400,000 two years later and reached 800,000 in 1971. By 1978 the total numbers had fallen somewhat and stood at about half a million. This export of surplus labour helped the introduction of economic reforms in Yugoslavia and

Table 4.3 Number of foreign visitors to Bulgaria: total and number of visitors from the West (selected years)

	Total	Number of Westerners
1960	200,000	40,000
1963	414,500	
1966	1,480,000	
1970	2,500,000	947,000
1979	5,120,000	2,222,500

reduced the pressures of unemployment. It also played a major part in securing the balance of payments through the contribution to the invisible trade account. In 1979 total remittances by Yugoslav guest-workers abroad approached 2 billion US dollars, having nearly doubled during the decade (see Table 4.4). Precise figures were not available for the other countries in the region, but some with acute labour shortages made use of contract labour. The construction industry in the DDR used Polish workers until 1975 when labour shortages at home led to the arrangement being phased out. Bulgaria also provided labour. Nowhere, however, had the process gone so far as it had in Yugoslavia which was the only state officially to acknowledge the existence of unemploy-·ment. Elsewhere labour shortages were becoming a major constraint during the 1970s on the economies of individual states. The worst crisis was in the DDR where by 1980 labour shortages arising from the country's peculiar demographic structure were becoming steadily more acute. The rational and economical use of labour was becoming as important as careful control of investment.

The 1970s saw a massive expansion of the indebtedness of the eastern European countries to Western and OPEC states and to the USSR. In perhaps the most striking development of the decade by 1980 certain

Table 4.4 Yugoslavia: income from remittances from Yugoslavs working abroad and from tourism, and total Yugoslav exports: in millions of US dollars for selected years during the period 1972–9.

	1972	1974	1976	1978	1979	1981
Remittances	984	1,620	1,415	1,714	1,710	2,800
Tourists	462	650	725	930	1,028	1,500
Exports	2,237	3,804	4,878	5,671	6,522	10,513

states had placed themselves in serious difficulties with concomitant economic and political consequences. The process began on a large scale in about 1974. It took two forms. Investment capital was acquired either through joint ventures or through bank loans. Trade deficits had also to be funded. This was done either by export credit guarantees offered by Western governments or by private banks often encouraged by their governments. This was especially true of West German banks as the federal government saw financial aid as an important element in its *Ostpolitik*. Credits financed purchases of raw materials and investment goods. By 1977 the mushrooming of debt in eastern Europe was giving cause for concern, and the position in certain countries had become acute.

One source of capital was the newly rich OPEC states. Reports of joint investment projects in 1975 referred to 350 million US dollars of Iranian investment in Polish paper mills and food-processing industries. Unspecified sums of Iranian investment were mentioned in connection with cement, machine tools and oil-related industries in Romania. That country was also reported to be the recipient of approximately 500 million US dollars of Kuwaiti investment. In 1975 Kuwait agreed to provide 40 million US dollars for an oil pipeline from Bakar in Yugoslavia to Bratislava, passing through Hungary, and additional credits were subsequently extended both to Romania and Hungary. Such projects were made possible by the steady relaxation of regulations throughout the region permitting the establishment of joint ventures in which the foreign partner was allowed to hold 49 per cent of the capital and either to repatriate profits or freely export the products in lieu. Such relaxations occurred in Hungary in 1972, in Romania in 1971, and in Bulgaria and Poland as well. Probably the major role of credits was in the financing of trade deficits. Those with Western countries were largely provided by private banks which by 1980 were calculated as covering approximately 60 per cent of all debts by eastern European states. The worst case was that of Poland, whose government had enormously expanded the national debt in the course of its attempt during the 1970s to sustain growth. By the end of 1981 its debts were calculated at nearly 30 billion US dollars and far exceeded those of other states. In 1980, for example, the DDR had approximately 8 billion dollars of debts and Czechoslovakia about 3 billion. The short-term nature of Poland's debts exacerbated matters, for one-third were scheduled for repayment in the near future. Persistent rumours suggested that Romania too was beginning to encounter payment difficulties. Its precise indebtedness was a matter of some dispute. Official figures of some 6 billion dollars debt were set against estimates ranging between 10 and 14 billion. The Romanian case was eased, however, by its membership of the IMF, which it joined in 1972. Even so, during 1982 its economy displayed familiar signs of distress as the availability of goods became limited, energy supplies restricted and queues lengthened.

The other source of credits was the USSR. The enormous increase in oil and other raw material prices during the 1970s had its effect on countries compelled as a consequence of their massive expansion of heavy industry to import substantial quantities of metal ores and fuels. So striking was the increase in world prices and so marked the disparity between them and those obtaining between Comecon members that it was agreed in 1975 to use free market prices in a modified form to replace the fixed prices hitherto used in trade between members. After 1975 prices were recalculated annually and based on the world average price for the previous five years. The effect was to shield Comecon countries from the immediate effects of price increases but at the expense of steadily rising prices which put great pressure on the national economies of individual countries. As the principal supplier of industrial raw materials and especially of oil, the USSR was compelled to extend substantial credits to its eastern European partners. In the case of Poland, for example, these accumulated trade credits amounted to about £700 million at the end of 1980. Other countries too were to a greater or lesser extent dependent on the USSR for credits to sustain their imports of vital raw materials, a particular example being the DDR. Obviously this new dependence provided the Soviet government with an important lever in the event of political disagreement with other communist governments or developments of which it disapproved.

Agriculture during the 1960s and 1970s

The debt problem was made worse by the persisting weaknesses in the agricultural system of the area. The DDR had been a food-importing country for some time, buying from the USSR and from Bulgaria. But the other states suffered periodic shortages in foodstuffs required to feed the large urban population. Probably the best record of expansion of agricultural production during the 1970s was in Bulgaria and Hungary, where private production was especially important. Elsewhere things were much worse. A measure of the problem was the reintroduction of food rationing in Poland and Romania in 1981. This was particularly striking as these two countries, the largest in the region, ought to have been best able to meet their own requirements. Moreover, they had radically different patterns of organisation, the former with a largely privately owned agriculture, the latter with a fully fledged system of state and collective farms. In Romania it was officially claimed in the early 1970s that the collectivised sector accounted for by far the greater part of its agricultural output and subsequent deficiencies could not plausibly be ascribed to private agriculture.

Part of the continuing problems of the area arose from climatic conditions. The extremes of temperature that typify continental climates

Table 4.5   Net material product: sectors of origin in eastern European countries, excluding Yugoslavia: percentages deriving from agriculture and from industry (selected years)

	1950		1958		1963		1967		1975		1980	
	Agric.	Ind.	Agric.	Ind.	Agric.	Ind.	Agric.	Ind.	Agric.	Ind.	Agric.	Ind.
Bulgaria	52.0	23.7	42.5	43.7	33.3	44.8	28.3	49.2	21.9	51.3	16.7	60.8
Czechoslovakia	34.3	48.5	19.5	58.8	14.0	66.8	11.1	67.3	8.3	64.4	7.3	75.5
DDR	20.1	53.6	13.0	61.5	9.7	66.0	9.7	65.4	10.0	62.2	8.5	75.1
Hungary	37.5	41.9	28.1	50.8	19.7	59.1	15.5	63.3	16.3	47.0	15.8	60.1
Poland	43.3	34.6	29.9	44.6	23.5	49.8	19.6	53.5	12.6	52.1	15.3	64.0
Romania	50.8	23.8	36.4	38.8	29.8	46.9	25.7	54.7	16.6	57.1	15.2	68.6
UK*	5.8	41.1	4.2	40.6	3.9	39.4	3.2	38.8	2.6	33.4	2.2	26.5

* UK figures are for gross domestic product, and are given merely to indicate the general trend and permit overall comparison. The conceptions of NMP and GDP are very different and cannot be used for precise comparison.

were exacerbated by water problems. Droughts and floods were not uncommon. Extensive flood control and irrigation programmes were undertaken in Romania, Bulgaria and Yugoslavia, and extensive flooding in the first in 1975 had serious effects on agricultural production for several years thereafter. Other states also suffered similar setbacks. There were, for example, droughts in Yugoslavia in 1950 and 1952, in the DDR in 1953 and in Hungary between 1945 and 1947. Climatic conditions produced bad harvests in the DDR in 1955 and in Poland between 1973 and 1975 and again in 1980. There were considerable variations in crop yields from year to year. Polish experiences were typical. In 1981 the yield of grain crops increased by approximately 2 million tonnes over those of the preceding year while the potato crop was up from 26 million tonnes to 42 million and the amount of sugar extracted from beet was almost one-third more, at 1.6 million tonnes. Such wide variations in yields and climatic problems compounded the basic weaknesses in the region's agriculture and necessitated heavy purchases of foodstuffs abroad with consequent effects on the balance of payments. Given the rigid parameters within which the national investment programmes were constructed this had serious effects on the national economies of the region, and added to the already heavy borrowings made to finance the industrial development programme.

The agricultural sector continued to produce a major if declining part of the national material product of countries in the region (see Table 4.5). At the end of the 1970s it constituted 9.1 per cent in Czechoslovakia, 9.5 per cent in the DDR, 16 per cent in Hungary and Poland, 16.3 per cent in Romania and 18.4 per cent in Bulgaria. Agriculture and forestry were still large employers of labour. Certain specialist items of food were significant items in foreign trade. Even if they were scarce at home they were well known abroad. Bulgarian, Romanian and Hungarian jams, Hungarian and Yugoslav wines, Polish ham and bacon products and bottled and canned vegetables and vegetable oils were familiar. Moreover an important and increasing amount of land was devoted to industrial crops. Sunflowers, rape-seed and other oilseed crops and fibre plants such as flax and hemp had a significant part to play in providing raw materials for the industries of the area.

Overall agricultural performance was disappointing. Extremely uneven growth rates were recorded during the 1950s, varying from 1.9 per cent per year in Hungary to 2.4 per cent in Poland, 5.2 per cent in the DDR and 6.2 per cent in Bulgaria. The best achievement was in Yugoslavia, where the annual average reached 8.1 per cent. However, given the steep decline in agricultural output recorded during the war and the late recovery in Yugoslav agriculture after 1945 the figure was less flattering than it appeared. Precise comparisons were made difficult by varying practices in estimating yield, but the overall unevenness was apparent (see Table 4.6). The governments of the area periodically

Table 4.6   *Annual percentage growth/decrease in agricultural output in eastern Europe (selected years)*

	1956	1961	1964	1968	1973	1976	1970–7‡	1978	1980
Bulgaria	− 5.0	− 3.5	11.4	−8.7	0.7	4.1	1.5	4.3	−4.9
Czechoslovakia	3.0	nil	3.0	3.6	4.7	− 2.4	1.0	1.5	6.0
DDR	1.0		6.0	1.0	−0.6	− 4.9	0.9	1.4	0.2
Hungary	nil	0.7	6.0	1.0	6.7	− 2.7	1.9	2.0	2.6
Poland	6.0	10.4	1.3	4.4	7.3	− 1.1	0.2	4.1	−9.6
Romania	−15.0	8.0	6.3	−3.6	0.7	17.3		3.4	−5.0
Yugoslavia		− 3.0†	5.9	−3.0	7.0	4.8*	5.3	−6.4	−2.0

* Figure for 1977.
† Figure for 1962.
‡ Yearly average.

admitted their disappointment. Part of the difficulty lay in the relatively low priority accorded to agriculture. Firm believers in state ownership of the means of production, communist governments were ambivalent in their attitudes towards collectives. Consistent pressure was exerted in favour of ever-larger units in which the direct connection between farmer and land was eroded and decisions taken by professional managers. It was probable that the eventual outcome would be the transformation of collectives into state farms, and the process seemed well advanced, especially in Bulgaria and Hungary. Governments differentiated in favour of state as opposed to collective farms, and deliveries of machinery and fertilisers were greater in the case of the former than of the latter. Despite this, however, average productivity was not commensurately higher on state farms.

Total investment did not match requirements. During the later 1950s agriculture received a markedly increased share of total capital investment, but its percentage subsequently declined until by the later 1970s it was generally at or below the levels recorded between 1951 and 1956. Even in Poland and Romania it was only marginally higher (see Table 4.7). It was too low to compensate for the years of neglect and for the low levels of capital input commonplace before 1939. It did not make up for the drift from the land, and low morale among agricultural workers compounded the difficulties. The share of agriculture in total capital investment during the 1960s and 1970s varied between 11 and 15 per cent in Czechoslovakia and 12 and 14 per cent in the DDR. Rates were higher in Hungary, and highest in Bulgaria which was alone in allocating over one-quarter of its capital investment to agriculture in the decade after 1956. As important as the rates of investment was the use to which it was put. There were striking advances in the numbers of tractors, providing increased motor power and reflecting the growth in the machine-building capacity of newly industrialised economies. The number of units available in the DDR increased from about 90,000 in 1961 to approximately 140,000 in 1975, while in Poland it grew from about 71,000 at the earlier date to over 570,000 at the end of the 1970s. Given the much greater size of Poland, the earlier discrepancy in numbers was of considerable significance. It was probably true that by the end of the 1970s adequate numbers of tractors were generally available though the position was probably least satisfactory in Romania and Yugoslavia. In some countries, notably Czechoslovakia, there were indications of a fall in the total number of tractors used, though their average power increased.

A similar picture emerged with regard to the utilisation of fertiliser. Even in the industrialised DDR where there were adequate supplies of nitrogen, potash and calcium and where the chemical industry was relatively well developed, fertiliser production was inadequate to meet demand until production facilities were expanded about 1956. It took

Table 4.7 Fixed capital investment in eastern European countries (excluding Yugoslavia): percentages devoted to investment in industry and agriculture (averages over period)

	1951–6		1956–60		1961–5		1966–70		1971–5	
	Agric.	Ind.	Agric.	Ind.	Agric.	Ind.	Agric.	Ind.	Agric.	Ind.
Bulgaria	19.3	44.1	31.6	41.5	25.1	47.5	17.0	45.8	15.8	41.5
Czechoslovakia	11.2	41.1	16.4	40.2	15.1	44.2	11.9	39.0	11.5	36.8
DDR					13.5	48.4	14.1	51.0	12.6	53.4
Hungary	14.5	41.7	14.8	36.5	17.7	37.4	20.2	39.8	13.0	36.9
Poland	10.0	45.8	12.6	40.6	13.7	41.7	15.9	40.2	14.0	43.8
Romania	11.0	57.7	17.6	41.1	15.5	53.2	12.5	56.3	14.4	50.5

considerably longer to expand production elsewhere. The overall result was that whereas the quantity of fertiliser used in the DDR increased by approximately two and a half times between 1948 and 1971, in Czechoslovakia it increased over seven times and in Hungary by about twenty-four times. As with the provision of tractors, such agricultural investment goods benefited directly from burgeoning industry and could therefore be seen as an offspin of industrial growth. When agricultural and industrial requirements were in direct competition, however, as in the demand for electrical power or for building materials for new construction works, it was agriculture that was neglected. The overall result was a lopsided investment programme that left the needs of the countryside unsatisfied in important respects, and had especially serious repercussions for animal husbandry where inadequate accommodation reduced the numbers of animals kept and adversely affected their quality.

The continuing drain of manpower from the land to industry was another important factor. Dependent on high levels of recruitment to the industrial labour force, the investment programmes of eastern European governments required the large-scale movement of labour from the land. Given the gross overpopulation present everywhere this was desirable. Yet the recruitment of the young and the enterprising removed from agriculture too many active and energetic workers and left an ageing and largely female workforce. The inducements offered to move to industrial employment were as seductive for peasants in Poland's private agriculture as they were for those in the collective farms of Czechoslovakia, the DDR or Hungary. Much of the appeal of work in industry lay in the social opportunities offered by town life compared to the relative dullness of the villages, and the contrast was undoubtedly sharpened by the intrusion of wireless and television into the countryside. A significant part was also played by the relative neglect of the rural world, where social services, educational opportunities and overall living standards were less well funded than those in the towns.

The prices paid for agricultural goods also acted as disincentives to agricultural production. Only in Poland and Yugoslavia was there a steady increase in the prices paid to farmers for their produce, rendered necessary by the steady rise in the prices of manufactured inputs required by agriculture. In Yugoslavia regular increases in the wholesale prices paid by the government were a feature of the 1970s. While there were far more substantial increases in the prices paid to farmers in Poland than there were elsewhere in eastern Europe there were persistent complaints that wholesale prices did not cover the cost of inputs, with the prices paid to milk producers being an especial cause of irritation. Elsewhere the stable prices paid to collective farms for their produce were matched by the stable prices paid by them for fertilisers, farm equipment and services. These official prices did not, however, offer an adequate incentive to the peasantry to improve its productivity. The possibilities for increasing yields were illustrated by the levels achieved on the private garden plots of members of collectives. Free to sell the produce of these on the unregulated, private market, peasants relied on them for a substantial portion of their incomes. In Hungary, for example, they accounted for approximately half of the incomes of peasant households in the mid-1970s and for over one-quarter of the total net agricultural output in 1974. In particular, half the animals and 90 per cent of all small animals were bred on private plots and half the grapes and fruit came from them. By specialising in the production of fruit, vegetables and animal products such as eggs, poultry, ham and bacon, private peasant plots made a disproportionate contribution to eastern European food supplies. The prices they commanded on the private market were significantly higher than those in state-controlled retail outlets. Despite the chronic food shortages in the cities of Poland during 1981 it was generally possible to secure reasonable supplies in rural areas, and similar considerations probably lay behind the decision of the Romanian government to restrict rationed foodstuffs to those living in urban areas or engaged in non-agricultural work. The peasantry of eastern Europe could feed itself from its private plots.

The traditional prejudices and suspicions of urban-based Marxists often led them to place the management of state and collective farms in the hands of Party members from a non-agricultural background. While they were politically reliable and trusted by their superiors they were sometimes totally devoid of knowledge of agriculture and were often regarded with considerable suspicion by the peasantry. In many cases the result was a lack of understanding and sympathy, which led to tensions and inadequate responses to the daily problems of agriculture. There was an almost total absence of skilled agronomists able to offer technical expertise in scientific farming. The quality of management, however, improved after the early years, and by the late 1970s the flow of trained and skilled manpower had gone a long way towards meeting demand. However, there remained a division between the technically educated and scientifically minded products of modern colleges and institutes and the great mass of the rural workforce, which remained poorly educated and distrustful of novelty.

A further symptom of the distrust and suspicion of central authorities for collective farmers was the adoption of the machine tractor stations first devised in the USSR during the 1930s. Tractors, combines and other machinery was not allocated to the individual collective farm, though it was to state farms which were much more directly under governmental control. Instead, governmental agencies were set up that held the machinery, and these machine tractor stations rented them and their operators and mechanics to individual collectives. In addition to the undoubted political and ideological motivation for the creation, there may well have been more purely economic considerations. Machinery was scarce in the early years of collectivised agriculture. It was essential to make the fullest use of what existed, and there were few peasants skilled enough to maintain or even properly to operate agricultural machinery. Few collectives were financially sound enough to be able to build up their own pools of equipment. Yet the advantages of the system were outweighed by the wastefulness of maintaining a substantial stock of idle capacity which had to be reserved well in advance before the essential information necessary for its use was available. It was extremely difficult to deploy the machinery held in the stations to meet the rapidly changing patterns of seasonal requirements. When the crucial harvesting period opened, there were loud complaints at the lack of machinery or at the deficiencies of a system that made it impossible to make the best use of satisfactory harvesting conditions. Machine tractor stations were first disbanded in Yugoslavia in 1950, though it was not possible for private peasant farmers to buy tractors until the late 1950s. Once the decision to wind them up was taken in the USSR, eastern Europe followed its lead during the later 1950s. However, as late as 1960 over half the farm machinery remained in the stations and it was not until the end of the decade that their role dwindled to that of repair and maintenance facilities. The collectives purchased the machinery and became its controllers. Even then, Romania remained an exception. There machine tractor stations held nearly three-quarters of the available agricultural equipment in 1972.

Conclusion

By the early 1980s the centralised, state-dominated economy was clearly on the threshold of a period of further change. The first, heroic epoch of crash development and growth had come to an end, and the heavy industrial infrastructure was in place. The emphasis on coal and steel in the 1940s, on chemicals in the 1960s, on oil and energy in the 1970s and the belated interest in electronics by about 1980 showed communist planners to be following developments in the non-communist world rather than undertaking initiatives to establish their states as pace-setters in new developments. The rather old-fashioned industrial development strategies laid down in the immediate post-war years had probably been unavoidable, given the dominance of Soviet economic thought. Yet its legacy tied up the resources of eastern European states in obsolescent industries making it difficult to release those needed for the development of new technologies. Command economies had also failed to come to grips with the problems of agriculture. While there was no reason to think it was inherently impossible for the communist economic system to accommodate the special requirements of farming it was manifest that it had as yet failed to do so. There was, moreover, reason to question whether communist governments recognised these special needs as legitimate, tending instead to see them as tiresome and old-fashioned.

There were indications of the system's capacity to adapt and change. Greater political security and self-confidence among the ruling parties permitted the relaxation of the rigidities of central control and allowed experiments with individual initiative and private economic activity. Individuals selling their services and skills in their spare time were a vital adjunct to the insufficient and unreliable repair and servicing facilities provided by the state. Frowned upon and periodically denounced, they were in fact tolerated. The black economy, dependent on a well-established system of syphoning off spare parts and equipment from state enterprises, provided the plumbers, electricians, mechanics, car repairers, dentists and handymen otherwise only obtainable after long delays, if at all. It was not a vehicle for tax avoidance but an integral part of the economic system. In a more regularised and legitimate form private initiative was accepted in Hungary, Poland and Yugoslavia, where increasing opportunities were being opened up to individuals to operate small service facilities, creating a new group of small-scale businessmen. It filled a gap that the cumbersome centralised economic system was never able to plug. That such innovation and flexibility was prized and that the system might be on the verge of a further bout of organisational change freeing its economic joints was suggested by the pointed public comments of Andropov, the new Soviet First Secretary, who by early 1983 had identified the Hungarian economic system as worthy of close examination by Soviet economists and officials.

Further reading

1. *General works:*
Berend, I.T., and Ranki, G., *Economic Development in East-Central Europe in the Nineteenth and Twentieth Centuries* (Columbia University Press, 1974).
Kaser, M.C., and Radice, E.A., *The Economic History of East Europe, 1919–1975*, vol. 1 (Oxford University Press, 1982).
Nove, A., Hohmann, H.H., and Seidenstecher, G. (eds), *The East European Economies in the 1970s* (Butterworth, 1982).

2. *Economic problems after the Second World War:*
Royal Institute for International Affairs, *South Eastern Europe* (1940).
Warriner, D., *Eastern Europe after Hitler*, Fabian Research Series no. 50 (1940).

3. *Specific aspects:*
Brabant, van, J.M., *Socialist Economic Integration* (Cambridge University Press, 1980).
Ellmann, M., *Socialist Planning* (Cambridge University Press, 1979).
Gamarnikow, M., *Economic Reforms in Eastern Europe* (Wayne State University Press, 1968).
Haraszti, M., *A Worker in a Workers' State* (Penguin, 1977).
Hohmann, H.H., Kaser, M.C., and Thalheim, K.C. (eds), *The New Economic Systems of Eastern Europe* (C. Hurst, 1975).
Kaser, M.C., *Comecon* (Oxford University Press, 1967).

Wellisz, S., *The Economies of the Soviet Bloc* (McGraw-Hill, 1964).
Wilczynski, J., *The Economics of Socialism*, 4th edn (Allen & Unwin, 1982).

4. *Individual countries:*

Balassa, B., 'The Hungarian Economic Reform', *World Bank Staff Working Paper no. 506* (1982).
Dobrin, B., *Bulgarian Economic Development Since World War 2* (Praeger, 1973).
Donath, F., *Reform and Revolution. The Transformation of Hungary's Agriculture 1945–1970* (Corvina Press, 1980).
Hare, P.G., Radice, H., and Swain, N. (eds), *Hungary: A Decade of Economic Reform* (Allen & Unwin, 1981).
Horvat, B., *The Yugoslav Economic System* (International Arts and Sciences Press, 1976).
Leptin, G., and Melzer, M., *Economic Reform in East German Industry* (Oxford University Press, 1978).
Montias, J.M., *Economic Development of Communist Romania* (MIT Press, 1967).
Murgescu, C., *Romania's Socialist Economy* (Bucharest, 1974).
Singleton, F., and Carter, B., *The Economy of Yugoslavia* (Croom Helm, 1982).
Stolper, W.F., and Roskamp, K.W., *The Structure of the East German Economy* (Harvard University Press, 1960).
Taylor, J., *The Economic Development of Poland, 1919–1950*, 2nd edn (Greenwood Press, 1970).
Tsantis, A.C. (ed.), *Romania. The Industrialization of an Agrarian Economy under Socialist Planning*, a report to the World Bank (1979).
United States Congress, Joint Economic Committee, *East European Economic Assessment*, 2 vols (1981).
Zielinski, J.G., *Economic Reforms in Polish Industry* (Oxford University Press, 1973).

5

COMMUNIST SOCIETY

The objective of the new communist regimes was to mould a new world. Inspired by the nineteenth-century belief first enunciated by Marx, they saw the industrial proletariat as the standard-bearer of a better, more just and more humane world. Industrial workers were seen as revolutionaries, fired by idealistic concerns and actively committed to the achievement of socialism. The industrialisation process and its accompanying social upheaval had therefore a moral purpose. From it would emerge a new, socialist individual, tolerant, deeply conscious of obligations to others, collectivist not selfish in outlook. Such people would uphold equality of opportunity and place a high value on culture and self-improvement. The changes needed were of a once-and-for-all nature, throwing a generation into the melting pot before a new social order emerged and settled into a pattern radically different from any that had gone before. Between the establishment of communist governments and the early 1960s the dynamics of social change were fuelled as governments used their coercive powers to the full to drive through a revolution in eastern European society. Once the process of change had been completed newly mature industrial societies required governments devoted to orderly administration. Where the process had not been completed, as for example in Romania, the earlier governmental commitment to change and activism, to the propagation of new social values, lasted longer. Established, static societies posed different problems for governments than revolutionary, changing ones, and it was necessary to adapt to new circumstances.

It was difficult to chart the process of change since the independent academic discipline of sociology and the empirical science of opinion polling as opposed to government-sponsored surveying were not encouraged. In the early years university departments were closed down and publication of information suspended, and it was only after 1954 that social investigation began to make a slow recovery, first in Poland. The perils confronting sociologists were well illustrated in Czechoslovakia, where the discipline was not re-established until 1964 and was promptly purged after the Warsaw Pact invasion in 1968. Poland, Hungary and Yugoslavia remained relatively free of restrictions and published far more information than did other states in the region, while the relative poverty of data relating to the DDR was to some extent compensated by the massive effort made in the Federal Republic to elucidate developments in the other German state.

Growth of urban population

Whatever the shortage of hard, factual information there was no doubt that the collectivisation of agriculture and mass industrialisation wrenched the population of the area from its traditional social roots and hurled it into a process of social modernisation familiar from other states' experiences of similar phenomena. In twenty-five years eastern Europe passed through an accelerated process of change of profound intensity.

Apart from Czechoslovakia and eastern Germany, the majority of the population of the region in 1950 was composed of peasants. At least half the labour force was employed in agriculture: even in comparatively advanced Czechoslovakia the figure was approximately 38 per cent while in the DDR it reached one-quarter. Thereafter numbers employed in the agricultural workforce fell dramatically (see Table 5.1). In Bulgaria the crucial change came between 1955 and 1965 during which period the percentage of the population actively engaged in agriculture fell below 50 per cent and continued to drop. By 1978 percentages for Czechoslovakia and the DDR had fallen to 13 and 10 respectively, while elsewhere too substantial falls had been recorded. Hungary was well on

Table 5.1   Percentage of the labour force employed in agriculture

	1950	1960	1970	1980
Bulgaria	73	57	47	23.8
Czechoslovakia	38	26	19	12.6
DDR	24	18	13	10
Hungary	49	37	25	20.6
Poland	56	47	39	26.1
Romania	74	66	49	29.8
Yugoslavia	70	58	50	33.4
UK*	5.5	2.1	1.8	1.6

* Excludes the self-employed and employers working their own land.
Source: J. Triska and C. Gati (eds), *Blue Collar Workers in Eastern Europe* (Allen & Unwin, 1981) p. 31; figures for 1980 from UN, *Economic Survey for Europe, 1981*; figures for UK from Central Statistical Office, *Annual Abstract of Statistics*.

the way to achieving a modernised, industrialised workforce, with 20 per cent of its labour force engaged in agriculture. In the other states at least one-third of the labour force was engaged in agriculture. The highest percentages were in Romania and Yugoslavia, where 40 per cent of the labour force was still working the land. These figures marked substantial reductions from the 74 per cent and 70 per cent so engaged in 1950. Eastern European society had become industrial. Everywhere a majority of the population was engaged in producer industry or the service industries and peasant society was obsolescent. The figures reveal the magnitude of the change. The most obvious feature was the enormous growth in the urban population. As with all industrialising societies, the process was accompanied by a huge influx of former peasants into the burgeoning industrial centres. While definitions of 'urban' varied from state to state, the censuses of all eastern European states revealed increases in the percentage of the population so classified (see Table 5.2). In the case of Bulgaria, for example, less than one-quarter of the population was classified as urban in 1945. By 1968 one-half lived in urban centres and the proportion was growing quickly. The same was true for Poland, while over half the population of Hungary lived in urban communities by the mid-1970s. While neither Romania nor Yugoslavia had reached similar levels the process of urbanisation was well advanced and it was only a matter of time before they did so. The highest levels of concentration were recorded in the DDR and Czechoslovakia.

Table 5.2   Percentage of the population classified as 'urban' in accordance with national classifications (selected years)

Bulgaria	24.5 (1946)	33.5 (1956)	50.0 (1968)	62.1 (1980)
Czechoslovakia	51.2 (1950)	47.6 (1961)	62.0 (1970)	66.7 (1974)
DDR	70.8 (1950)	72.9 (1964)	75.4 (1974)	76.2 (1980)
Hungary	36.5 (1949)	39.7 (1960)	45.2 (1970)	54.0 (1980)
Poland	39.0 (1950)	48.3 (1960)	51.5 (1968)	58.5 (1980)
Romania	23.4 (1948)	31.3 (1956)	38.2 (1966)	48.6 (1978)
Yugoslavia	16.1 (1948)	28.4 (1961)	38.6 (1971)	
UK	80.3 (1951)	78.3 (1961)	76.9 (1971)	76.2 (1981)*

* England and Wales only.

Definitions of 'urban' varied. Although in Czechoslovakia, the DDR and Yugoslavia a minimum population of 2,000 was specified, in these three countries as elsewhere population was not the only criterion. Urban status was a legal definition, giving a particular administrative position. Though everywhere the rate of increase in such localities was considerable, overall distribution was not as concentrated as this might suggest. Almost unique was the position in Hungary, whose capital, Budapest, was the largest city in eastern Europe and only outstripped by Leningrad and Moscow among Soviet cities. By 1980 Budapest and its suburbs accounted for nearly 40 per cent of the population of the country. This was only partly the result of post-war developments. Like Vienna, it was a former capital city of the erstwhile Dual Monarchy and had catered for a state far larger than Hungary was after 1919. In the other eastern European countries capitals still played a primary role in national life, though they did not dominate to the same degree. Sofia came nearest, housing 12 per cent of the population of Bulgaria in 1978, while Prague, Bucharest and East Berlin had between 7 and 8 per cent of their respective populations. Governments were aware of the problems caused by disproportionate expansion of capital cities and imposed limitations on ingress, as for example with Budapest during the 1960s and Sofia in the mid-1970s.

Capitals apart, there was a striking lack of really large cities. It would take time for traditional urban centres to expand and for new ones to develop to become large enough to offer a thoroughly urban environment, sufficiently provided with the amenities and generating the attachment among their citizens necessary to offer a counter-weight to

Map 4   Czechoslovakia, German Democratic Republic and Poland.

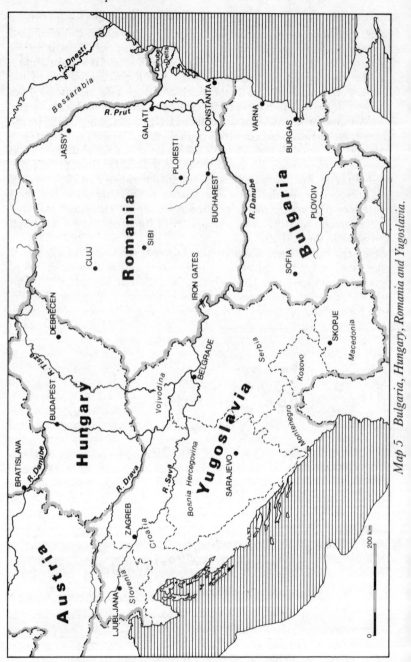

Map 5   Bulgaria, Hungary, Romania and Yugoslavia.

those of the respective capitals. By 1980 this process was probably most developed in the DDR, inheritor of a long urban tradition. Berlin apart, Leipzig, Dresden, Karl-Marx-Stadt (formerly Chemnitz), Magdeburg, Halle and Rostock were sufficiently large to meet these criteria, and there were a further seven cities with populations of more than 100,000. At the other extreme stood Yugoslavia, where the national capital, Belgrade, and the Croatian capital, Zagreb, were approximately the same size and offered similar facilities. Among other provincial capitals Skopje, devastated by earthquake in 1963 and later rebuilt, Sarajevo and Ljubljana were the only large cities and only a further four exceeded 100,000 in population. In Romania the ten cities with populations of 100,000–200,000 and nine of 200,000–300,000 could not counter the attractions of Bucharest, with nearly 2 million, though provincial capitals were important focal points for cultural, administrative and social services, enhanced when they were also centres for the significant Hungarian minority, as were Cluj and Turgu-Mures. Poland too had large urban concentrations. Warsaw grew very little and major provincial centres such as Wroclaw, formerly Breslau, Lodz, Poznan and Krakow all exceeded half a million in population and disposed of a range of amenities rivalling those of Belgrade and Zagreb. Only Leipzig and Dresden of non-capital cities were as significant and the population of both these cities was slowly declining.

The typical eastern European urban centre was small, ranging up to 90,000 in population – the size of such western European cities as Troyes, Esslingen and Rotherham. After 1960 governmental planning policies favoured smaller centres. Restrictions on migration to the biggest cities were coupled with an emphasis on decentralised industrialisation, as for example in Romania. There was a marked tendency for urban centres with less than 20,000 inhabitants to stagnate and for those with 20,000–100,000 to grow. By 1980 the generality of eastern European cities were rather small. The 'typical' urban centre that accommodated the majority of town dwellers in highly urbanised Czechoslovakia and the DDR as well as in Yugoslavia had less than 50,000 inhabitants at the end of the 1970s. Such relatively small centres went some way to offset the effects of urban development, for towns with less than 50,000 citizens were probably not large enough to generate the full range of social, cultural and economic facilities. Most eastern European cities were more accurately equated with western European market towns liable to be characterised as slower-paced or provincial.

Population: vital statistics

This change in occupation and habitat took place at a time of rapid population growth. Not only did the relative proportions between urban and rural change, so too did the absolute numbers involved (see Table 5.3). The population of Bulgaria, for example, increased from just over 7 million in 1948 to nearly 9 million in 1978, while that of Czechoslovakia grew from 12,339,000 in 1948 to over 15 million in 1978. Most spectacular was the growth in the number of Poles, from just under 24 million at the earlier date to just over 35 million at the later one. The DDR was the only exception. There the population fell, a reduction caused in part by the massive exodus to the Federal Republic, ending only with the construction of the Berlin Wall in 1961, and compounded by low birth

Table 5.3   Population of eastern European countries: rounded to the nearest thousand, in thousands (selected years)

	1948	1958	1968	1980
Bulgaria	7,130	7,728	8,370	8,862
Czechoslovakia	12,339	13,474	14,361	15,318
DDR	19,066	17,355	17,084	16,737
Hungary	9,158	9,882	10,275	10,713
Poland	23,980	28,770	32,426	35,578
Romania	15,893	18,056	19,721	22,268
Yugoslavia	15,901	18,018	20,029	22,344
UK*	50,026	51,842	55,282	55,888

* UK figures are given for comparison.

and high death rates which produced negative growth each year after 1969. Populations expanded because of buoyant birth rates and a sharp fall in the death rate, which declined more steeply than the former. The number of older citizens living on beyond retirement grew appreciably. Indeed, were it not for the lengthening life expectancy in the DDR the fall in its population would have been even more marked. The most spectacular achievements were in the states with the greatest room for improvement. In Romania, for example, a death rate of 19.3 per thousand population and a life expectancy of 42 years during the late 1930s changed to 9.6 per thousand and 66½ for men and 70½ for women respectively (see Table 5.4). Overall population patterns became virtually indistinguishable from those of other advanced industrialised countries. Eastern Europeans had smaller families, their children survived infancy in large numbers, they lived until their early seventies and the men died before the women. Such general comments ought not to be allowed to mask the occasional regional divergencies. The case of the DDR was exceptional. There the death rates per thousand inhabitants remained higher than elsewhere in the region as its population was noticeably older. At the other extreme in some countries individual regions still retained their traditionally higher birth rates while enjoying the advantage of steeply falling mortality rates. The result was a marked growth in the population of certain ethnic groups. The best example was the Albanian population in the Kosovo region of Yugoslavia. Unlike the more advanced industrialised regions of the country, Kosovo retained a relatively high birth rate. The resulting increase in the Albanian population and its growing percentage share in the population of the Kosovo region helped fuel traditional animosities between Albanian and Serb inhabitants and gave new confidence and power to the former in the demands for increased shares in government and culture facilities.

Social and national cohesion

As populations grew and economic policies took effect, the enormous regional diversities traditional in eastern Europe began to decline. In part this was the inevitable consequence of the downgrading of agriculture and the peasant way of life, for modern industrial societies used technology to overcome many of the factors that formerly influenced living standards and circumscribed prosperity. The natural fertility of the soil, difficulties of water supply, access to markets for agricultural goods, information about scientific techniques and a sense of involvement in a wider national community could all be transformed. Chemical fertilisers, irrigation machinery, new metalled roads and motor transport, better educational provision and agronomical experts and radio and television were the fruits of industrial society. All helped break down regional diversities and end local isolation. Whereas traditionally eastern Europe had consisted of distinct, isolated communities, enjoying wide variations in their standards of living and often remote from other villages only a few miles away, there now occurred an enormous levelling of living standards. A distinct sense of national identity emerged, linking Hungarians, Poles, Bulgars and Germans. The traditional animosities of contending ethnic groups and wide differences separating regions within one country lessened.

This homogenisation process was the result of deliberate policy decisions. The new communist governments were determined to end the established rivalries that had divided so many ethnic groups from each other and had, for example, set Croats against Serbs or Czechs against Slovaks. They saw economic development as the common denominator that would heal wounds by raising the living standards of the disadvantaged areas. The wealthier regions would mark time while the less developed advanced quickly. Thus the policies of discrimination in economic matters, designed to quicken investment in such backward regions as Macedonia, Montenegro or the Kosovo region in Yugoslavia, or in Slovakia, or in the less developed regions of Romania, had important social implications. The social indicators, such as educational provision, availability of medical services, cultural facilities and well-paid jobs narrowed perceptibly as previously less favoured regions began to catch up. The overall consequence was to create for the first

Table 5.4 Vital statistics of population: birth and death rates per thousand inhabitants and infant mortality rates per thousand live births (selected years)

	1948			1958			1968			1980		
	Birth	Death	Inf. mort.	Birth	Death	Inf. mort.	Birth	Death	Inf. mort.	Birth	Death	Inf. mort.
Bulgaria	24.7	12.6	118.2	17.9	7.9	52.2	16.9	8.6	28.3	14.3	10.7	19.9
Czechoslovakia	23.4	11.5	83.5	17.4	9.3	29.5	14.9	10.7	22.2	16.2	12.1	16.6
DDR	12.1	15.2	94.0	15.6	12.7	44.2	14.3	14.2	20.2	14.6	14.2	12.1
Hungary	21.0	11.6	94.1	16.0	9.9	58.1	15.0	11.2	35.8	13.9	13.6	
Poland	29.4	11.2	110.7	26.2	8.4	72.7	16.2	7.5	33.4	19.5	9.8	21.2
Romania	23.9	15.6	142.7	21.6	8.7	70.5	26.7	17.1	59.5	18.6*	9.9*	31.6*
Yugoslavia	28.1	13.5		24.0	9.3	86.4	19.1	8.7	58.6	17.0	9.0	32.8
UK	18.1	10.9	36.0	16.8	11.6	23.3	17.1	11.8	18.6	13.1*	12.1*	12.9*

* Figure for 1979.

time in eastern Europe truly national societies that lacked the enormous regional variations previously so characteristic. Yet the process did not bring an end to regional problems. Paradoxically, greater homogeneity did not end awareness and the identification of economic development as the vehicle to end well-entrenched hatreds did not prove entirely successful. The process of favouring less well-developed areas aroused the resentment of the formerly more highly developed ones. Thus the Hungarian and German minorities in Romania which traditionally enjoyed higher living standards than the mass of the inhabitants of the country saw their privileged position eroded, as did the Slovenes in Yugoslavia. The result was a sense of grievance and the emergence of a conviction that government was hostile. Even the favoured regions had not lost their sense of separate identity. If anything, the sense of separate identity of Slovaks within Czechoslovakia seemed to have been strengthened by the remarkable progress made by Slovaks in levelling the differences between themselves and the Czechs.

The ending of regional variation and the erasing of animosities was most successful in those states enjoying a high degree of ethnic cohesion. In Hungary, the DDR, Bulgaria and Poland national societies characterised by common living standards and common values emerged. In multi-national Yugoslavia and in Romania the process had not gone as far by 1980. There were certainly far fewer differences in living standards or social structure than there were formerly, yet such differences did still exist and the strong sense of national identity and difference that had always characterised the varying ethnic groups in both countries persisted. As for Czechoslovakia, even if there were few regional or social variations, a strongly felt sense of cultural identification among Czechs and Slovaks remained. In addition, the smaller states found it easier to ensure equality of provision of social services than the larger ones. Sheer size made it more difficult for Poland, Yugoslavia and Romania to provide the basic infrastructure that underpinned social homogeneity than for the substantially smaller Czechoslovakia, Bulgaria, DDR or Hungary. In the drive to smooth out the differences previously commonplace, the smaller, ethnically discrete states enjoyed a substantial advantage.

Social mobility

The political and economic revolution initially offered opportunities for and demanded a degree of social mobility hitherto unequalled. In the course of about twenty years society experienced a concentrated restructuring. By the early 1970s a new social structure had emerged everywhere, with the possible exception of Romania. It was geographically settled, and upward mobility within it ran in recognised, established channels. Upheaval and rapid social change were largely things of the past as eastern European industrial society assumed many of the characteristics of its western counterparts. In the early years, however, the situation was very different. The destruction of the former elites removed the whole stratum of decision-makers and controllers. Whether in the administration, the armed forces, the police, industrial management or lower level white-collar occupations in all aspects of national life, new openings appeared by 1950 as the previous office-holders fled, were imprisoned or merely dismissed. On top of this came the dramatic programmes of industrial development and the creation of command economies. All demanded new people to operate, control or work in them. If initially the test for the holders of the top posts and for many of those in key positions at lower levels of the political and economic system was political reliability, the social consequence was the rapid formation of a new hierarchy in which the upper strata were composed of holders of managerial and decision-making posts, the number of which was expanding rapidly. Other new sectors emerged. The increase in the bureaucracy called into being a newly expanded white-collar sector of clerks and lower-level officials, while the programme of industrial growth led to a huge increase in the numbers of industrial workers. All three social groups were new in composition. The vast majority of their members had moved upward socially. Industrial workers under the pre-communist regimes were politically favoured by the new arrangements and found themselves occupying responsible managerial posts previously occupied by the representatives of the bourgeoisie. Some clerks or lower-ranking officials came from the former privileged classes but most came from the literate urban or rural population. As for the proletariat, its recruits were drawn from the peasantry, especially the younger, predominantly male and more geo-graphically mobile sectors. Of all the social groups, the one whose members were not newcomers was the peasantry. While other sectors of society drew into their ranks men and women previously of different social groupings, the peasantry continued to be drawn from those who had always been peasants. Yet the peasantry too changed in its overall profile, for it lost a disproportionate number of young men. Increasingly the rural workforce came to be composed of the old, of women (who by 1980 made up a very substantial percentage), and of the adolescent population which by 1980 made an important contribution to the rural labour force. Under the impact of economic change the whole society of the region underwent important changes affecting every grouping in vital if different ways.

The magnitude of the change was charted best in Poland, Hungary and Yugoslavia where surveys during the early 1960s showed the results of this social process. In Yugoslavia, for example, of those engaged in white-collar occupations, in 1960 30 per cent were of peasant and manual worker origin, and the figure rose to 49 per cent for those in highly qualified posts and to 62 per cent for those in managerial positions. The 1971 census revealed that over 40 per cent of the population had moved from its place of origin, and that 30 per cent of the urban population was of peasant origin. Similar data emerged from a special inquiry held in Hungary in 1963, which revealed that rates of social mobility ranged as high as 60 per cent. The same results emerged from surveys in Poland at approximately the same time, where a mobility factor of approximately 50 per cent was recorded. The implication of these high figures was given graphic form by figures collected for individual factories in Poland in 1959. These showed that in newly established factories only one-fifth of the workforce had had experience as industrial workers before 1939. Some 30 per cent were first-generation migrants from the countryside and up to half were less than 28 years old. Throughout the region a very substantial percentage of the population was by 1960 engaged in work different to that of their parents and located away from their place of origin. The process was divided broadly into two stages. Those of peasant background were attracted to the urban centres to man the expanding industry and became industrial workers, and those of urban background were drawn from the ranks of the proletariat and moved into non-manual, white-collar and managerial posts. The opportunities were greatest for the geographically mobile and for the young and adventurous, and for those from a politically reliable social background.

Worker-peasant families

In addition to this profound change, there emerged throughout the region a new social phenomenon, that of the worker-peasant who kept in contact with both the traditional world of the countryside and with the new urban, industrial community. In many respects such individuals and, crucially, their families gained considerably from their novel position. Peasant families able to secure industrial employment for at least one of their members while maintaining their rural base could take advantage of membership of the collective farm and thus secure the private plot allocated to all its members as well as maintain the family dwelling, of considerable significance in a region where the housing stock only belatedly began to improve in quantity and quality during the 1970s. At the same time connections with the industrial economy brought access to the higher money incomes paid in industry as well as to the urban areas with their better shopping and improved educational and medical facilities. In addition familiarity with urban ways was of considerable advantage to peasants in a society where power was urban based. More murkily, there were the personal connections that allowed freer, if dubiously legal, access to many otherwise scarce items, especially those vital to building and electrical work. Both sides benefited and the resulting higher standards of living could be shared by the family as a whole. The phenomenon was not characteristic of either the DDR or Czechoslovakia, where the extent of social change had been less dramatic, but elsewhere it was of considerable significance. In Yugoslavia the 1960 census showed that 44 per cent of the agricultural labour force had connections with the urban, industrialised world while in the later 1960s in Poland one-third of the country's farmers had a member of their family working in industry. The link between rural and urban worlds was assisted by the widespread practice of commuting to and from work. This produced 'mixed' settlements in which a high percentage of the population was engaged in industrial work even though the settlement itself was located in the countryside. By the mid-1970s there were approximately 1 million such commuters in Hungary while in Yugoslavia about one-quarter of those living in rural areas and of working age were commuters. Finally, governmental policy changed after about 1960, as for example in Romania where a determined effort was made to establish manufacturing industry in rural areas especially on the fringes of the Carpathian mountains. The location of industry in rural areas led to an interpenetration of urban and rural values, and helped stem the influx into overcrowded towns. It also had important political overtones, as with the deliberate selection of the site for the new town of Nowa Huta in Poland. Located near the historic cultural and religious centre of Krakow, it was intended that the influx of industry would assist in the establishment of communist power in this rural region.

This increasing population and the enforced changes in its domicile made large and increasing demands on the social services. Housing, education, medical services, pensions, transport facilities and the provision of public utilities such as piped water, sewerage facilities, electricity and gas supplies came under sustained pressure. Given the monopoly over such items assumed throughout the region by the new communist regimes the populations were totally dependent upon the governments for the provision of these services. Yet the new regimes were dedicated to the massive diversion of investment capital to heavy industry. The provision of social services came far behind on the list of priorities. In the early years state plans included little provision for investment in consumer goods as a whole, including public facilities. It was not until the later 1950s and especially the 1960s that eastern European governments began to release more investment funds to meet the enormous demands placed upon groaning social services. Expenditure increased on housing, pensions, medical facilities and passenger transportation services which all lagged behind demand.

Low priority afforded to the peasantry

The population movement from country to town and the expansion of industry accorded well with pre-communist intellectual prejudices in eastern Europe. The peasant world had been condemned as backward, a stagnant and superstitious backwater whose values and attitudes were a millstone around the neck of the nation. Such contemptuous dismissiveness downgraded peasants and led to a social climate in which many non-communists regarded the bulk of the nation with the same jaundiced eye as did communists. For the latter, however, the values of the urbanised and educated were reinforced by ideological considerations. Viewing the peasantry as the bastion of property-consciousness, addicted to individual family effort and wedded to the old ways, communists had additional reasons to seek to destroy it. If the goal of a socialist society without private property and based on community effort through a redistribution of income leading to the egalitarian society of the future were to be built, it could only be done on the basis of an industrialised society. Social and economic investment in rural areas were of low priority. The stream of former peasants seeking work in the new industries of the region was welcomed. The spread of modern communications, and especially of wireless and later of television, brought the urban world to the village, and emphasised the advantages of industrial work and urban life. It was not until the 1960s that a change set in and governmental attitudes began to modify. If the decade of the 1960s saw an increasing awareness of the role and importance of agriculture in national life, the 1970s were to witness a major adjustment in policies as the social amenities of urban life were increasingly extended into the countryside and the rural world invested with a new dignity.

The early years of communist governments were bleak ones for the peasantry of eastern Europe. The collectivisation of agriculture and differential economic policies required substantial deliveries of foodstuffs at low, fixed prices and were accompanied by an almost total neglect of the provision of social benefits and public amenities. Basing themselves on the theoretical proposition that the peasantry constituted a separate social class, governments persisted in regarding them as the owners of private property and thus outside the network of state provision as extended to those working in the socialised sectors of the economy. This view persisted even after the completion of collectivisation. The granting of private plots to each member household in the collective formally enshrined the principle of the qualitatively different nature of rural society. If the official ideology of the state emphasised the union of worker and peasant the latter was not a full partner but a distinctly second-class one.

Social payments to collective farmers
The concrete effects of this were seen for example in the provision of social services and benefits. Where there was virtually no private sector and the collectivisation of agriculture was achieved more or less rapidly, the extension of social benefits occurred more quickly than in countries in which the process was lengthier and more disputed. A good indication of the variation was provided by the inclusion of collective farmers or

independent peasants within the old-age pension system. In the case of Bulgaria collective farmers were included within the state retirement pension scheme in 1957 and in Hungary in 1958, the offer of pensions constituting a major element in the campaigns in both countries to bring peasants within the collectivised system. At the other extreme was the case of Poland. There the offer of pensions to a largely uncollectivised peasantry was only made in 1968, on condition that the recipients assign their land to the state. Exactly ten years later retirement pensions were extended to all peasants, thus finally ending the gap between socialised and non-socialised sectors of the community. There was a similar pattern in the provision of other social security benefits. In the Polish case health cover was not extended to the peasantry until 1972. Before then private peasant farmers had had to purchase insurance for themselves and their families. In Hungary the retirement age for collective farm workers was not standardised with those in industry until 1980, while lower rates of family allowances were paid to co-operative farmers until 1975. There was a similar discernible differentiation in the provision of public amenities. Metalled roads, electricity supplies, piped water, mains sewerage or septic tanks, and gas supplies, either mains or bottled, were much slower to reach into the countryside than they were in the towns. In Bulgaria during the 1970s the sixth and seventh Five-year Plans included the deliberate objective of improving the living standards of the countryside with especial emphasis on the provision of electricity and mains water. By 1980 this had been achieved and virtually all households had access to both. A somewhat similar situation pertained in Hungary. There the needs of the countryside had been recognised somewhat earlier and the 1960s witnessed a considerable expansion in the provision of amenities in the rural areas. By 1970 electricity was available in all villages, though 12 per cent of houses were still unconnected in that year, and every village enjoyed a metalled road linking it with the rest of the country. As for sewerage, only 5 per cent of village housing had mains sewerage in 1970, though a further 45 per cent had septic tanks. Mains water was connected to 10 per cent of village homes and while piped gas was virtually unknown, nearly half had access to bottled gas. After 1970 the position improved further. In both Bulgaria and Hungary the drive to close the gap between rural and urban areas by the provision of amenities and the extension of the social security system to cover all citizens began about 1960, had made headway by 1970 but was only intensified during the 1970s. Similar progress was made elsewhere. In the DDR and Czechoslovakia the gap was not so great and the process of equalisation between urban and rural made somewhat more rapid headway, in the case of Czechoslovakia being closely associated with the drive to equalise conditions between the Czeck and Slovak areas of the country, the latter being the more rural in character. In the other three countries progress was less rapid and there remained significant differences during the 1970s between the opportunities afforded by government to rural and urban citizens.

Agricultural incomes

The discrimination practised against the rural community was also manifest in the payments made to those working in agriculture. The prices fixed by central government for the deliveries made either by peasants or collective farms were low. Where comparisons could be made directly with the prices on the uncontrolled market it was clear that governments required the agricultural sector to provide goods at prices far below the 'true' or free market levels. The difference was made up by the allocation of private plots to collective farmers or by permitting independent peasants free use of the surplus left after compulsory deliveries had been met. In both cases peasant private sales of foodstuffs found a ready market and made some contribution to unnaturally depressed income levels. The cost was born by the peasant who, in addition to meeting the obligations to the collective, had to provide many additional hours of labour on the family plot. Long hours of work for poor levels of remuneration did little to attract the young to agriculture as a career. As in so many areas of policy a change was discernible during the 1960s. Agricultural incomes rose as the prices paid by the state were increased. Between 1955 and 1970, for example, money wages on Bulgarian state farms increased by 85 per cent while on Czechoslovak and Hungarian ones they more than doubled. The burden of work was reduced somewhat by the increased provision of machinery and fertilisers for the collective farms. In Poland and Yugoslavia predominantly private agriculture was progressively freed of restraints placed upon it and the prices paid by the state for deliveries of produce increased slowly. Once more the process quickened after 1970 and in Hungary and Poland especially new economic policies designed to increase agricultural yields if anything rather favoured the agricultural sector. As farmers' incomes increased and greater prosperity reached the countryside, complaints could be heard that the regimes were favouring the peasantry at the expense of the industrial proletariat. Attempts to counteract this by intervention to redress the balance and restrict farm incomes led to substantial reductions in the quantity of foodstuffs available and, in Hungary, to a rapid turnabout in policy. Refusal to make such an adjustment in Poland led to shortages, demands for food rationing and increasing queues in the run-up to the 1980 disturbances.

Modifications in governmental policy and the generally apparent concern to improve conditions and raise peasant living standards was due in no small part to an emerging awareness of significant problems in the countryside. As the young and energetic left the land for work in industry in urban centres labour deficiencies appeared. Agriculture required trained manpower to farm the land, whether privately or collectively owned. It could no longer rely on the old, on women or the adolescent. These unskilled and often physically weak groups could not offer the human resources necessary for a healthy agriculture. Paradoxically, modernising regimes decrying the peasant world and its values had succeeded too well and by the mid-1970s it had become necessary for them to backpedal by emphasising the attractions of rural life.

Education

After the upheavals associated with the first five years of the communist regimes the process of social change and mobility between different strata became formalised. No longer was political reliability and social origin by itself enough. Competence and skill therefore became more important and education became the major social determinant. The key to occupation in a social system from which almost all other status-determining factors had either been removed or were state controlled, education in effect determined social position. The direct link between jobs on the one hand and qualification and training on the other placed education at the centre both of economic and social policy. By 1950 it had become apparent that the way to get ahead in the new socialist system was through skill. This social importance of education was reinforced by two further considerations. All the new communist governments were bent on rapid growth and industrialisation, which required a huge effort to promote technical education at all levels. Trained manpower was at a premium and its ranks needed to be swollen as quickly as possible. Moreover, the new regimes were committed to the dissemination of socialist values and to the creation of citizens who accepted their social obligations and conformed to the new, socialist, morality. Not only was education desirable for its technical elements, it was vital for its non-materialistic influence. There resulted an enormous emphasis upon educational provision for all age groups. With time the importance of educational provision grew rather than lessened as the success of industrialisation produced technically advanced economies dependent upon the skills of their workforce. As education became prized as the key to better living standards, regime objectives and citizen preferences came to correspond.

The communist inheritance varied widely. In the DDR and Hungary there was virtually no illiteracy. Elsewhere rates fluctuated, increasing steadily in the larger and more rural countries, and were at their highest in Poland, Romania, Yugoslavia and Bulgaria. Men were more likely to be literate than women, the young rather than the old, urban inhabitants rather than rural ones. In Bulgaria, where pre-communist governments had a reasonably good record in the provision of education, about 24 per cent of the population was illiterate in 1946, while in Yugoslavia one-quarter was illiterate in 1953. A massive drive was launched to convince the population, aimed as much at adults as at children. Literacy classes to cater for the whole population mushroomed and citizens were reminded that it was their socialist duty to attend. The results were spectacular. Illiteracy rates reportedly fell markedly. By 1960 the Polish government claimed that no more than 5 per cent of its population remained illiterate. Progress was least rapid in Romania where about 10 per cent were still illiterate by 1960, and especially in Yugoslavia where in 1961 only four out of five inhabitants satisfied a literacy test, a figure that had risen to 85 per cent in 1971. Over all, however, by the 1970s eastern Europe had been wrenched from its traditional ignorance.

The spread of educational provision was crucial to the breakdown of peasant society. Historically, peasants had not appreciated the advantages of school education, unassimilated to their life-styles or cultures. The school curriculum was not relevant to the needs of rural society while many teachers lacked contact with the countryside and tended to condemn peasant ways. School and home were antipathetic. Peasant children attended school intermittently and left long before completing the full elementary course. Where peasant political parties or self-help movements had succeeded in devising educational systems to which peasants could relate, education had made greater impact. Elsewhere it had always been a battle to secure attendance, as it still was in parts of Yugoslavia in 1980. Communist governments extended and enforced elementary educational provision with the same determination used to attack all their objectives. Elementary education was made compulsory for boys and girls beginning at age 6 or 7. The period of time was subsequently lengthened until by the 1970s elementary education everywhere took at least eight years, and provided a full course of instruction. Once students ended their elementary courses they were offered the opportunity to continue to secondary education. This was not compulsory though strongly recommended, and facilities were initially split between vocational and general schools. The former equipped their students for technical careers and were closely geared to the requirements of different sections of the national economy. The latter corresponded closely to the prestigious *gymnaziums* of the pre-communist regimes, and were the key to entry to the higher educational institutions such as universities or higher technical institutions. The *gymnazium* had always enjoyed considerable social prestige, and this pattern of preference persisted. In Poland, for example, traditional preferences for non-vocational secondary education and for the broader, humanistic university training led to great over-demand for places in such courses during the 1960s and left many vacancies in institutions of vocational training, causing the government great concern. In response, governments moved over to a system of so-called polytechnic education which introduced a unified secondary system and became widespread during the 1970s. This removed many social distinctions and opened the way generally to higher educational facilities. By the late 1970s secondary education still remained optional, though very heavily subscribed, enrolling for example 95 per cent of the appropriate age cohorts in Bulgaria. At the highest level there was an enormous increase in student numbers (see Table 5.5) and tremendous emphasis was placed throughout the region on the provision of technical and scientific educational facilities. There was an enormous expansion in the number of students graduating in technical and engineering subjects, and a corresponding decrease in the numbers graduating in the humanities. There was also a considerable increase in the number of teacher-graduates. Taken together, those graduating in technical and peda-gogical subjects amounted to as much as 80 per cent of the total number.

Apart from the DDR, the demand for educational facilities was greatly enhanced everywhere by the rise in the number of children and this produced great strains. The case of Poland was exceptional. There nearly 30 per cent of the population was aged 15 or under throughout the 1950s and 1960s. If the figure was not as high elsewhere, it was still considerable, amounting, for example, to 24 per cent in Hungary by the early 1970s. Large numbers of teachers were needed, especially since many of those in posts when the communists came to power were found to be politically unreliable and were dismissed. This was especially the case in higher educational bodies, but everywhere the combination of pressure of numbers and the test of political reliability required the creation and maintenance of a large pool of teachers. Many of them were women and the teaching profession, especially at the elementary level, came to recruit substantially from among the female population. The extension of compulsory, universal elementary education and the en-couragement of other levels also demanded a substantial increase in buildings and equipment. Inevitably it proved more difficult to extend secondary schooling to the countryside, and there was a lag between the provision of suitable facilities in rural as opposed to urban areas. It was, for example, more difficult for the Polish government to meet the demand for secondary education in rural areas than for that of Bulgaria. Once more, size had its influence. In the absence of adequate local facilities the availability of boarding accommodation permitted peasant children to take advantage of secondary schooling. If such facilities were not easily available, the presence of a relative in an accessible urban centre permitted the rural child to attend secondary school there at minimal cost to the parent. This latter tendency, especially noticeable in Poland and Yugoslavia, was a further example of the advantages to families of having urban- and rural-based members.

If governments were eager to expand their educational provision and to increase educational levels, it was not automatically made available to all citizens. During the early years access to higher educational facilities in particular was very selective, with preference given to children of peasant and worker background. The offspring of the former privileged

Table 5.5   Number of students at universities and in institutions of higher education per thousand population (selected years)

	1960	1970	1974
Bulgaria	6.4	10.7	12.2
Czechoslovakia	6.9	9.1	9.3*
DDR	13.2	17.8	17.2
Hungary	4.5	7.8	9.8
Poland	5.6	10.1	11.9*
Romania	3.9	7.4	6.8*
Yugoslavia	8.4 (1962–3)		
UK	2.5†	3.8†	4.0†

* Figure for 1973.
† Figures related to university students only.

Second column first-part years:

	1960
Bulgaria	7.0 (1948)
Czechoslovakia	4.4 (1949)
DDR	2.7 (1950)
Hungary	4.6 (1949)
Poland	3.7 (1953)
Romania	2.9 (1949)
Yugoslavia	2.0 (1950)†

sections of society were shut out of universities and technical institutions. Such restrictiveness died out during the 1950s and early 1960s as the internal strains faded, but politically inspired controls on access remained. In particular, membership of the appropriate youth organisations was *de rigeur* and practising membership of a religious organisation deeply suspect. After internal upheavals and purges of the Party the children of purged members found it hard to secure admission. During the 1970s such controls were applied most stringently in Czechoslovakia and the DDR though elsewhere in the region they had been substantially reduced. Internal tensions continued to have repercussions at the higher levels of the educational system. The close correlation between educational attainment and occupation and living standards ensured that such policies were of considerable importance for the individuals excluded and that the threat was an effective instrument of pressure.

In addition to the network of free schools and institutions of higher education there evolved a parallel system of educational facilities for adults. The impetus came from the urgent need to increase the numbers of experienced industrial workers with technical education able to assume positions of responsibility at the intermediate level in expanding industries. Crash programmes trained skilled workers on the job or at special technical schools, attendance at which was either part time or full time for short, intensive periods. Universities also provided courses for the rapid training of suitable skilled workers as engineers. This effort produced impressive results and the numbers of those regarded as qualified increased steeply. The training was inevitably less thorough than might have been desirable and produced specialists of rather narrow outlook whose skills were not readily transferable to other sectors of the economy. But, crucially, it provided adequately equipped skilled manpower in sufficient quantity to meet the immediate requirements of the first stages of industrialisation. Subsequently the whole emphasis switched to provide continuing education for adults. For those who had only completed elementary education a network of part-time secondary schools allowed adults to enhance their educational and career prospects. This facility was augmented by correspondence and extra-mural courses. Finally, at all levels intensive specialist instruction was established to raise the level of specific technical knowledge in precise areas of the national economy. Closely attached to specific vocations, diplomas and certificates validated competence in every area of economic life, from forestry to catering, engineering to collective farm work. Improvements in living standards or social position were allied to the acquisition of such qualifications, and every effort was made to enhance the opportunities for eastern European workers to acquire additional skills.

The investment in educational services at all levels was illustrated by a comparison between the sums spent by each state in 1961 and in 1970. The greatest increase was in Yugoslavia, which in 1961 spent considerably less on education than did the other states. By 1970 the sum involved had been expanded nearly fivefold, from approximately 100 million to 585 million US dollars. Elsewhere the rise was less spectacular as the amounts expended in 1961 had been considerably greater. The increase ranged from just over 80 per cent in the DDR to over 123 per cent in Bulgaria. On a per capita basis expenditure on education in Czechoslovakia and the DDR was substantially higher than elsewhere. The amounts spent in Poland and Hungary were almost identical, while between 1961 and 1970 Bulgaria outstripped Romania. In both years Yugoslavia spent least. These sums were spent on a service that was not intended to leave students wholly free to choose their future careers. Education was devised as a training mechanism for particular vocations and those undergoing it were expected to appreciate this. Manpower requirements were as much a part of the Five-year Plans as every other raw material input.

Employment

Government declared that unemployment did not exist and guaranteed work to all capable of it. Indeed a requirement was laid on all citizens to take employment, and non-fulfilment led to accusations of parasitism. In some states imprisonment followed failure to find work. Yugoslavia apart, there were either legal provisions ensuring work, as in the 1961 Labour Code in the DDR, or it was guaranteed in the state's constitution, as in the 1971 Bulgarian Constitution. Regulations governed the length of the working day, fixed at a five-day week of forty-two and a half hours in the Bulgarian Constitution, and at forty-four hours in Hungary in 1970. Elsewhere the working week could be longer: in Romania, for example, a six-day week totalling forty-eight hours was introduced in 1973. One of the demands of striking workers in Poland in 1980 was for a five-day working week. The guarantee of employment could be double-edged. By the terms of the 1961 law in the DDR a free choice of occupation was given according to the individual's qualifications and to social need. The latter provision originally meant in practice the compulsory allocation of individuals to places of work, though the interpretation was subsequently abolished in favour of persuasion to secure the satisfactory distribution of the available labour force. The power to allocate citizens to particular jobs remained, however, and could be invoked to neutralise persistent critics. It was not easy to ensure full employment. In Poland the Five-year Plan introduced in 1970 originally envisaged ending the work guarantee and assumed employment of approximately half a million in 1975. This provision was later removed. The exception in the area was Yugoslavia, where unemployment was a fact of economic life. The first admitted unemployment was in 1952 when 2.6 per cent of the non-agricultural workforce was officially so designated. The problem of unemployment was alleviated by work in the expanding economies of western Europe which absorbed many Yugoslav guest-workers during the 1960s. After 1973, however, the openings provided by the capitalist economies progressively lessened and by 1980 unemployment was running at over 800,000, more than 7 per cent of the labour force. The danger that similar difficulties might surface was one consideration underlying opposition among workers to economic reform in Hungary where attempts to approximate to world free market conditions required some accommodation with the overmanning that had come to characterise the area. The shake-out of labour that greater productivity involved led in Hungary to the relaxation after 1979 of regulations to permit the firing of personnel, the substitution of part-time for full-time labour and the introduction of job-sharing. Elsewhere the strains of maintaining full employment were most apparent in Romania. Even in the DDR where labour shortages remained as a consequence of the country's demographic peculiarities, complaints were sometimes voiced that economically unnecessary jobs were created to cater for newcomers to the labour market, while the age profile of the Polish population demanded a rapid and sustained expansion of jobs throughout the 1970s as the large juvenile population reached employment age.

Housing

Economic change and the burgeoning industrial sector placed a serious strain on housing stocks. Inevitably there were major differences in housing provision in different states and, especially, striking variations within them. The major distinction was between housing in rural and urban areas, as the latter in particular failed to keep pace with demand. Over all, housing was originally given low priority and little capital was released for it. Of all the basic elements affecting living standards, housing was the most universally neglected and was probably the major single cause of social strains in eastern European cities.

In the aftermath of the communist takeover the new regimes assumed powers over national housing stocks. As was normal in continental Europe, private owner-occupation of individual dwellings in urban areas was wholly exceptional and rented apartments in tenement blocks were the norm. Perhaps surprisingly, these were not necessarily nationalised. In Poland, Czechoslovakia and the DDR private owners of tenanted buildings in multiple occupation were not sequestered. As they were simultaneously subjected to rent freezes, lost their right to choose their own tenants and dispossess occupants, the right of ownership was more a burden than an advantage. The allocation of housing in urban areas became and remained a major element in political patronage, dependent on the Party's local representatives. Mounting maintenance costs far outstripped rental income with the inevitable consequence that the quality of housing stocks fell. Where the state did assume ownership, as in Romania, similar problems arose, but at the government's expense. Whereas under the former system private owners subsidised their tenants, in the latter case it was the state. Repairs went undone and maintenance work lapsed, and the physical quality of the housing stock everywhere declined. By the mid-1960s the problem had become inescapable.

It was especially severe in the urban centres. In those countries devastated by war the sheer volume of reconstruction work placed a huge burden on government. In this respect Poland and the DDR were particularly badly hit, and serious if localised damage affected both Romania and Hungary. To compound the problem, governments were unwilling or unable to allocate adequate funds to construction work, while the mass influx of workers into the developing industries added a new dimension to the problem. Governments sought to regulate the inflow by requiring permits for residence in urban areas and by encouraging commuting. They did not substantially increase their provision of housing. Instead they encouraged industrial enterprises and local authorities to assume a larger part of the burden and after 1960 began to experiment with co-operative and private initiatives. The push to provide adequate housing did not, however, gather real momentum until the 1970s when governments began to devote substantially greater sums to house construction and launched a major drive to meet demand.

The housing stock in eastern Europe depended overwhelmingly on buildings constructed before 1945. Even in the war-torn DDR only one-fifth of the housing stock in 1968 had been constructed after 1945, and well over one-half had been built before 1914. A similar situation pertained in Czechoslovakia, where in 1961 over three-quarters of the housing stock had been constructed before 1945. Indeed during the early 1960s, Czechoslovakia shared with Poland the dubious distinction of having the highest population density per room in Europe and with Portugal the unimpressive achievement of the lowest housing construction rates. Other countries also had poor performances. The house construction rates in Romania declined annually until 1954. During the next five years only 16½ per cent of all new construction was provided by the state, and it was not until after 1959 that its percentage share rose. Given that only the state built housing in urban areas, the statistic was resonant with implications as the urban population expanded. Fewer housing units were completed in Budapest during the 1960s than in the 1890s. The gloomy picture had serious social implications. Overcrowding, lack of amenities and inadequate standards of repair influenced low factory morale and poor performance levels among schoolchildren.

New housing was provided by enterprises as well as public authorities. A legitimate charge on the income of enterprises was the provision of accommodation for its workers. This was often regarded by management as a useful addition to the incentives available to attract and keep adequate supplies of qualified labour. The quantity of housing accommodation involved could be considerable, and after the economic reform of the 1960s the increased scope offered to management was utilised by some to undertake fairly comprehensive housing programmes. Although these began to tail off by the later 1960s some enterprises remained active, such as the Bourgas petrochemical works in Bulgaria which had provided some 4,000 housing units for its staff by 1979. Elsewhere enterprises sometimes played a leading part in the allocation of housing constructed by the local authority, as happened in Yugoslavia. In all such cases the manner of allocation was a source of great interest to the labour force and could lead to serious disputes with the management.

One source of possible construction remained private initiative. After the mid-1960s governments showed increasing readiness to encourage such developments, in part as a very successful method of removing surplus spending power from a population whose disposal income and personal savings were growing quickly. Private house construction simultaneously saved the government scarce investment capital, satisfied a deep-felt social demand and relieved some of the pressures leading to disguised inflation (see Table 5.6). The preferred form of private construction was the housing co-operative, which had emerged everywhere by 1970. Members of the organisation were required to make a

Table 5.6   Percentage share of the state in new housing construction in eastern Europe (selected years)

	1961–5	1967	1969–70	1980
Bulgaria	20		28	50*
Czechoslovakia	37		17	39
DDR		64		51
Hungary	37		36	34
Poland	52		24	18
Romania	35		62†	94†

* Figure for 1979.
† Includes construction by housing co-operatives.

substantial downpayment and the balance of the construction cost came from state loans, repayable over a term of years at very low or nil rates of interest. By 1970 such co-operatives were the largest single source of new construction in Czechoslovakia and Poland. In addition, private house building also became steadily more common. In rural areas private housing had always been the norm. Individual families in collective farms retained their houses and immediate outbuildings, and new construction and repairs of rural housing were more easily accomplished. This was especially true during the early 1950s when building materials and labour were more easily obtained in rural than urban areas. In Romania, for example, between 1953 and 1964 over 70 per cent of all new housing was constructed in rural areas, and 96 per cent of it was private construction. The drift from the countryside which put pressure on urban housing stocks also reduced pressure on rural ones. It ought, however, to be noted that despite this, population densities per room were higher in the rural areas of Poland than in urban ones throughout the 1950s and 1960s. By the mid-1960s individual provision was officially favoured, despite the ideological complications involved. The 1971 Bulgarian Constitution confirmed the right of citizens to own houses, flats and villas. It had become increasingly common throughout eastern Europe for the more affluent sectors of society to construct country holiday homes. The overall effect was that private residential construction was encouraged. Stiff qualifications on eligibility for subsidised housing were introduced in Hungary in 1970 and in Poland in 1974, and the controls on house construction were loosened and the acquisition of permits simplified. In Romania state-owned property was sold off and building plots provided cheaply.

Though the 1970s saw a substantial effort to make good some of the previous neglect, housing provision in 1980 remained more satisfactory in the countryside than in urban areas. The position was probably best in the three smallest countries. The government of the DDR launched a major programme of construction and renovation in 1971 and stepped it up in 1976. Even then it was not expected to be completed until 1990. The Bulgarian government made 1983 its target date for providing every family with its own housing unit. Conditions in Czechoslovakia on the other hand stagnated, with waiting lists in 1976 of between six and eight years for young couples seeking the allocation of housing. The problem was worst in Poland and was growing rather than diminishing. Waiting lists had lengthened to ten years and were still growing, and only one-fifth of the country's young married couples had their own apartment. Three-quarters had to make do with one room, frequently shared with others.

The position of women

War and post-war upheaval distorted the population balance in eastern Europe. In the DDR and Poland in particular there was a striking imbalance between the sexes, with women forming over 55 per cent of the population of the former in 1950 and 55 per cent in Poland in 1945. Less extreme variations existed elsewhere. In the DDR the imbalance persisted and in 1979 still over 53 per cent of the population was female. The mobilisation of women was a major objective of communist governments. While it would be excessively cynical to attribute the regard paid to female equality to a major drive to harness women for the labour force, there can be little doubt that the demonstrable concern to provide maternity leave, crèches, kindergartens and other enterprise-based facilities led to mothers continuing to go out to work. The most assiduous provision of such amenities was in the DDR, where the labour of women was crucial to the national economy.

The pace at which women were recruited into the industrial workforce was striking as a high percentage of women became involved in the full range of industrial activities and service industries. By 1954 one-third of the labour force in mining and manufacturing industries in Czechoslovakia, Poland and Hungary was composed of women who were finding their way into heavy industry. In Poland, for example, they constituted nearly one-quarter of the workforce in non-ferrous metallurgy, mining and in the lumbering and wood-working industries. Similar figures were recorded in Romania, where despite the lower demand for labour one-quarter of the total workforce in 1953 was female. The percentage of women in the national labour force continued everywhere to grow. By 1975 48 per cent of the Czechoslovak workforce was female, and by the mid-1970s over half that of the DDR. In the case of Yugoslavia the percentage of women rose steadily: from 18 per cent in 1940 to 24 per cent in 1952 and over 31 per cent in 1971.

Particular sectors of the economy came to rely on women. This remained true of agriculture throughout the region, whether private or collectivised. This was not surprising, given the close traditional involvement of peasant women with farm labour and it was natural that as peasant men left, the gap created would be filled by their womenfolk. The overall effect, however, was radically to change the nature of agricultural work. In peasant societies agricultural activities were clearly divided into male and female spheres. The sharp differentiation left the field-work by and large to the men while women assumed responsibility for work in the house and immediate garden area and with the animals. This division according to sex went with the heavy demands placed upon the rural female workforce, so that although there was nothing novel about women taking a leading part in agricultural work, there was a fundamental. change that by 1960 marked a radical break with the social work patterns of the traditional peasant world and brought to an end the established division between male and female. Paradoxically, the reverse process emerged in non-agricultural work, where clear differences arose between the spheres of work of men and women. Certain occupations became heavily dependent on women. This was especially true of education, the health services and social work, of the retail trade, of tourism, of finance and insurance, and of certain branches of light industry. The most detailed information came from Yugoslavia, where in 1970 women constituted 54 per cent of the workforce in the social services as a whole, including 71 per cent of social workers and 68 per cent of those in the health services, 53 per cent of those working in schools and over 61 per cent of those engaged in finance and insurance. Women constituted an absolute majority of those in the textile, leather and shoe and tobacco industries, and nearly half of those in tourism and the retail trade. Similar patterns were clearly discernible elsewhere.

Although women played such a crucial part in the labour force, with the concomitant opportunities and advantages opened to them, there were marked discrepancies in the levels of remuneration between men and women and the occupations with substantial female components enjoyed rather low social esteem. Thus medical doctors and school teachers were not well paid. Moreover, the least well-paid occupations were universally those in which women formed a majority of the workforce, as was well illustrated by information gathered in Czechoslovakia during the 1960s that showed that occupations paying substantially below average wages included elementary school teachers, hospital nurses, shop assistants, domestic servants, and nurses in crèches and kindergartens. School teachers and medical doctors in general practice regularly scored rather low in opinion polls designed to explore the social esteem attached to various professions. Popular esteem and levels of remuneration were closely linked. Though women's pay was low, averaging in Czechoslovakia in 1968 two-thirds that of men, their earnings had come by the 1970s to form a major part of family budgets, whether urban or rural. Even lump-sum maternity allowances and the substantial graded family allowances did not compensate for the drop in income and living standards attendant upon women leaving work to start a family. In addition to rather low pay and poor esteem, women were also strikingly underrepresented in the higher managerial and directing posts, whether in the economy or in politics. This was the more surprising as women shared equally in the great expansion of educational facilities. Elementary education made compulsory by 1950 for girls as well as boys acted as a mechanism of social mobility for women as well as men. By the 1970s girls were taking advantage of secondary and higher education on equal terms with boys, girls were as likely to enter secondary education as were boys, and more did so in Czechoslovakia, while it was common for at least 40 per cent of university students to be female. In such circumstances it was surprising that women did not play a more significant role in the higher reaches of the decision-making process.

In the domestic sphere, however, the position of women changed as family cohesion became seriously weakened by 1980. The impact of education and social mobility had led to the virtual disappearance of the old peasant family structure. More serious was the increasing rate of divorce (see Table 5.7) and the growing laxity in sexual relationships. This was aided by the easy availability of abortion, by far the most common form of birth control in the region. Contraceptive devices were rather uncommon even in 1980, though the contraceptive pill had been

Table 5.7 Divorce rate in eastern European countries, per thousand inhabitants (selected years)

	1957	1966	1967	1973	1975	1980
Bulgaria	0.9		1.16		1.27	1.4
Czechoslovakia	1.07		1.39		2.18	2.2
DDR	1.33		1.66		2.47	2.7
Hungary	1.81		2.06		2.46	2.6
Poland	0.55		0.85		1.21	1.2
Romania	1.86	1.35	nil		1.63	1.6
Yugoslavia	1.14		1.05		1.18	1.0
UK*	0.52		0.88	2.14		2.7†

* UK figures given for comparison.
† Figure for 1979.

available in limited quantities in Hungary, Poland and Czechoslovakia by 1970. Such devices were frowned upon in the early days of communist regimes. None were made in Hungary until 1954 and even during the 1960s and early 1970s it was not uncommon for them to be available only on medical prescription. In strongly Roman Catholic areas traditional religious sanctions reinforced governmental attitudes. In the circumstances the relatively liberal attitude to abortion was striking. Commonplace everywhere by the mid-1960s, it only slowly began to give way to mechanical contraceptive devices after 1970 when the impact of industrialism began to have its effect even in rather old-fashioned Serb areas of Yugoslavia. Abortion, however, remained a fact of life for most women in the region. An example of its spread could be seen in Czechoslovakia, where abortion was legalised in 1958 for health or social reasons such as inadequate housing. By 1968 the abortion rate was over half that of live births in the country. A similar burgeoning in the rate led to concern in Romania, where the law had been liberalised in 1956 and where a decade later the incidence had mushroomed. The government's alarm led in October 1966 to the ending of legal abortion except in abnormal circumstances, the sole example of restriction in the area.

The other striking development after 1950 was the steep increase in the incidence of divorce. The leaders of the new communist regimes set an example. Many of them were divorced, some more than once. Where Tito and Djilas, Ulbricht and Honecker led others followed, and eastern European divorce rates during the 1950s increased steadily. This was especially so in Czechoslovakia, the DDR, Hungary and Romania. In another markedly aberrant development, the Romanian government tightened up on divorce procedures in 1966, reducing the rate to nil in 1967 whereafter a slow rise by the mid-1970s brought the rate back to that of 1965. Elsewhere divorce rates in Poland were abnormally low, as they were in Bulgaria and Yugoslavia, where in another marked variation from the regional norm they fell steadily between 1948 and the mid-1960s before a new increase began, apparently associated with the stresses on family life caused by husbands working abroad. However, by the mid-1970s the rates of 1948 had not been equalled.

Medical services

In addition to expanded and enhanced educational opportunities and equality between men and women, a third major element in the social transformation of the area was the expansion of free medical facilities with the accompanying implications for life expectancy and levels of health. As with other areas of social expenditure, the improvements did not come instantaneously, for it was not until the later 1950s and early 1960s that governments began substantially to increase the sums allocated to the medical services and to expand them throughout each country. The statistical information showed impressive rates of progress in the physical provision of doctors and hospital facilities (see Table 5.8) but hid significant variations. In the case of Hungary, for example, in 1972 there were 7.5 doctors for every 10,000 inhabitants in the country-side but 36 in towns and 46.4 in the capital, Budapest. Once more, there was a disproportionate provision between town and countryside with the latter noticeably disadvantaged. Thus in 1969 80 per cent of Romanian doctors lived in urban areas leaving many country districts without any provision at all, while in 1972 half the villages in Hungary, containing 20 per cent of the rural population, had no resident doctor. After 1970 efforts were made throughout the region to correct the imbalance between town and country, in accordance with the general policy of improving living standards in the latter and making life more attractive. The process was based on the establishment of a network of centres, one for each settlement system. These offered a range of medical facilities. Doctors working at polyclinics rarely made home visits and patients were not guaranteed the opportunity of seeing the same adviser on each visit, though both might be secured by payment of a fee. Treatment had been free to all workers in the socialised economy and to their families since the beginning, but the position of the self-employed and private peasant farmers was less favourable and they were not universally included in the system until the 1970s. A major priority was always the care of mothers and children, the success of which was reflected in the tumbling infant mortality rates (see Table 5.4). Many formerly endemic diseases such as tuberculosis and malaria were eradicated and the overall level of public health substantially improved so that by 1980 the difference between the life expectancy figures and overall death rates per thousand inhabitants in eastern and western Europe had narrowed appreciably.

Table 5.8   Number of physicians (A) and hospital beds (B) per 10,000 population in eastern European countries (selected years)

	1948		1960		1970		1977	
	A	B	A	B	A	B	A	B
Bulgaria			17.0	82.5	18.6	77.5	22.6	87.0
Czechoslovakia	9.0	58	17.5	78.1	20.0	103.0	25.3	123.5
DDR			12.2	119.0	16.8	117.6	18.9	106.4
Hungary	10.0	52	15.3	87.2	19.2	81.3	23.0	87.7
Poland	3.5	28	12.7	70.3	15.2	76.3	16.5	76.3
Romania		28	13.5	72.5	12.1	83.3	13.6	91.7
Yugoslavia			7.1*		10.0	56.5	13.0	60.2
UK†			12.0		12.7	94.3	15.8	112.4

* Figure for 1962.
† UK figures based on different definitions are not directly comparable.

Retirement

Healthier, longer-living populations saw a steady increase in the proportion of the population past retirement age. By the end of the 1970s life expectancy exceeded 70 and was greater for women than for men and the number of pensioners to be supported by national economies was growing. Significantly this was the one section of the populace readily afforded permission to leave the DDR for the Federal Republic. It would, however, be misleading to think of pensioners as retired, for in both Hungary and the DDR efforts were made to persuade citizens to work on after the retirement age by offering them financial inducements. Pensioners everywhere played an important role in the agricultural labour force though they continued to be economically active in a wide variety of other occupations also. For many families the presence of pensioned relations able to devote a substantial part of their time to the household plot was the key to extracting the maximum benefit from it. The position of the retired in urban areas was by and large worse than in the countryside, for there was little opportunity to supplement income by produce grown at home and the opportunities for part-time work were more restricted in urban than in rural areas. The really poor inhabitants in eastern Europe were urban pensioners dependent entirely on state pensions. Surveys during the early 1970s suggested that such pensioners lived in less satisfactory housing, were dependent on the state food supply system and could not afford to supplement this by purchases on the private market, and had restricted access to cultural opportunities. Despite the advent of the industrialised society, for the old in eastern Europe it was still highly advantageous to be part of a family with roots in the countryside, having children strategically placed in both industrial and agricultural sectors. Without the support of a family, life for the retired in eastern Europe was difficult.

The provision of pensions by the communist regimes reflected the same pattern of evolution as other social services. Initially made available only to those engaged in the socialised sector of the economy, their rates during the first years were little more than the bare minimum necessary to bring the aged above the poverty line. As with other sectors of the social security network, the rates of pensions were raised progressively during the 1960s and 1970s and their eligibility extended to cover the previously excluded sectors of society. By the 1970s it was standard in eastern Europe for the retirement age for men to be 60 and for women 55 years. Those who worked in especially dangerous or demanding industries, such as mining or heavy metallurgy, retired earlier, as did women who had given birth to large families. As in the West, it was normal for members of the police and armed forces to retire earlier. The rate of pension was linked to length of service and to average earnings during the past five or ten years of work. Despite the increase in the numbers of pensioners the percentage of national income paid out in

Table 5.9   Social consumption funds: distribution of payments between various social services in selected eastern European countries, in percentages, for 1970, 1979 and 1980

	1970				1979				1980			
	Pensions	Education and culture	Health	Other*	Pensions	Education and culture	Health	Other*	Pensions	Education and culture	Health	Other*
Bulgaria	52.3	25.0	15.2	7.5	44.2	22.6	15.3	17.9	47.2	22.3	15.1	15.4
Czechoslovakia	57.6	18.7	16.4	7.3	48.6	21.1	15.5	14.8	48.8	21.0	15.6	15.6
DDR	44.2	26.8	12.9	16.1	36.1	22.5	17.8	23.6	37.1	21.7	17.9	23.3
Hungary	44.9	23.0	21.7	10.4	57.0	21.0	14.0	8.0	58.0	20.0	14.0	8.0
Poland	39.2	27.4	24.7	8.7	44.1	N.A.	N.A.	N.A.	44.9	N.A.	N.A.	N.A.

N.A. Figure not available.
* Includes expenditure on housing maintenance.

pensions did not increase substantially, and although the major effort to improve rates during the 1970s was accelerating at the end of the decade, the percentage of social expenditure devoted to pensions was falling (see Table 5.9). Improvements of 7–8 per cent annually in Bulgaria were similar to those in Czechoslovakia with Romanian rates somewhat less. Very substantial increases were paid in 1980 in the DDR, Hungary and Poland, though in the latter two cases they probably barely compensated for large price rises. Over all the position of pensioners relative to other sections of society did not greatly change. Income levels were, however, an insufficient guide to the relative living standards of pensioners for they benefited from the low level of rents, low prices for electricity, gas and other public amenities and from low official food prices, all subsidised by governments. The availability of these varied markedly, and often required a substantial input of personal effort.

Living standards
Overall standards of living were a compound of social and private expenditure. The two elements were incorporated within the overall national plans and were subjected to the apportionment of resources in accordance with the decisions of national governments. Given the scale of priorities of the latter, it was not surprising that living standards fell sharply in the early years of the communist regimes, began to recover during the later 1950s, faltered during the 1960s and recorded notable improvements during the earlier 1970s before, by 1980, showing signs of faltering once more. The improvements of the later 1950s and 1960s were by and large associated with increasing resources being allocated to social services and especially to the education and health services, while those of the 1970s more closely reflected increases in the levels of national product allocated to private consumption. In 1979 the highest percentage so distributed were in the DDR, where it was 68.8 per cent and Hungary at 65 per cent. The lowest was in Bulgaria, where 53 per cent of national product was allotted to private consumption. The share of social consumption was a mirror image, ranging from 22.8 per cent in Bulgaria and 21.6 per cent in Czechoslovakia to 11.2 per cent in the DDR and 11 per cent in Hungary. Hungary, Romania and the DDR were countries in which private consumption played the more significant role in 1979, while the reverse was true in Bulgaria and Czechoslovakia.

Social expenditures varied in scale and incidence from state to state but also from region to region and, increasingly importantly, from enterprise to enterprise within individual countries. The economic reforms of the 1960s had left greater freedom of action to enterprises to decide the overall pattern of expenditures within the global sums laid down by the central planning agencies, and the inevitable result was variations in the scope and intensity of investment in social facilities. Cultural and leisure-time activities financed from the earmarked funds of enterprises reflected the decisions of management and also the relative prosperity of the individual organisation. Given the important role of such provision within the overall standard of living of the workforce, such variations could be of considerable importance. Central government policy towards the level of subsidy by the national economy also played a crucial part. The record of different states varied. In the DDR, for example, there was a relatively large and increasing level of subsidy that amounted to 12 per cent of NMP in 1976, increasing gradually to 13½ per cent in 1980. Prices remained virtually unchanged. Between 70 and 75 per cent of the total subsidy was spent supporting food prices. Elsewhere the pattern was much less consistent. In Poland steep rises in food prices, the most recent in 1981 when they increased by over one-quarter, alternated with prolonged periods of stability, while in Hungary the first moves to reduce subsidies and permit domestic prices to rise to world levels were made during the early 1970s. Public reaction led to the process being discontinued for five years until mounting economic problems after 1979 led the government to renew the process, ensuring virtually static living standards and a price rise of over 9 per cent in 1980. In Yugoslavia, on the other hand, a pattern more familiar in western Europe emerged. Substantial price rises led to high rates of inflation during the 1960s and 1970s, increasing from 9.4 per cent in 1976 to a remarkable 22 per cent in 1979. Rates remained high in 1980 and 1981. They contrasted markedly with the 4 per cent recorded annually in Bulgaria between 1976 and 1980, or the average 1.4 per cent in Romania between the same dates. Even in badly affected Poland the rate of increase had only reached 8.7 per cent in 1980, though it climbed steeply in 1981 and 1982.

In addition to overall governmental planning policy and to social and private consumption, which reflected the decisions of the planners, albeit in a frequently imperfect form, various marginal elements could and did affect living standards appreciably. Access to opportunities for spare-time employment, the possession of scarce or highly prized skills, or the availability of surplus produce from private household plots could all be turned into income on the admittedly small private market at rates far higher than those pertaining in the state-controlled sector. Access to rewards and privileges such as private shopping amenities, special hospital and medical care facilities, foreign travel to other socialist or, even more valuable, to capitalist countries, the opportunity to secure preferential allocation of residence permits for capital cities and to procure favourable treatment in the distribution of new residential accommodation with modern conveniences at nominal rents, the reserved hotels and restaurants of superior quality available only to designated groups and the exclusive clubs and resort areas at favoured holiday centres were all items that weighed far more in the maintenance of high standards of living than money income. The favoured created for themselves a network of subsidised facilities and special opportunities for members of their families which it was easy for the outsider to overlook unless they became too glaring, as was the case with President Tito's flamboyant palaces. Yet such special opportunities were the bedrock of the life-style of many eastern Europeans and mattered far more than cash incomes. It was therefore all the easier for them to regard with equanimity the substantial increase in cash incomes obtained by certain sectors in the 1970s by private economic activity. Successful peasants in Hungary or Poland or skilled experts able to utilise their spare time to act as repairers or builders were often able to secure for themselves surprisingly large money incomes. As these could not be invested or used to secure significant property and as there were major restrictions on the availability of consumer goods, in line with the decisions of the planners, large cash incomes were in fact of marginal overall importance. While they created ill-feeling among the population at large they were of no continuing importance given the absence of the machinery necessary to turn money into power. In that respect access to power was still the prerequisite for high living standards and that was still firmly in the hands of the Party.

Consumption

In private consumption the major element was the purchase of food. It acquired disproportionate importance given the relatively low cost of housing and public amenities. As a consequence, the population was extremely sensitive to increases in official food prices. Very large proportions of income were devoted to the purchase of food, drink and tobacco. In Czechoslovakia in 1962 such purchases accounted for over half total private expenditure, and the overall levels of expenditure on food remained high throughout the 1970s. Significant variations between the expenditures of worker, peasant and non-manual worker households continued to be evident in 1979 (see Table 5.10). As the relative economic performance of the various countries improved there was a steady though unspectacular improvement in the quality of foodstuffs consumed in the region. In 1950 potatoes played a conspicuous part in the diet in Poland and the DDR, while grains of various types predominated in Bulgaria and Romania. Everywhere consumption of fats, meat and meat products and dairy products was restricted, with the highest per capita consumption of such items being found in the DDR, Czechoslovakia and Hungary. As living standards rose so did the consumption of protein-rich foodstuffs with per capita meat consumption being a rough guide to the relative improvement in living standards (see Table 5.11).

Alcohol consumption also increased, leading to excessive drinking, an established feature of all communist societies. Consumption per head was extremely high, and individual countries had the dubious distinction of boasting some of the highest levels anywhere. By the mid-1970s

Table 5.10   Percentage of family income expended on foodstuffs: 1970 compared with 1980 (selected countries)

	1970			1980		
	Worker families	Peasant families	Non-manual worker families	Worker families	Peasant families	Non-manual worker families
Bulgaria	33.9	34.8	29.1	36.8	41.4	34.9
Czechoslovakia	33.3	26.4	29.5	27.0	26.0	24.4
DDR	27.1*	28.2		27.1*	26.5	
Hungary	33.8	32.8	27.7	33.8	35.9	28.0
Poland	46.7	53.9	N.A.	40.9	42.7	N.A.
Romania				45.6	62.7	N.A.
UK+	25.7	(35.0)		22.7	(30.5)	

N.A. Figure not available.
* Includes non-manual worker families.
+ All families, figure in brackets includes alcohol and tobacco as well as foodstuffs.

Table 5.11   Consumption of meat and meat products in selected eastern European countries in kilograms per head (selected years)

	1950	1967	1973	1980
Bulgaria	21 (1952)	43	50	61.2
Czechoslovakia	28.9	63	77.3	85
DDR	25.6	62	74	89.4
Hungary	34.3	52	63.2	70.5
Poland	42.7	56 (1966)	62.5	74
Romania	16.1	31 (1963)	45 (1975)	62
UK*	51	70.4	68.4	71.2

* UK figures given for comparison.
Sources: Adapted from G.R. Feiwel, *Poland's Industrialization Policy* (Praeger, 1972) vol. 2, p. 647, table 67; J.M. Montias, *The Economic Development of Communist Rumania* (MIT Press, 1967) p. 51, table 1.15; UN, Economic Commission for Europe, *Annual Economic Survey of Europe*; Central Statistical Office, *Annual Abstract of Statistics*.

Poland had the highest per head consumption of spirits in the world, Czechoslovakia the second highest consumption per head of beer, with the DDR also among the world leaders, while Hungary vied with Poland in consumption of spirits and occupied third place in the world table of consumption of wine. There were major problems associated with drinking by the young. Over half of those aged 18 or under in Bulgaria drank regularly, rates in Czechoslovakia were higher and not very different in Poland. Not surprisingly there were high levels of alcohol addiction. Despite the absence of precise statistical information, the repeated warnings as well as major efforts to sponsor sobriety pointed to drink as a major social problem in Bulgaria, Hungary and Poland. Everywhere drink was an important component in the commission of crime, especially cases of murder, sexual assault and general unruly behaviour subsumed under the overall heading 'hooliganism'. In Hungary it was generally believed that over-drinking was closely associated with the suicide rate, one of the highest in the world.

Governmental concern to lessen the consumption of alcohol and its anxiety to increase exports of foodstuffs to pay for essential imports of raw materials and machinery and meet the burden of foreign debt payments grew. They sought therefore to encourage their populations to switch their consumption to manufactured items and away from food-stuffs, manipulating prices to promote the purchase of consumer durables. This objective was relatively unsuccessful, however, and by 1980 food requirements in eastern Europe remained high, placing con-siderable strain on the national economies as planners sought to satisfy both internal demand and the projected export requirement. The increasing pressures produced the phenomenon of the shopping expedition to neighbouring socialist countries in search for foodstuffs less readily obtainable at home, with the relatively well-supplied Hungary and Bulgaria favourite destinations attracting large numbers of visitors from the wealthier DDR and Czechoslovakia. After events in Poland in 1980 and 1981, the impetus towards which was greatly assisted by food shortages, it was scarcely surprising that other governments were showing signs of unease at food supply difficulties and at the predations of citizens from friendly neighbouring states. Restrictions on travel were applied, initially in the DDR and Czechoslovakia and subsequently elsewhere.

Provision and consumption of durable, manufactured goods followed a similar pattern, except that governmental decisions and planning targets were all important. There was no private manufacturing facilities to supplement the state-controlled ones, as was the case with agricultural products. Given the early emphasis on the production of heavy industry and of plant, machinery and other 'producer' goods as opposed to 'consumption' goods, the availability of industrial products to the private citizen was adversely affected. Indeed until about 1955 the position was worse than it had been in much of the region during the immediate pre-war years. Matters began slowly to improve after the politically unnerving events of 1955 and 1956, as governments recognised that offers of spectacular consumption levels in the future were insufficient to secure popular acquiescence in the present and that it was necessary to expand that proportion of the national plan allocated to private consumption. Throughout the region between 1955 and 1960 there were modest but discernible improvements in the supply of cloth, both cotton and woollen, of shoes and footwear, and of other basic items. In the mid-1960s the pattern of consumption began to change as populations began to seek a wider range of goods. Ownership of wireless receivers and later of televisions increased substantially, with a widening of cultural and educational horizons, as well as opportunities for more politically inspired instruction. The boom in wireless acquisition preceded that of televisions by about a decade, as television services became generally available, the latest ones opening in Romania in 1957 and Bulgaria in November 1959 (see Table 5.12). Later still came ownership of motor vehicles. Passenger motor cars were extremely rare in the region after the war, and ownership remained largely in the hands of official and economic organisations. Motor-vehicle construction plants concentrated on production of commercial vehicles and public passenger-carrying conveyances. Ownership of bicycles and motorcycles was relatively widespread, but by the early 1960s the acquisition of a private motor car was a major status symbol, much sought and requiring a substantial downpayment as a deposit against

Table 5.12   Ownership of wireless receivers and television sets, in thousands (selected years)

Wireless receivers					
	1949	1959	1968	1973	1979
Bulgaria	205		2,245	2,266	
Czechoslovakia	2,229	3,050	3,200	3,110	3,778
DDR		5,061	5,940		6,290
Hungary		1,775		2,533	2,590
Poland	1,055	5,000		5,800	8,560
Romania	226		3,030	3,100	3,200
Yugoslavia	220		3,171		4,600
Television sets					
	1958	1961	1968	1973	1978
Bulgaria		31	620	1,381	2,047*
Czechoslovakia	328		2,600	3,400	4,048†
DDR	318		4,170		5,630†
Hungary		605‡		2,199	2,630
Poland	1,883§			5,670	7,710
Romania		245‖	1,200	2,100	3,600
Yugoslavia				2,245	4,200
UK	8,900	12,789‖	15,506	17,293	18,268†

* Figure for 1980.
† Figure for 1979.
‡ Figure for 1964.
§ Figure for 1959.
‖ Figure for 1963.

delivery, often delayed by four or five years. As governments came to acknowledge the popular demand they either expanded their indigenous manufacturing facilities, as with the Wartburg enterprise in the DDR or Skoda in Czechoslovakia, or entered into arrangements with foreign capitalist concerns, as did the Polish government with the Fiat company. After 1970 private ownership increased dramatically as eastern Europe joined the car-owning industrial world (see Table 5.13). A similar delay accompanied the extension of telephone facilities and long delays before connection to the telephone system were normal throughout the 1970s. Unlike motor vehicle production, governments did not greatly expand the facility to meet increasing public demand and access to a private telephone continued to be one of the more valued prerequisites of office and political influence (see Table 5.14).

Table 5.13 Number of inhabitants per private motor car, including taxis, selected eastern European countries (selected years)

	1950	1955	1960	1970	1974	1979
Czechoslovakia				18.7	11.9	7.7
DDR	242.2	143.5	54.1	14.7	10.0	6.6
Hungary	715.3		319.3	43.0	21.3	11.7
Poland	771.2	677.6	253.0	67.8	36.6	19.0*
Yugoslavia	2,562.9	1,388.0	339.2	28.3	15.9	11.8*
UK+	21.1	14.0	9.2	4.8	4.0	3.7

* Figure for 1978.
+ UK figures given for comparison.

Table 5.14 Number of telephones per one hundred inhabitants: eastern European countries, 1970 and 1978

	1970	1978
Bulgaria	5.6	11.6
Czechoslovakia	13.8	19.6
DDR	12.3	17.6
Hungary	8.0	10.7
Poland	5.7	8.8
Romania	3.2	
Yugoslavia	3.6	7.1*
UK+	25.1	41.5

* Figure for 1977.
+ UK figures given for comparison.

If access to wireless, television and motor vehicles was of great importance in widening the horizons of social life, the acquisition of household durables was of equal significance in easing the work-load on the private sphere. This was especially important for working women, who continued to bear the brunt of the traditionally female areas of housework and care of children. Here too a great improvement set in from the mid-1960s as completion of the first stages of industrialisation permitted greater provision of investment capital and provided the necessary steel and engineering capacity for the manufacture of consumer durables. The general availability of adequate electricity supplies was another essential prerequisite for modern household equipment. Production of washing-machines, vacuum cleaners, refrigerators and electric and gas stoves and other equipment grew from the early 1960s and reached a plateau about 1975, whereafter it levelled off. The availability of such items grew sharply (see Table 5.15). As in other respects, the position was best in the DDR and Czechoslovakia. By 1980 in the DDR at least, such equipment was virtually a standard feature of all households. Elsewhere the position was less satisfactory, though Hungary was fast achieving the same density of provision as that obtaining in the DDR and Czechoslovakia.

Any attempt to draw up a balance sheet of relative standards of living in eastern Europe was fraught with difficulties. It was certainly true that there had been a progressive improvement in the region beginning everywhere at some point during the mid-1950s and accelerating especially after 1970. Food rationing, a fact of life since 1945, had been progressively dismantled everywhere though the possibilities of its re-introduction remained, as was best illustrated in the case of Poland where rationing was reintroduced in 1951 and again in 1980. In the case of Yugoslavia the ending of rationing in 1951 was only made possible by substantial and continuing food aid from the USA, an advantage not available to other governments in the region. Overall food supplies were usually adequate after 1950 to meet basic nutritional requirements, though diet remained in 1980 less varied and more limited than was normal in western Europe and harvest failure and distribution blockage could still produce localised shortages. As the experience of both Poland and Romania in 1980 showed, food supply could still be precarious at times and the traditional dependency on agriculture as a principal component of the national wealth though reduced remained not inconsiderable. Industrial production had been steadily diversified and after 1960 especially had come to have greater regard for the domestic consumer as provision of household goods and domestic equipment had grown to meet the clear demands of the population. In the more advanced economies such provision was nearing the stage of meeting requirements. In Romania and Yugoslavia that point was still some way off in 1980, while the position in Bulgaria was in advance of that of the other

Table 5.15 Availability of washing-machines and refrigerators in eastern European countries, excluding Yugoslavia, per one hundred households (per one thousand inhabitants) (selected years)

	1965		1970		1975		1980	
	Washing-machine	Refrigerator	Washing-machine	Refrigerator	Washing-machine	Refrigerator	Washing-machine	Refrigerator
Bulgaria	23	5	50 (141)	29 (81)	50 (176)	61 (174)	(217)	(233)
Czechoslovakia	67	30	86 (276)	56 (177)	110 (363)	79 (260)	(411)	(305)
DDR	28	26	54 (205)	56 (215)	73 (277)	85 (322)	(328)	(423)
Hungary	37	8	55 (179)	32 (103)	67 (228)	64 (220)	(300)	(293)
Poland			81* (185)*	47* (70)*	92 (217)	73 (162)	(253)	(269)
Romania			(46)	(54)	(68)	(96)	(102)	(156)
UK+			65	66	75	91	78	93

+ UK figure is the percentage of households possessing the relevant equipment.
* Figure for 1971.

two Balkan states. Housing in 1980 remained unsatisfactory. A great effort had been made and was continuing, but even where the best quantitative improvements had occurred the overall quality of the housing stock still left much to be desired. It was difficult to choose between Romania, where the targets set in the 1975 Five-year Plan were only 65 per cent achieved but where average floor area of each unit was 75 square metres, and Czechoslovakia where the achievement level was nearer to 90 per cent but each unit averaged only 48 square metres. Provisions of modern conveniences varied widely. Best in the DDR and Czechoslovakia where virtually all new housing had central heating, indoor sanitation and bathrooms and piped water, the position was less satisfactory in Hungary and much less so in Romania. Increasing provision of free educational and health services had had positive beneficial effects by 1980 and better educated youngsters and longer living oldsters were making increased demands on items such as public transport, vacation resorts and cultural amenities, all of which were oversubscribed. Eastern Europe was experiencing a rise in expectations with growing prosperity, a measure of the success of governments in bringing their peoples into the industrial, consumer-oriented world.

Despite the domination of public provision, by 1980 the role of private activity and individual enterprise remained of some importance, especially so for the individuals involved. Private activity could make a significant impact on the margins of social conditions by supplementing and cushioning the overall national provision. Increased income permitted access to private sales of agricultural produce or to the 'commercial' shops in Poland where goods not generally available were sold at higher prices than the subsidised ones in ordinary stores. Access to convertible currencies from relatives abroad or remittances permitted purchases in special shops reserved for foreigners or holders of convertible currency. Private enterprise continued to play a vital role in the provision of repair and handicraft facilities even in the DDR and Czechoslovakia where such activities were disapproved. In reality there was probably little to choose between the importance of such private activities in any country in the area. The process of encouraging it had gone farthest in Hungary, Yugoslavia and Poland, where during the 1970s official approval had been extended somewhat erratically. It had led by 1980 to the emergence of small private operations in the service sector embracing petrol filling-station franchise holding, bar and restaurant operation, and small-scale retailing. It had been more successful in Hungary and Yugoslavia than in Poland.

Whatever indices were taken to compare the overall standards of living in the individual countries of the area, very similar results emerged. In Western calculations of gross national product in US dollars per capita in 1978 the DDR headed the list with $5,660, followed by Czechoslovakia, Poland, Hungary, Bulgaria with Romania and

Yugoslavia at the bottom of the table. Calculations based on life expectancy, availability of medical facilities, GNP per capita and the number of students as a percentage of the total population made by Yugoslav scholars in 1974 revealed the same ranking order, with the transposition of Poland and Hungary. Ownership of consumer durables, availability of housing, production of electricity with its indirect importance for living conditions, provision of child-care facilities and other indicators of social conditions reinforced a picture that had changed little in relative rank order over the years between 1950 and 1980. The DDR headed the list, followed by Czechoslovakia. Then came Hungary, Poland, Bulgaria and Romania and Yugoslavia. Of these, conditions in Hungary and Bulgaria seemed to be improving most rapidly, while the plight of Poland in 1980 sent shock waves throughout the area, and Romania too was experiencing serious internal difficulties. In each state there had been very considerable improvements during the thirty years, but their relative standing had not changed.

Popular attitudes
By 1980 the welfare society that governments had introduced over a quarter of a century had struck root. Surveys and opinion polls suggested the industrial workforce were appreciative of the moral aspects of the new society, valuing the security provided by full employment and state provision of medical care and insurance, and stressing its egalitarian nature. In particular the ending of formal divisions between employee and worker, symbolised by separate canteens and restrooms in places of work, and the creation of a sense that all were working and dependent for their livelihood on a common employer seemed to have struck root. Certain differences in attitudes were discernible between newcomers to industry and those long settled and adjusted, with a strong correlation between newcomers and unskilled workers. These tended to be more concerned with immediate improvements in living standards and to be less impressed by the more abstract considerations of security and equality. There was also a strong correlation between skilled workers and Party membership. Workers no longer commented on the division between themselves and management or national political leadership on the grounds of taste, cultural preferences or language but discerned clashes of interest based on control, subordination and material possessions. As town and country were also closely connected it was legitimate to anticipate that such attitudes would gradually permeate an homogeneous society. Given the overall objective of communist governments to shape a new socialist man with 'positive' attitudes to society and social duties and obligations as opposed to 'negative' individualistic traits, there was every reason for quiet governmental satisfaction in the more advanced states of the region. It was noticeable that only in Romania did the government still anxiously urge the need to work together in a spirit of unity stressing the

behaviour expected of socialist citizens and decrying egotism which restricted the influence of society upon the individual. Such revolutionary puritanism was a thing of the past elsewhere by 1980.

The spread of socialist attitudes bore with it, however, some dangers for regimes whose outward commitment to welfare provision and vociferous claims to be egalitarian were deceptive. In particular, despite claims to the contrary, the system was not based on equal treatment. Indeed the very marked privileges available to restricted circles and dependent upon Party membership, occupational status or individual activity did provoke ill-feeling among the populace at large, as did the higher salaries of white-collar workers and administrators. To the extent that socialist attitudes spread, such inequalities would become less acceptable, and the demands of industrial workers at times of internal political upheaval in Poland, Hungary and Czechoslovakia suggested that, paradoxically, socialism could be a danger to communist governments. Intellectual criticism of an unequal system might be reinforced by the personal experiences of workers. Moreover, it was striking that the profession of politics was poorly regarded throughout the region. Surveys were unanimous in revealing a considerable degree of popular cynicism in eastern as in western Europe as to the motives and honesty of politicians. Greatest public esteem attached to the occupants of posts requiring considerable educational preparation or training and roughly definable as purveyors of welfare services to the community: university professors, specialist medical personnel, engineers, scientific research workers and certain skilled workers such as miners or skilled engineering workers.

If the picture of a society accepting approved attitudes towards and deriving its values from social action was comforting, there was undeniably an important recalcitrant minority. Frequent exhortations to observe socialist discipline at work and to respect social property reinforced the impression that there was considerable absenteeism and petty pilfering. The incidence of such offences in the courts and sentences for misdemeanours comprised the second largest category of crime after the rather imprecise one of political offences, which covered a multitude of sins. Some evidence from Poland and Czechoslovakia suggested that when government demands upon workers overstepped the limits considered acceptable and proper by the latter the incidence of theft and decline in the standard of work increased. The creation of a suitably socialist attitude among workers laid equal obligations on government, implying an agreed level of work performance and behaviour in return for agreed levels of production, remuneration and social provision. By 1980 it was also reasonably clear that a further element in the relationship between government and population was a degree of disengagement from the political process. Apathy, lethargy and disinterest in politics and an increasing preoccupation with family, friends and leisure pursuits were discernible in Hungary, Czechoslovakia and Yugoslavia.

It was officially denounced, yet it was hard not to believe that such attitudes were tacitly accepted, especially when an interest in politics could produce the explosion that, after a decade of disinterest in public affairs, took place in Poland in 1980. Disengagement was preferable to activism if it led to disaffection. The exceptions were Romania, where the noisy campaign for an involved and concerned citizenry may well have been less successful than it sounded to be, and the DDR, whose disciplined citizens achieved a high level of participation in political campaigns, production drives, beautification schemes, friendship rallies and study groups.

The crime statistics of the region suggested some success. It was rather difficult, however, to draw precise parallels with non-communist society for the concept of crime was not readily assimilable to Western notions. The crime rate in the DDR, for example, was very low, those notified to the police amounting to about 640 per 100,000 population per year. These mainly related to traffic offences and to offences against socialist property. It was certainly true that the DDR was a markedly law-abiding society, but many matters that would have been regarded as crimes in Western society were covered by the system of parallel courts and informal social activity common throughout the region. Domestic matters, such as relations between spouses and between parents and children, problems of local significance, such as disorderly behaviour or aberrant conduct and other minor matters, usually fell within the purview of courts set up within individual enterprises, housing blocks, educational establishments, offices and other social and work units. Informal and non-professional in their composition, they came under the overall aegis of the appropriate Party unit and were entrusted with the function of rehabilitating offenders through comradely castigation and social supervision. Such institutions reflected the official view that crime resulted from confusion in the minds of the imperfectly socialised and was the product of cultural deficiencies that laid the offender open to the baneful influence of traditional ways and the insidious effects of Western capitalism. The natural conclusion to this theory was that offenders should be re-educated into socialist harmony, at the lowest level through popular disapproval and the continuing pressures of concerned citizens upon a local deviant, and at the highest by the beneficial effects of hard labour in company with other offenders in forced labour camps, under the improving knowledge that such work was of benefit to the community as a whole. Economic advantage and penal theory coincided.

There were, however, indications that modern, urbanised, industrial society had similar problems whatever its ideological basis. Hungary, which gave greater publicity to social and criminal problems than other eastern European states, provided details of its prostitution as well as its alcohol and suicide problems. Violence at sporting occasions was commonplace. Football hooliganism and outbreaks of fighting were a well-attested feature of the Hungarian and Bulgarian sporting scene. Similar troubles were reported in Czechoslovakia, where passions often ran high at ice-hockey matches. Other sparse details of social troubles emerged by the end of the 1970s in the DDR, where juvenile delinquency had emerged as a definite problem in its own right, including a sophisticated system of squatting in East Berlin to take advantage of the machinery for allocating residential accommodation, and in Poland where one of the consequences of the relaxation of censorship in 1980 was the revelation that there was a considerable drug problem among Polish youth.

Further reading
Many of the works listed at the end of Chapter 4 are relevant to social developments.

1. *General works:*
Faber, B.L. (ed.), *The Social Structure of Eastern Europe* (Praeger, 1976).
French, R.A., and Ian-Hamilton, F.E., *The Socialist City* (J. Wiley, 1979).
Grant, N.D.C., *Society, Schools and Progress in Eastern Europe* (Pergamon, 1969).
Horvat, B., 'The Welfare of the Common Man', *World Development*, vol. 2, no. vii, 1974, pp. 29ff.
Obrebski, J., *The Changing Peasantry in Eastern Europe* (Schenckman, 1976).
Pundeff, M.V., 'Education for Communism', in S. Fischer-Galati (ed.), *Eastern Europe in the Sixties* (Praeger, 1963).
Triska, J., and Gati, C. (eds), *Blue Collar Workers in Eastern Europe* (Allen & Unwin, 1981).
Volgyes, I. (ed.), *Social Deviance in Eastern Europe* (Westview Press, 1978).
Volgyes, I. (ed.), *The Peasantry of Eastern Europe*, vol. 2 (Pergamon, 1979).

2. *Individual countries:*
Byrnes, R.F. (ed.), *The Zadruga. Essays by and in Honour of P.E. Mosely* (University of Notre Dame Press, 1976).
Chirot, D., 'Social Change in Communist Romania', *Social Forces*, vol. 57, no. ii, 1978, pp. 457ff.
Donath, F., *Reform and Revolution. Transformation of Hungary's Agriculture 1945–1970* (Corvina Press, 1980).
Enyedi, G. (ed.), *Rural Transformation in Hungary* (Akademiai Kiado, 1976).
Ferge, Z., *A Society in the Making. Hungarian Social and Societal Policy 1945–75* (Penguin, 1979).
Hale, J., *Ceausescu's Romania* (Harrap, 1971).
Halpern, J.M., and Halpern, B.K., *A Serbian Village in Historical Perspective* (Holt, Rinehart & Winston, 1972).
Jambrek, P., *Development and Social Change in Yugoslavia* (Saxon House, 1975).
Krejci, J., *Social Change and Stratification in Postwar Czechoslovakia* (Macmillan, 1972).
Krejci, J., *Social Structure in Divided Germany* (Croom Helm, 1976).
Lane, D., and Kolankiewicz, G., *Social Groups in Polish Society* (Macmillan, 1973).
Salzman, Z., and Scheufler, V., *Komarov, a Czech Farming Village* (Holt, Rinehart and Winston, 1974).
Szczepanski, J., *Polish Society* (Random House, 1970).
Volgyes, I., 'Modernization, Stratification and Elite Development in Hungary', *Social Forces*, vol. 57, no. ii, 1978, pp. 500ff.

6

CULTURE IN EASTERN EUROPE

In the revolution in people's attitudes to which communists were committed, culture had its part to play along with economic change and political power. Communist ideology gave prominence to culture and leisure-time activities that were seen as far more than merely recreational. They had a key role to play in shaping the new socialist citizen. Relationship to place of work and the forces of political control and social organisation would be supplemented by reading materials, games played, theatrical and cinematic performances, by wireless broadcasts and television pictures. Such ambitious objectives were consistent with the deeply moral nature of early communist enthusiasts seeking to change people's attitudes and, with them, the world. Idealistic and Utopian, they fully subscribed to the objective of a social re-education which to less sympathetic minds looked very much like brain-washing. They also believed that throughout history culture and access to cultural facilities had been the prerogative of the wealthy and propertied. In the new people's democracies music, theatre, art, sport and literature were to be commonly available, and were to be offered to all thereby opening opportunities for self-enrichment and cultural enhancement. As a symbol of this commitment there appeared through-out the region new Palaces of Culture, modelled on those in the USSR and often the gifts of the Soviet government. As an earnest of the importance attached to culture and to the responsibilities of communist citizens to achieve new levels of self-enhancement, eastern European leaders were pictured as lovers of music and literature. Their tastes in these matters were moreover as conservative and respectable as any latter-day bourgeois traditionalist could wish.

Provision of cultural facilities
Throughout the region there occurred an impressive explosion of material provision. More books were written, more translated from foreign languages and more classics revived, and they were printed in

greater quantities and sold more cheaply than ever before. Libraries mushroomed. However defined, the achievement was substantial: in Bulgaria, for example, there were 10,305 libraries in 1979 and in that year 43.4 million copies of books were printed. Sports facilities were modernised, hugely expanded or newly built. High priority was given to, and large sums of money invested in, training establishments. In Yugoslavia, for example, the extreme variety of the cultural traditions of the peoples who constituted the state was recognised by the creation of three Academies of Dramatic Art, with associated schools of music and dance, at Belgrade, Zagreb and Ljubljana. A similar function was served by the two Institutes set up in Romania, one located at Tirgu-Mures specifically to cater for the Hungarian minority while the other at Bucharest covered the whole state. These and similar institutes elsewhere had the rank of Institutions of Higher Education and issued diplomas that were the key to entry to the appropriate profession. They offered an all-round education and ranked in esteem with scientific, educational and research institutes of similar standing. Closely associated with this was the creation of other educational institutions for the other arts and for sports. From them emerged during the 1950s the first in an increasing flow of trained gymnasts and film cameramen, stage managers, designers and athletes, composers and sports coaches who by 1980 had made their mark internationally.

As the state became in effect the sole patron of artists and sportsmen it began to become clear that as with all patronage systems there was a price to be paid for material security and an assured market. Patrons demand conformity to the cultural standards and ethics of their own moral and political codes. As the only source of patronage, the new monopolist regimes were able to pressurise their artists and technicians into producing works that in style and content conformed to the values proclaimed uniquely acceptable. For sportsmen the price of conformity was less serious. The content of athletics or games was not moral or political in itself, while personal success was none the less gratifying for being jubilantly welcomed by governments as a sign of the superiority of the communist political system. Nor was the satisfaction derived from the availability of and access to sporting opportunities for wide circles of citizens diminished by governmental proclamation that such bounty illustrated the concern of communist governments for the well-being of their citizens. In the creative arts, however, it soon became apparent that close supervision over content and style had debilitating effects for they were crucial for the artistic value and attractiveness of the works produced. This was as true for wireless and television programmes as it was for the theatre and literature. It could indeed be argued that criticism of and dissatisfaction with the *status quo* were essential ingredients of worthwhile creativity producing inner tension, psychological insight and critical assessment while offering the audience food for thought.

Inevitably it was creative artists and those engaged in the production and circulation of their works· who got into difficulties. Given the emphasis placed on the social and political responsibilities of the arts and the power inherent in monopoly patronage it would have been expecting much to ask communist governments to indulge critics or license views at variance with Marxism–Leninism. After all, they had not displayed similar benignity in political or economic matters. The problem was compounded by the important role traditionally played in eastern European social and political life by creative artists. This was especially true of Poland, where during the long years of foreign occupation after the partitions the traditions and values of Polish national life had been self-consciously kept alive by her writers and musicians. Indeed, in 1919 the first President of newly re-established Poland had been the distinguished concert pianist Paderewski. Similar traditions played their part elsewhere, and it was generally the case that the literary journal and cultural appreciation circle had been two basic units of national life under foreign domination, be it~German, Hungarian, Russian or Turkish. It was not surprising that this tradition continued.

In the immediate circumstances of post-war eastern Europe the tradition of opposition among creative artists and performers probably worked to the advantage of communist governments. There was no immediate clash between them. Communists were able to tap the idealism and radicalism that flourished in the cultural life of the region and that had been enhanced by the war. Many of its leading figures could be relied upon for support. Communist or fellow-traveller·Polish film-makers and avant-garde playwrights of the theatre of the absurd, German authors and dramatists, Bulgarians associated with the Workers' Literary Front during the 1920s were distinguished examples of a common phenomenon. Compelled to leave their countries during the 1930s they returned home after 1945 and their sympathy and active support enlisted behind the new communist regimes. They were joined by others who had taken part in resistance movements. A distinguished body gathered in the Soviet zone of Germany. Most eminent was Brecht, but Zweig and Anna Seghers also returned from exile, as did the well-known film director Wolf. They constituted a considerable coterie of talent. Artists accustomed to think of themselves as committed commentators on their societies and as standard-bearers of national life were also broadly 'progressive'. They did not doubt that reform and social and economic development were essential. Far from there being automatic suspicion between governments and the artistic community there was every reason to think the process started by the communists would evoke warm co-operation and sympathy.

From the outset governments displayed considerable willingness to recognise the major contribution that creative artists could make and harness it to the common cause. Organisations were set up to incorporate those engaged in every branch of the arts. Writers' Unions, organisations of painters and sculptors, and for those engaged in the film industry were set up and those involved in the appropriate activity required to join. Self-regulating bodies, they became controlling organisms that produced their own journals and operated studios and publishing houses. They were also subjected to the *nomenklatura* process. It rapidly became apparent that governments were highly appreciative of the role of the artist in the broadest sense, depicted as the progressive champion of popular enlightenment. Authors were assured that their books would be printed and playwrights that their works would be staged. Very considerable material rewards were offered. The successful enjoyed high living standards and great social prestige. As economic recovery increased national prosperity the rewards grew. By 1980 it was normal for those engaged in cultural work of all types to have access to special retreats for creative endeavour, to enjoy special restaurants, to be eligible for grants and loans to assist in temporary adversity and to share in preferential holiday and medical facilities. Although one of the few groups still self-employed, they were early included within the scope of state social insurance schemes and were assured of regular employment as, for example, translators. State prizes such as the Hungarian Kossuth Prize or the Bulgarian Dimitrov Prize carried with them not only great prestige but financial reward. Individual cities such as Wroclaw, Warsaw and Krakow also awarded their own prizes. Royalties paid to authors were extremely generous and they were guaranteed large print orders. For the especially favoured royalties accruing abroad in 'hard' currencies were available. Most satisfactory of all was state support for the performing arts. Music, theatre and film-making were all expensive activities and the enormous increase in the output of each testified to the willingness of the state to make available the necessary resources. By the late 1960s, for example, 70 per cent of the budget of Romania's theatres was provided by state subsidy.

Socialist realism

As in politics and economics, communist governments were heavily influenced by developments in the USSR. Coincident with the emergence of communist governments in eastern Europe during the later 1940s there was a marked tightening of Soviet attitudes as pressures were intensified in the campaign associated with Zhdanov. Soviet limitations on freedom of expression required creative artists to subordinate their works to the demands of *partiynost*, the requirement that everything produced should advance the cause of the Party. In August 1948 the World Congress in Defence of Peace proclaimed this to be the norm to which creative artists should approximate. The Party called for them to take an active part in the building of socialism by using their skills positively. Eastern European governments rapidly followed the Soviet lead. In Romania in 1948, in Poland and Czechoslovakia in 1949 and in the DDR in 1951 Writers' Unions and other professional associations of creative artists solemnly agreed that it was their members' duty to follow the guidelines known as socialist realism. Attacks were made against prominent communists such as the distinguished philosopher Lukacs in Hungary in 1949. Accused of providing an unacceptable view of communism he was anathemised, along with the author Dery who showed too great a sympathy for non-communists. Calling upon artists to wage war against false, bourgeois prejudices and conceptions and back constructive ideas, socialist realism laid stress on the tangible and earthy. While interested in human relationships, it required that the conditions for the solution of contradictions in them be depicted. Showing how the fate of man can be controlled by common, social effort, it decried individualism and demanded a sturdily optimistic picture of human achievement. Reformed drunkards, liberated women, peasants joyfully reconciled to collective agricultural labour and tongue-tied workers able to offer the fruits of their experience to guide well-intentioned young experts were all led to better and more fulfilling lives by the Party. Social action and joint, communal responsibility was stressed as was the necessity of work and labour. All who denied the beneficent effects of communal action were possessed of moral flaws; those who recanted and perceived their errors were 'objectively' communists even when most opposed to the Party, which in the resolution of the plot they joyfully joined. Party members were without weaknesses, even when logic suggested that they were frankly incapable and unworthy of the roles they occupied. With bad and good clearly defined, the outcome of the story ordained and much of the incidental momentum of its development prescribed, there remained little for the artist to do and only a restricted scope for his invention. As the demands of socialist realism were reinforced by increasingly tight censorship many creative artists felt the restrictions placed upon them were derogatory to their genius and resented the suspicions of government. Worst of all the most obvious source of artistic endeavour was stopped as the criticism central to all worthwhile cultural products was stilled.

Although much of the artistic output of these early years was frankly poor, works of merit were produced. The horrendous impact of Nazi occupation and persecution afforded a common bridge between governments and artists and it became a valuable function of the latter to assist their peoples to come to terms with the experience and place it within the shared memory of their society. The remarkable, moving short stories of Borowski, a survivor of both Auschwitz and Dachau, probed relationships within and the psychology of the death camps and were published in a collection entitled *This Way for the Gas, Ladies and Gentlemen*. It was a monument to Polish literary genius, as was the vivid depiction of the chaos and moral collapse immediately after the end of the war given in Andrzejewski's *Ashes and Diamonds*. The problems of post-war adjustment were also the theme of probably the best Polish film of this period, Ford's *Five Boys from Barska Street*. In the DDR Apitz's *Naked amongst the Wolves* made a valiant attempt to bring home to German readers the realities of life in a concentration camp while the film *The Murderers Are Amongst Us* made by Staudte in 1946 stressed the need to purge German society of those guilty of war and atrocity. In Czecho-slovakia short stories by Drda appraised community reaction to collab-oration with the German occupier, while Lustig depicted life in the ghetto at Terezin, of which he was one of the few survivors. More remarkable was the novel *The Cowards*, written by Skvorecky at the height of the campaign for socialist realism. Although its publication was delayed until 1958 the portrayal of the liberation of Czechoslovakia showed Soviet troops in a less than idealistic light and was testimony to the critical and artistic powers of eastern European novelists. Life under German occupation and the activities of the partisan movement was a rich source for Yugoslav writers such as Isakovic, Marinkovic and Kranjec. Despite these examples, over all the rigid application of the canons of socialist realism deadened artistic output and led to works of dreary monotony whose unremitting optimism increasingly rang hollow. By the mid-1950s the artistic community was stirring in revolt.

In the eastern European tradition, 1954 and 1955 brought an upsurge of periodicals and literary debating circles that served as focal points for demands for reform of wider than merely artistic significance. The *Deutsche Zeitschrift fur Philosophie* in the DDR and the periodical *Po Prostu* in Poland became major vehicles for radical comment, while the 'Crooked Circle' society in Warsaw and the 'Petofi Circle' in Budapest brought together critics of the dead-weight of Stalinism. After 1953 such developments stimulated and channelled discontent. Previously loyal communists such as Brecht and the Pole Wazyk wrote poems critical of their governments. The sensation caused by these developments became part of the general reaction to the destalinisation campaign begun by Khrushchev in the USSR. Although gradually brought under control after 1956 as editorial boards were purged, journals closed and clubs wound up, the unrest among creative artists produced an important relaxation in the application of rigid guidelines.

Cinema

The cultural renaissance of the mid-1950s was especially associated with the cinema. Throughout the region very considerable efforts had been made to increase the number of cinemas and develop indigenous film industries. The pre-communist tradition had varied. In Czechoslovakia and Hungary, as well as Germany, film-making had begun by 1900 and by 1914 there were flourishing industries in all three countries. In Poland the establishment of a film industry came with independence after 1918, though it never achieved financial viability. Yugoslavia had been an intermittent producer of films, with a strongly marked regional variation, while neither Bulgaria nor Romania had any industry worth the name before 1945. Czech, Hungarian and German film-makers and technicians had international reputations. Indeed, it had been the Korda brothers who after leaving their native Hungary had revitalised the British film industry during the 1930s.

Recovery was inevitably slow after 1945. The enormous destruction of studios and film manufacturing and processing plant was only slowly made good. Ironically the film industry in Czechoslovakia gained from the war, for the principal Nazi production facilities had been concentrated there. Between 1945 and 1948 the industry was nationalised in each country, and by 1948 a start was being made to reopen production. In Poland the first steps were taken by the Army Film Unit attached to the USSR-based Polish Army which formed the nucleus for the future. Resistance units in Czechoslovakia and the partisans in Yugoslavia had been able to maintain film units that became the nucleus of later production bodies. Pre-war left-wing producers such as Wolf and the Bulgarian Dodow in the DDR, or Zaninovic in Yugoslavia, played a major part in re-establishing the industry in their own countries, as did the Society of Devotees of Artistic Films, or START, organisation of left-wing film-makers in Poland. Over all, however, the talent available was as limited as were the production facilities and it was not until the new film schools began to produce their first graduates that eastern European film began to make significant progress. By the mid-1950s the rebuilding cf production facilities and the flow of graduates alike had reached the level where major production could be undertaken. It coincided with the first fruits of the liberalising in cultural controls. The output of feature films increased steadily while the growth in the number of cinemas provided large audiences.

By the mid-1950s the achievements of eastern European film-makers in the field of documentaries, often of an educational nature, had attracted international attention. Bulgarian popular science documentaries and the output of Polish and Czechoslovak studios were well known. So too were the cartoons that had been part of the Czech film tradition before 1939 and the animation techniques that had been an important element in pre-war Yugoslav output. To these was added a new Romanian speciality, puppet films. Interesting as these were, they had not made the same impact on the international scene as substantial feature films. After 1954 this changed. The most impressive productions came from Poland where a new, talented generation of film-makers graduated from the Polish higher educational establishment at Lodz. The first fruits of the expansion of film and cinematographic institutes, directors of the calibre and creativity of Munk, Wajda and Kawalerowicz made a major international as well as domestic impact. This new wave concentrated initially on historical themes. Wajda's series of films relating to the war, the problems of occupation and the underground resistance paralleled the similar preoccupation of writers. His films *A Generation, Canal* and *Ashes and Diamonds* made an immediate impact between 1954 and 1958. A similar preoccupation with the past led in 1960 to the most successful Polish film of the post-war years, Ford's *Knights of the Teutonic Order*, which drew more Polish cinema-goers than any other film. The interest in the politically relatively safe theme of the past gave way to greater willingness to comment on issues of contemporary relevance to Poles. Here Munk led the way with his films *Man on the Track* in 1957 and *Bad Luck*, made in 1960. After his death in 1961 a new generation of directors emerged. The best-known were Polanski, who soon left Poland to become a major Hollywood director of the 1970s, and Zanussi. Together with Wajda the latter became the most prominent and outspoken director of the 1970s and was if anything even more significant as a producer of films for television. Wajda's *Man of Marble* and *Rough Treatment* and Zanussi's *Camouflage* dealt with corruption and the misuse of power by those in authority and illustrated the plight of the well-intentioned seeking to tell the truth when faced by pressures and crushing force. They established a genre that lasted throughout the 1970s and culminated in Zanussi's *Contract* and *The Constant Factor* and Wajda's *Man of Iron*. Such works bore eloquent testimony to the courage and skills of Polish film-makers. They also illustrated both the high quality of the training in state film schools and the relatively wide freedom given to Polish artists after the mid-1950s. This permitted controversial and delicate political issues to be treated. It was another striking example of the difference between Poland and most other eastern European communist regimes.

Apart from Poland, directors in both Hungary and Czechoslovakia were able to make significant and important films. The recrudescence of the Hungarian industry began in the later 1950s as graduates of the Academy of Cinematographic Art began work. Once more the themes of war and its responsibilities were a major element, especially in the early works of Kovacs who played a crucial role in establishing the new cinema. A preoccupation with historical themes drawn from the repression of Hungarian revolutionaries after 1848 and 1919 led to Jancso's *Round-up*, *The Red and the White* and *Silence and Cry*, all made between 1965 and 1968. However, in Hungary too the themes of post-war development, the disruption and disorientation caused by the socialist revolution and the problems of personal adjustment to socialism produced films such as Fabri's *Twenty Hours* in 1964, Szabo's *Father* in 1966 and Makk's *Love* in 1970. By avoiding the narrow stereotypes and transcending the unremitting optimism so characteristic of the early productions of socialist realism they marked the coming of age of the

Hungarian post-war industry. A similar renaissance in the Czechoslovak film industry was of shorter duration and did not lead to the same sustained quality. The increasingly less restrictive atmosphere of the later 1950s and 1960s was abruptly brought to an end by the tightening-up after the abortive Prague Spring. However, for a brief period graduates of the Film Faculty of the Prague Academy of Performing Arts emulated their Polish and Hungarian peers. The director best-known abroad was Forman, whose *Peter and Paula* of 1963 and *A Blonde in Love* of 1965 found especial favour in the West. The picture of ordinary men and women coming to terms with the realities of everyday life and recognisable dilemmas of human social behaviour was presented with wry humour.

Elsewhere in the region films continued to present the preoccupation with successful adaptation of men to socialism, the triumph of social action and the problems of working people successfully meeting the challenges of improved working techniques. Such optimistic present-ations enjoyed large captive audiences. Yet if there was an overwhelming emphasis on working-class themes in the output of film studios in the DDR and Romania, it was also true that during the 1960s and 1970s the treatment of contemporary problems became more' humane and sympathetic and also less idealistic. An especial genre of films relating to the problems of the young growing up and living in socialist societies began to emerge. Probably the best-known came from the DDR, where the 'new wave' film-maker Plenzdorf showed a teenage drop-out in *The New Sufferings of Young W.*, made in 1972. If the film enjoyed a suitable ending with the invention of a new paint-spraying technique to give posthumous social relevance to the rebel's life, the main theme of the film was none the less one of adolescent alienation. Remarkable in a different way was the appearance in 1973 also in the DDR of the first communist soft-porn film, *The Legend of Paul and Paula*. By the late 1970s the monumental caricature and crude depictions of early socialist realism had given way to more sophisticated and convincing portrayals that suggested that the preferred artistic style of communism was capable of development and depths of insight into the human predicament.

Television

As in western Europe, after 1960 the availability of television grew steadily. In 1960 only in Czechoslovakia and the DDR, and to a lesser extent in Poland, was there a significant degree of television ownership. Indeed, services had not begun until the 1950s – in Czechoslovakia in 1953 and in Romania and Bulgaria in 1957 and 1959 respectively. By 1960, however, the era of mass television ownership was on the point of beginning. All eastern European countries, with the exception of Yugoslavia, were members of the Intervision system, enabling them to share programmes and facilities. By 1980 television ownership had become nearly as widespread as in the West (see Table 5.11) with similar consequences for attendances at live theatrical performances and at cinemas. Between 1960 and 1980 audience figures at the former fell by 40 per cent in Czechoslovakia and by one-third in the DDR, while in Poland they declined by one-quarter. Cinema attendances fell even more steeply: by over 60 per cent in Czechoslovakia and the DDR and over 55 per cent in Hungary and Poland. By 1976 surveys of career ambitions of Bulgarian schoolchildren revealed that the most favoured occupation was that of television technician. The television era had arrived in eastern Europe.

The advent of television permitted a high degree of penetration of citizens' cultural lives, and was eagerly embraced by governments. Programme output closely followed that already foreshadowed in other cultural media. There was a high didactic content, with a substantial news and current affairs output. Discussion programmes resembled lectures or party political broadcasts rather than genuine exchanges of deeply held opinions. Only in times of domestic crisis did they reveal real clashes of opinions on basic issues, as was the case for example in Poland during 1981. When not utilised for purposes of political education, such 'discussions' enabled social tensions to be aired. Mild criticism of the performance of institutions previously targeted by government or Party acted as escape valves for popular sentiment. Sports events too were given considerable coverage, while innocent and whimsical children's television programmes were frequently of very high quality. Quiz programmes were virtually unknown, and members of the public degrading themselves in return for cash mercifully absent. More surprisingly, there were few programmes based on the powerful and well-established eastern European tradition of cabaret. Such light entertainment as was offered was to Western eyes anaemic and staid. In place of fictional war films, soap operas and police and hospital-based melodramas, there was a striking tendency towards commemoration of Second World War anniversaries and an emphasis on the requirements of contemporary national defence.

Literature

The flowering of the new cinema was paralleled by similar developments in literature. From the mid-1950s authors began to develop themes touching extremely sensitive areas of recent experience. Cautiously at first and then with increasing boldness, hitherto taboo subjects were broached. By 1960 four broad strands of criticism had emerged. One related to the realities of building socialism and to the failures of economic policy, especially in the countryside. A second commented on the forced labour camps and the prison camps, often by authors with the benefit of first-hand experience, in the same vein as the Soviet writer Solzhenitsyn. The third pointed to the misuse of power and the pressures of a totalitarian system on its critics. Its medium was either the historical scenario or, by the mid-1960s, direct themes of contemporary relevance. Allied to this was an awareness of the effects of power on those who held it. Finally there was a body of literature that depicted problems of disorientation, loneliness and lack of purpose. Such authors challenged the operation of the communist system and officially approved views as to its success. They denied claims that socialism eliminated individual unhappiness by ensuring group action that supported each and every citizen and submerged individual frailty and psychological disquiets under the glowing strength of social solidarity and cohesion. Governmental reaction varied from state to state, but everywhere by the early 1970s the criticisms of the late 1950s and 1960s had been tamed and a modified form of socialist realism re-established as the preferred art form.

The destalinisation campaign made possible the publication of accounts of prison and labour camps with the tacit consent of governments anxious to shift responsibility for events in the recent past. The Polish author Chacinski, the Hungarian Lengyel and the Czechs Pecka and Kundera produced accounts of prison life in which the bare details of the camps were matched by the trivial nature of the offences that led to the punishment. The best-known of these works in western Europe was Kundera's *The Joke*. There was a growth too in literature with historical themes treating power, its misuse and effects. In the DDR Heym's *The King David Report*, in Hungary Dery's presentation of St Ambrose in *The Excommunicator* or the Pole Andrzejewski's portrayal of Torquemada in *The Inquisitor* were presented as critiques of religious figures, while the Hungarian Hay's *Attila's Nights* and the Pole Bochenski's *Julius the God* took figures from the ancient world as pegs on which to hang discussions of the effects of power on those who wield it and of its abuse on those subject to it. They had striking contemporary relevance. By the late 1960s the same themes were being openly applied to communist society, most notably in Czechoslovakia where Kundera's *The Joke* and Mnacko's *The Taste of Power* emerged as powerful critiques of the communist system. Similar themes emerged in the poetry of the area. The Czech poet Holub, the Pole Herbert and the Hungarian writer Csoori took as their themes the realities of the socialist economic system and of the transformation of society. In particular they showed the tensions, harassments and shortfalls. Finally, there also emerged a significant body of literature that commented adversely on the public state of mind. Far from the optimistic assessments of socialist realism were the poetry of Biermann in the DDR and the short stories of many Czechoslovak writers of the 1960s. They revealed a world in which disenchantment among young people, and a general and pervasive sense of isolation and loneliness characterised society. Drunkenness, divorce, delinquency and adolescent rebelliousness combined with cynicism and absence of warmth in human relationships evoked an image of society totally at variance with the official view. From such spiritual desolation it was a short step to the depiction of the revolutionary communist movement as being pervaded from its inception by cynical manipulation and the ruthless sacrifice of individuals to a cause paying lip-service only to such human values as loyalty, decency and honest dealings. The fierce reaction in Yugoslavia to Kis's *A Tomb for Boris Davidovich* when it was first published in 1976 illustrated that the theme struck a nerve in even the least rigid communist state.

Modified socialist realism and renewed restrictions

Confronted with the growing volume of critical writings, whether explicit or implicit, the reaction of every government was to tighten controls over artists and dramatists without returning to the extreme rigidities of the Stalinist years. However disturbing the criticisms, the consensus of opinion favoured a flexible form of official guidance on cultural matters. The role of the creative artist was reaffirmed, as was his importance in the creation of the new socialist society. He was, however, expected to immerse himself in the life of the people, preferably by living and working with them so as to discover the contradictions of real life affecting the mass of the population. Condemning as contrived and artificial many of the preoccupations of the artistic community, its responsibility to combat anti-socialist values and to assist society in its historically determined evolution was restated. The artist was to uncover the real abuses of power and to devote himself to the correction of defects affecting the lives of ordinary people. He was not to question the sincerity or honesty of the Party, its members or public officials nor to give unreasonable and undue prominence to the defects of individuals unable to adapt to socialism. The most severe measures were taken in the DDR. Calls for writers to base their work on these principles were repeated in 1964 and again at the Eighth Party Congress in 1972. This modified form of socialist realism may have given a wider canvass to creative artists and reduced the restraints of Stalinist cultural policy, but the overall objectives and conceptions were retained and the government of the DDR reinforced them by coercive measures. In 1965 a sustained attack was launched against critics, the most notable victims being Havemann, Heym and Biermann. Christa Wolf was dropped as a candidate member of the Central Committee of the SED after being too outspoken in her defence of artistic integrity and freedom of expression. Havemann was placed under house-arrest and subjected to continuous surveillance. He was later fined in 1978 for alleged currency offences relating to his foreign earnings. Biermann was deprived of his right of re-entry to the DDR while on a tour of the Federal Republic in 1976, and other leading critics were given long-stay visas to remain abroad indefinitely. In 1979 it was made illegal to publish outside the DDR without prior permission. In the same year Heym and eight others were expelled from the Writers' Union and thus in effect deprived of the right to work as authors. Heym was also fined for currency offences. This combination of virtual exile, official harassment and professional excommunication was a potent combination, followed elsewhere. After the replacing of Dubcek, Party control over culture in Czechoslovakia was tightened by measures similar to those used in the DDR. Among others, the Jewish authors Lustig and Grossmann went to Israel, and Skvorecky to Canada. Others were denied the right to publish. Mnacko's *The Taste of Power* was not published in full in Czechoslovakia and neither were the later novels of Kundera while the plays of Havel were neither reprinted, published nor performed after 1969. In Romania too Party control was reaffirmed after 1971, though there had been few signs of critical comment and the most notable Romanian author, Dumitriu, had decamped to western Europe with his family in 1960. However, in 1971 and 1972 increasing emphasis was laid on the requirement that authors should write in a positive manner and avoid the 'problematical' aspects of socialism. Writers who refused were accused of opting out of society and condemned, and in 1972 the Writers' Union acknowledged the new directives and accepted them as Union policy. While Bulgaria had not experienced significant difficulties with its artistic community, in both Yugoslavia and Hungary there was a noticeable hardening of official attitudes. Indeed in Yugoslavia the Croatian separatist sentiment that led to the crisis of 1971–2 had largely taken the form of a recrudescence of nationalist cultural self-assertion. A major part was played by the Croatian Writers' Union after 1967 and by the nationalist cultural organisation the Matica Hrvatska whose journal *Kritika* began publication in 1968. During the crisis both societies were purged, and *Kritika* and another cultural journal, *Praxis*, closed down. It became more difficult for critical authors to secure publication, a problem that confronted Kis when he tried to publish *A Tomb for Boris Davidovich*. In Hungary, on the other hand, the position never became so critical. The government was able to maintain its overall authority during the 1960s and succeeded in integrating critical currents. In part this was the result of its willingness to imprison critics, as it had demonstrated by the prison sentences passed on Dery between 1957 and 1961 and Hay between 1957 and 1960. It was also probable that the memory of Soviet action in 1956 was a brake on too open criticism. In Poland alone was a different course discernible. The dismissal of Gomulka and the advent of Gierek ushered in a decade of less stringent censorship and more relaxation in cultural matters which permitted Polish creative artists to be more forthright. It was symbolic that Polish universities purged for their criticisms in 1968–9 remained untouched until 1982.

Whatever the trials and tribulations of creative artists critical of certain aspects of the system, the majority – and usually the great majority – were not disaffected and were uncritical. The confines of socialist realism were not challenged by all artists of standing. Anna Seghers, for example, found them acceptable and her substantial output constituted one of the major literary achievements of the DDR. Other writers such as Strittmatter were able to develop themes such as peasant reaction to collectivisation and the transformation of the countryside into substantial works without rejecting official artistic guidelines. Moreover, the exclusivity of the art of creative writing was also under attack. Governments leant over backwards to identify and foster talented amateurs from different social backgrounds and encouraged their activities and published their works. The social exclusivity of writing was denied and newcomers drawn into Writers' Unions. The government of the DDR went to greater lengths than other communist regimes, but the process was common to all states. It was perhaps not surprising that those offered such opportunities found little of which to complain in the system that recognised their merits and rewarded them so handsomely.

Drama and music

It was in the interrelated areas of establishing and satisfying a new mass audience for cultural activity and creating machinery for collective involvement and group presentation that communist governments were most successful. Nowhere was this more apparent than in the performing arts. There, political calculation and cultural objectives coincided and the particular strengths of group-oriented skills and activities characteristic of all areas of communist life came into their own.

The anxiety to make available drama and music as widely as possible, both to audiences and for amateur involvement, led to a massive expansion in the numbers of professional performing companies. Theatre, opera and musical companies increased greatly. Communist governments quoted with pride the sheer quantities made available. In the DDR, for example, there were fifty-one dramatic, forty-five music, and forty-one ballet companies operating in 1965 while in Bulgaria in 1980 twenty-three professional musical companies of all types provided a focus for the amateur ensembles which numbered over 1,100. Everywhere the buildings available for theatrical productions increased sharply. At the very least by 1980 every significant town in eastern Europe had its own theatre company, and all really large centres were also locations for music and opera companies. The needs of country districts were met by visits from touring groups, and the total number of such performing groups was completed by specialist theatrical companies: puppet theatres, children's and youth companies and mime specialists. In comparison with pre-communist and pre-war cultural provision, there was a flowering of cultural opportunities and an ease of access to them that represented a major investment by the state in artistic endeavour. The concern displayed to foster the creation of amateur drama by encouraging the participation of workers and collective farmers in amateur dramatic groups was the counterpart of the interest displayed in discovering and promoting amateur writers and poets. Not only were groups established with Party encouragement at places of work, where they had ready access to the halls and assembly places provided by the enterprise, their productions were also given the benefit of advice from professionals working in the appropriate artistic area. Theatrical producers and stage designers and lighting experts were expected to offer help and encouragement to local amateur groups, while musicians and dancers were called upon to provide the skilled advice necessary to amateurs. In addition specialist journals were published to assist such groups. In Bulgaria, for example, a monthly journal of suitable plays, advice and assistance was published by a specialist state organ, the Central House of Folk Art, which supervised and co-ordinated amateur productions. The distinction between professional and amateur was thus blurred, and the structure of amateur perform-ances given added shape by the creation of national competitions. By the later 1970s it was commonplace for such competitions to culminate in regional and subsequently national finals, often held at one of the festivals of dramatic art which proliferated. At these, amateur groups vied with one another in the artistic equivalent of socialist emulation. The prizes for success were considerable. Participants were given leave of absence from work, travel expenses and subsistence costs were reimbursed and the successful groups could anticipate opportunities to travel abroad to cultural festivals as ambassadors of their country's artistic achievements. Visits to other socialist countries were attractive, but even more so was the prospect of visits to drama festivals in non-socialist countries. Not surprisingly it often became difficult to identify the point at which the amateur gave way to the professional. Indeed, as in the field of sports, the difference did not really exist, for the state monopoly of employment permitted great ease of movement from one category to another, and it probably made more sense to distinguish between part-time and full-time involvement in the performing arts.

At the heart of communist theatre stood the repertory company, a resident body performing as an entity, for communist theatrical companies discouraged the star system and excelled at ensemble and group work. The forerunners of such organisations were to be found in eastern Germany, where the best-known companies were the Berlin Komische Oper, founded in 1947, and Brecht's own creation, the Berliner Ensemble, set up in 1949. Both achieved international reputa-tions for their standards of production and acting. To them could be added the Dresden-based Staatskapelle orchestra which by the 1970s had acquired the reputation of one of Europe's best orchestras. In place of the stars around whom performances in the West were built, eastern

European companies concentrated on productions that were radical departures from the stylised and romantic presentations of the inter-war years. The theme of socialist realism as applied to the performing arts laid stress on realistic interpretation, with an overriding concern to penetrate the historical truth of the work and to emphasise its realistic message. As a consequence, productions seemed to unsympathetic eyes to be the shrillest form of political didacticism. There could be no question, however, of the influence that such realistic presentation of drama and music had on companies elsewhere. Producers and stage designers had an electrifying effect on western European audiences. Controversial operatic productions such as those given in London during the 1970s by the German producer Friedrich in collaboration with the Czech stage designer Svoboda made major contributions to the reinterpretation of Wagner's operas.

Such novelty sustained a reputation for innovation in the performing arts. Before 1939 there had been a well-established eastern European avant-garde in drama and music. Authors in Poland began a tradition of the theatre of the absurd, especially associated with Witkiewicz, which was continued after 1945 by Galczynski and later Mrozek. Elsewhere the Czechoslovak playwright Havel used similar techniques. In music, too, much pioneering work had been done by composers from eastern Europe. The Czech Janacek, the Hungarians Bartok and Dohnanyi, the Romanian Enescu and the Pole Szymanowski were among the foremost European composers of the inter-war years and the pattern of novelty and innovation they established was continued after 1945. The Polish composers Lutoslawski and Penderecki were especially prominent. Providing a bridge between the old and the new generation was the Hungarian composer Kodaly. Politically suspect after 1919 for his willingness to accept an official post during the abortive communist revolution of Bela Kun, Kodaly welcomed the new order after 1945. Until his death in 1967 he was the doyen of Hungarian music, filling many major public offices and winning all the major prizes at least once in a career that took him to the pinnacle of official recognition. It was, however, true that whatever the vibrancy of the avant-garde and however loaded with honours individual creative artists were, the mainstream of eastern European dramatic and musical life was more truly represented by different artists. In music and drama, as in literature, the official preference was for themes and styles that had immediate relations with working life. Ambitious to inspire audiences with the new, noble impulse of socialist construction, they wished to show that which could enrich and inspire by new and noble ideals, to paraphrase the official Bulgarian attitude. The results were theatrical and musical productions that duplicated their literary cousins, with the proviso that given the greater possibilities of state control over the theatre and the expense of theatrical production it was very much less common for critical works to see the light of day. When they did, as in Czechoslovakia in 1968, it was only briefly. Critical playwrights tended to write plays to be read, not to be performed. Among dramatists, preference was given to themes that presented a suitably encouraging picture of the construction of socialism and of the adaptation of man to the new conditions. Popular too were historical dramas that drew edifying lessons from previous epochs of national greatness or from the struggles of heroes with the repressiveness of either foreigners, such as the Turks or the Habsburgs, or of ruling elites of pre-communist times. The battle between old and new worlds, with a new generation coming to terms with the values of socialist society, inspired works such as the Romanian dramatist Lovinescu's play *The Crumbling Citadel*, in which a family was portrayed coming to terms with the new world and liking what it found, the German Strittmatter's *The Dutchman's Bride*, depicting the romance between the daughter of a day labourer and the son of a former landowner, or the Yugoslav Stojanovic's work *Dangerous Waters*, which showed the struggles confronting an old communist revolutionary coming to terms with the achievement of his ambitions. Successful examples of the collective action of society to redeem the socially ill-adjusted were also common subjects. The Yugoslav writer Casule treated such themes in several plays during the 1950s and early 1960s, while the Romanians Lovinsecu and Dorian respectively emphasised the social responsibilities of artists, in *The Death of an Artist*, and of members of collective farms, in *The Fifty-eighth Second*. Perhaps the best examples of the genre came from the DDR, where Sakowski's *Stones on the Road* showed the successful intervention of the collective farm which created the conditions to permit a woman to become independent of her husband. Women's emancipation, change in the countryside and the beneficial effects of united social action in liberating the individual were thus neatly gathered together into the modern equivalent of a medieval morality play.

Not surprisingly, the Yugoslav theatre was especially preoccupied with the war and German occupation. The playwrights Casule in *The Town-Hall Clock*, Arsovski with *Alexander* and *Both Sides of the River*, Djokovic in *Love* and Bozic with *The Righteous Man* wrote of the impact of war on individual human lives and on human responses to its strains while others, including Lebovic and Obremovic, were more concerned with the details of life in concentration camps or of day-to-day existence under the Germans. Over all the dictates of socialist realism had been abandoned relatively quickly in Yugoslavia and her playwrights preferred to deal with moral issues in an historical setting. Satires of life under the pre-communist regimes were everywhere fair fields for playwrights as they were for novelists and poets. Lapsed nuns and attacks on the more flagrant examples of religious ceremonial, dramatic portrayals of national epic stories mingled with presentations of legends and folk sagas. Such pieces enabled the strong nationalist sentiments in the region to be given a relatively safe outlet without running risks of adverse political consequences. It enabled communist governments to identify themselves with national traditions, as in Bulgaria where the national hero Ivan Shishman was the subject of a substantial play in the later 1950s.

In addition to these works by new communist authors, a substantial part of the repertory of eastern European companies was provided by classics from the past and by translations of foreign dramatists. Shakespeare was especially popular. The works of national dramatists of previous epochs were given frequent and often lavish productions, and wherever possible the progressive social and political implications they contained were highlighted. For such a treatment it was clearly desirable that the authors should have been in sympathy with politically advanced parties and opinions of their times, and if possible secured for themselves reputations as national heroes in their own right. The works of Vazov in Bulgaria, of Caragiale, Alecsandri or Petrescu in Romania, or of Cankar, Tucic, Begovic and Kosor in Yugoslavia were lovingly resurrected and frequent presentation served to emphasise governmental interest in preserving national cultural traditions. Flirtations with nationalism could on occasion be dangerous. The banning of a previously authorised production of Mickiewicz's famous nationalist play *The Forefathers' Eve* led to trouble in Warsaw in 1968. Yet over all the consequences of this cultural policy were positive. It allowed the Yugoslav government to emphasise its concern for the varying traditions of all the national groupings within the state by encouraging their indigenous theatrical traditions. Elsewhere a similar function was served by the establishment of theatres for national minorities whose cultural traditions, separate and distinct from those of the dominant nationality, were offered expression and given some safeguard against dilution. In Romania such theatres catered for the Hungarians, in Bulgaria for Turks and in the DDR even for the tiny community of Sorbs. In Yugoslavia Albanians, Turks, Italians and Hungarians each had their own theatres.

Sport

Nowhere were communist governments more successful in creating mass participation in cultural recreation than in spreading sport. They enormously expanded sporting and physical recreational facilities and made sustained efforts to encourage as great a rate of participation as possible in sporting activities of all types. Compulsory at school, physical recreation was also compulsory for one or two hours every week for students at university and other higher educational institutions. Called physical culture, sport was seen from the start as an integral part of the educational system and of social life in the widest sense. The proclaimed objective was to enrich the lives of the entire population by making available opportunities for widened physical experiences previously the prerogative of the wealthy and leisured minority. Leaders such as Ulbricht, Gomulka and Ceausescu were depicted as enthusiasts for sport, albeit of a dignified style and tempo suited to statesmen of advancing years. Swimmers and energetic walkers, they were shown playing rather sedate games of tennis or skiing.

As in so many other aspects of life in eastern Europe, the enthusiasm for mass participation had a less idealistic side. It was readily admitted that a healthy population, and especially a healthy young population, was a major military asset. Conscription for the armed forces and large trained military reserves required a high overall standard of physical fitness. The funds for providing sporting facilities and paying coaches and advisers came from various sources, but an important component was the defence and security budget, and the armed forces and security police were closely involved in the provision of facilities. Many of the elite sporting clubs of the region were specifically designed for members of the security police, as were their Soviet counterparts. All clubs bearing the name 'Dynamo', for example, were security police sporting associations, while army facilities trained a significant proportion of the region's leading athletes, many of whom were serving army officers. The pattern had already become apparent in 1956 when the Czechoslovak runner and army officer Zatopek made his mark at the Olympics. The mass physical culture movement was not the creation of the communists. It had a long tradition, political in inspiration. The earliest mass physical culture movement had been created in the Czech lands. Part of the Austro-Hungarian monarchy, at the end of the nineteenth century Czech nationalist politicians had sought ways of avoiding restrictions on mass activities and gatherings by using ostensibly non-political bodies. They had created the 'Sokol' movement, which had provided a network of clubs for mass calisthenics. Amateur and devoid of the apparatus of official organisation created by the communists, these early clubs had been remarkably successful in arousing popular national feeling. They created a tradition of mass physical cultural activity that continued in independent Czechoslovakia after 1918. The 'Sokol' movement spawned the *Spartakiads*, also subsequently taken over by communist governments. Periodic festivals of sporting and physical cultural displays and competition, the best talents among the children and youth of the Czech lands had participated. Expanded and refined, such gatherings became regular events throughout eastern Europe by the later 1960s and played an important part in screening potential champions and grooming future representatives for international sporting competitions. By the mid-1970s *Spartakiads* had everywhere become one of the principal stages in the creation of Olympic contenders.

Mass physical cultural organisations had also been politically oriented in Germany. There the sporting club or association had been a feature of every major political organisation in the Weimar Republic. The German Socialist Party and the Communist Party as well as the Nazi Party had used sporting bodies to buttress their cohesion and recruit the strong-arm squads that they maintained. After 1933 the Nazi government made efforts to encourage sport and extend sporting opportunities to the entire population, foreshadowing the course followed after 1950 by communist governments. The Nazis had also been aware of the propaganda value to be gained from staging the Olympic Games and made the most of the opportunity in 1936. Once more, they forged a path later followed by the communists. Enhanced national physical fitness for undisguisedly military reasons, the use of sport as a means of creating a sense of shared identity and purpose and the advantages to be gained from using international sporting occasions for enhancing national prestige, were all well established by 1939.

The original objective of communist governments may have been little more than the extension of sporting opportunities to the whole population. It rapidly became apparent, however, that whatever the virtues of freely available facilities, there was a concerted effort in every state to make sporting participation almost universal. Compulsory in educational institutions, it played a major part in the activities of young pioneers and mass youth organisations, and persuasion was applied at places of work and state propaganda apparatuses exerted moral pressure. It was questionable whether the ideal of a fit, committed public anxious for active participation was in fact anywhere achieved. By the later 1970s it was clear that the percentage of the adult population actively engaged in physical culture in the widest sense was probably not much higher than in the Western world. Fishing, occasional football, occasional swimming and walking fulfilled the public need for inter-mittent exercise. Indeed, with the spread of television vicarious involve-ment with sport as a spectator activity in the comfort of the home was probably as commonplace in eastern Europe in 1980 as it was elsewhere in the world.

Governments continued to attach high importance to sport, though the emphasis subtly changed from mass to elite achievement. Successful sportsmen were fêted and enjoyed opportunities and facilities reminiscent of those available to Western film stars, though it was continually emphasised that they owed their success to the system that moulded them. In the modified star system characteristic of the region top sportsmen were displayed as symbols of the success of communism, and their individual achievements subsumed into the common, collective achievement of the national sporting world. Medal winners and champions were merely the most outstanding figures in a galaxy of sporting activity at all levels and their fame was a reflection of the fame of communist physical culture. The returns were considerable. By the later 1970s such figures enjoyed the privileges available to the region's elite, though by the very nature of sports such enjoyment was for strictly limited periods as age and failing achievement inevitably brought eclipse. Foreign travel, luxury hotels, special diet, pocket money provided in foreign 'hard' currencies, purchases in special stores, special housing and all the other appurtenances of success were part and parcel of the lives of sports stars. They could look forward to financial security and good job opportunities for the rest of their lives, and the social prestige brought by success would linger on long after retirement from active competition. The enormous apparatus of coaching and administration in the eastern European sporting world offered many attractive openings for retired sports stars, and in suitably qualified cases the glamour of athletic achievement could advantageously be deployed to secure posts in the academic or political world. Sport and physical culture became by 1980 a ladder for personal advancement within eastern Europe. As with all other such ladders, it was strictly institutionalised and controlled.

By the later 1950s sport had become a major weapon in international prestige. The process had gone furthest in the DDR, but everywhere the object of communist sporting organisations became the creation of international champions and the winning of medals, gaining of records and securing of sporting prestige for the system. In the process the machinery of sport was turned from the provision of opportunities and facilities for the masses into a mechanism to identify and train a sporting elite. By the 1970s all the sophisticated mechanisms of modern medicine had been brought to bear. Computerised techniques were employed to predict the standards of achievement required of athletes in future competitions and the necessary appropriate physical characteristics calculated. Promising children who might be expected in due course to develop were identified, often as young as four or five years old, and then selected for special treatment. The educational system of every state included special sports schools where the selected potential champions were trained. In addition to general educational subjects there was an intensive programme of special sports training. As the establishments usually required children to board it was possible to ensure diet, rest and overall regime in accordance with scientific criteria to maximise possibilities of satisfactory development. At every stage the psychological as well as the physical attitudes necessary for future champions were encouraged and tested. Those not meeting the required standards were weeded out and returned to the ordinary educational system. There were persistent reports of manipulation of body chemistry. Drugs and especially steroids were provided for women athletes to develop muscle power. Field athletes were treated to increase body weight, track stars provided with strength-building drugs and potential gymnastic champions with puberty-retarding substances to enable them to retain their youthful suppleness. These brought science to the assistance of nature to breed champions whose function was to win success in international sport. There were surprisingly few objectors to the distortion of personality and physique entailed.

They were very successful. The best example was the DDR. Confronted initially by a virtual international boycott on recognition, the government turned to sport as one of the most promising media for compelling acceptance. The chosen area was the Olympic movement, which refused to accept separate German teams but permitted a single one, representing both the DDR and the Federal Republic. This lasted until the 1968 Games at Mexico, when those athletes from the DDR were permitted to use their own flag and anthem while remaining part of a common German team. By 1972 this had changed as a result of a sustained offensive in the governing body by the other communist states. At the Munich Games in 1972 the DDR fielded for the first time a separate, independent team and was in effect recognised by the sporting world as an independent, sovereign state. DDR athletes had a good record in the common team, and it was clearly judged vital for the international prestige of the DDR that it should make an immediate impression. This it did by winning sixty-six medals, including twenty golds, and at Moscow this grew further to 125, including forty-seven golds. This was a remarkable achievement for a small country with a restricted age cohort of young people for it was a close second to the USSR. Even making allowance for the absence of certain Western teams, it confirmed the international reputation of the DDR though at a price to the individual that many outside the DDR failed to appreciate.

Other countries made their mark on the international sporting scene. While none approached the DDR's single-minded pursuit of success they all contrived to make a mark in more restricted fields. A striking feature was the degree of specialisation as each state sought to establish a tradition of achievement in particular fields. By 1980 Bulgarian weight-lifters, boxers and field athletes, Romanian gymnasts, Hungarian fencers and water polo players, Czechoslovak ice-hockey players and bicyclists, Polish and Yugoslav footballers were all well known inter-nationally and individual sportsmen had established themselves in Western professional sport, especially tennis and football. For some Czechoslovak tennis stars this demanded permanent exile but the Romanian player Nastase was able to come to an arrangement with his government while Yugoslav sportsmen were in effect guest-workers abroad like so many of their fellow citizens.

The folk tradition

Governmental provision of facilities for popular participation fostered group consciousness by joint cultural activities. It also played an important part in helping reconcile sentiment among those whose lives had been disrupted by forced economic and social change. It permitted the expression of nationalism in a controlled manner that was politically acceptable. However much the realities of life changed, peasants could still cling to traditional folk culture, ostentatiously fostered by communist governments. Folk songs and dances and peasant traditions had been major factors in inspiriting eastern European peoples during the nineteenth century. They had shaped a sense of national identity and conservation of national feeling, and national language and custom had played a key part in the liberation of eastern European peoples from foreign rulers. Communist governments set up or expanded museums of folk art, conserved examples of peasant architecture and collected together exhibitions of various rural artefacts and agricultural machinery. Museums of ethnography were founded and folk dance groups and bands of traditional musicians sponsored and folk practices revived. Groups were encouraged in factories, schools and trade unions. In the process communist governments identified themselves with national traditions in the least embarrassing manner politically. At the very time when such policies were being developed, however, changes in the countryside were emptying folk traditions of their meaning and reducing them to displays to delight audiences. The courting and marriage dances or the sowing and harvesting songs were the product of communal activity. Through them and other manifestations of rural culture peasant societies had reinforced their ties of social cohesion and provided themselves with a ritualistic framework for their everyday economic activities and personal relationships. This was lost as those activities and relationships changed beyond all recognition with the impact of collectivisation and industrial growth. It was difficult to believe that the performance of Bulgarian folk music and dances by the Representative Group for Folk Dances of the 'Emmanuel Monolov' Trade Unions House of Culture in Gabrovo or Hungarian traditional dances given by the student members of Delep Sunshine Dance Group from Szeged possessed the same inherent meaning and significance for the participants as they had for the peasants who originally devised and performed them. The slow emptying of meaning from traditional dances, music and rituals was obvious by the late 1960s. It was an important theme in Kundera's *The Joke*.

A further advantage accrued from governmental support for traditional culture. A striking characteristic of pre-war culture in the Balkan countries had been the considerable divorce between the cultural attitudes and inspirations of the educated, governing elites and those of the peasantry. It had indeed been a point of honour for the educated to reject indigenous cultural traditions and look westward. Much of the impetus that made political radicals out of early twentieth-century devotees of national cultural revivals had come from the identification of the traditional governing class with foreign cultural patterns. This gulf had been much less important in Hungary than in Bulgaria, Romania or

Yugoslavia, and was virtually non-existent in Germany, Czechoslovakia or Poland. Where it existed, however, it had separated educated from non-educated, elites from the masses. Western European – especially French and German – influences had had a pervasive impact on the former. In addition, the presence of large Jewish populations in Poland, Romania and Hungary had also had an important influence on cultural life. In language and assumptions as much as in form and content the divide separating the masses from the rulers was considerable. It was the latter who provided the market for cultural productions, and their tastes and attitudes dominated the 'high' culture of the area. The mass, or 'low', culture was constituted by the private, celebratory world of the poor and uneducated. For every Bartok and Kodaly or Enescu using Hungarian or Romanian peasant music in their compositions and drawing it into the classical tradition, other composers produced works inaccessible to the majority of the population. Their inspiration came from German 'high' culture or from the French boulevards. Only after 1945 was this gulf progressively reduced. The process was helped by the virtually total removal of Jews either through wartime persecution or later emigration. As domestic revolution destroyed the old possessing, professional and governing classes it destroyed too the monopoly of the cultural medium they patronised. Moreover, the West was politically inimical, while the memory of German behaviour during the war had an inevitable effect on German claims to cultural superiority. By contrast, Russian cultural influences were energetically fostered. Often previously derided as Asiatic, they now became politically approved, as were native folk traditions.

A determined attempt was made to create a unified national culture. These conscious efforts, crass at first, gradually began to pay off. By the early 1970s persistence brought national tradition, folk culture and the work of acknowledged masters of the past together. In Poland, for example, the poet and playwright Galczynski fused everyday language and themes from folklore with the formal poetic traditions of 'high' culture and by his death in 1953 was the most popular poet in the country. After 1945 the Yugoslav government set out to foster the establishment of a body of theatrical works in the vernacular language of Macedonia, while enormous attention was given by the communist government in Romania to create a national operatic tradition. In painting, domestic artefacts and wood-working too the influence of peasant motifs and styles was everywhere marked by the early 1970s. At the same time a major effort was made to conciliate national minorities. In Czechoslovakia, for example, special cultural associations were set up specifically to encourage Slovak and Hungarian traditions and to ensure each was able to maintain and develop its own identity independent of the dominant Czech culture. In 1968 a similar body was set up to meet the needs of the small

German minority that remained. A similar organisation existed in Romania to cater for the Hungarian minority there.

Unofficial culture

These officially inspired and financed cultural activities excluded a genuinely unofficial, popular input by ordinary eastern Europeans as expressions of their own freely conceived preoccupations and attitudes. The folk culture of the region had ceased to be unofficial and instead had become approved. By the end of the 1970s there were signs that a new folk culture, associated with youth, was emerging. Its inspiration came in part from the West, where the effervescent 1960s had spawned a self-consciously separate, young people's culture whose moral radicalism had deeply shocked older western Europeans and Americans. Its example had spread. Eastern Europe was as much affected as other parts of the world, and the contemporaneous development of tourism assisted greatly. Young Western visitors brought their enthusiasm with them. Under these influences the contemporary equivalent of the former peasantry of the region sought their own cultural self-expression. Official reactions were fiercely hostile. In Hungary the wearing of US army-style insignia by young people was officially banned. Long hair and pop culture were the subject of outraged criticism in Poland and Bulgaria, where male Western visitors risked compulsory shaving or haircuts during the 1960s. Manifestations of a youth culture were denounced as pernicious examples of Western infiltration with potentially serious implications. Behind this condemnation may have lain the recognition that industrial society, whether capitalist or communist, was liable to be equally alien to workers who felt remote from the decision-taking and managerial process. The youth culture was as much a manifestation of this as the folk songs and traditions of the peasantry had been of the style and organisational relationships of the old rural society. The implications for communist ideological claims were important.

Governments proved themselves flexible enough to adapt and absorb some of the signs of a new popular culture. Jazz, the first vehicle of cultural protest, rock music, jeans and records of popular music were incorporated within the officially approved framework and allocated resources under the Five-year Plans. Reactions remained fierce, however, to those who refused to be incorporated. The best-known example was the case of the Czechoslovak rock music groups. Set up and permitted to perform during the period between 1966 and 1968, they were subsequently subjected to steady pressure and harassment. Their licences as musicians were withdrawn and they were not allowed to perform in public. Private bookings and performances were also harried. Finally, in 1976 most of the musicians were arrested, their equipment, records and books confiscated, and thirteen of them tried and sentenced to varying periods of imprisonment. At the centre of the indictment was the charge that their cultural productions violated approved canons of taste and were therefore indecent. Official judgement of the culturally acceptable inevitably brought official denunciation of the unacceptable, and the state as monopoly patron was not prepared to allow private patronage of art forms that it judged impermissible. Under the pressure of governmental harassment the Czechoslovak rock musicians were turned into political figures, regardless of their own intentions or desires. The treatment meted out to them inspired the publication of *Charter '77* with its call for the respect of civil and human rights. Once more culture served its long-established role as the conscience of eastern European public life and critic of government, and it did so as a result of governmental conviction that it should be subjected to official approval or outlawed.

Further reading

In addition to the works mentioned in the text, the following anthologies are of interest:

Becker, J. (ed.), *Old Land, New People* (Seven Seas Publishers, 1960).
Becker, J. (ed.), *A Pair of Mittens* (Seven Seas Publishers, 1961).
Gomori, G., and Newman, C. (eds), *New Writings of East Europe* (Quadrangle Books, 1968).
Koljevic, S. (ed.), *Yugoslav Short Stories* (Oxford University Press, 1966).
Theiner, G. (ed.), *New Writing in Czechoslovakia* (Penguin, 1969).
Wieniewska, C. (ed.), *Polish Writing To-day* (Penguin, 1967).

Theatre, cinema and music:
Csato, E., *The Polish Theatre* (Polonia, 1963).
Fuksiewicz, J., *Polish Cinema* (Interpress, 1973).
Hibbin, N., *Eastern Europe: An Illustrated Guide* (Zwemmer, 1969).
Manvell, R., and Fraenkl, H., *The German Cinema* (Dent, 1971).
Nemeskurty, I., *A Short History of the Hungarian Cinema* (Corvina Press, 1980).
Sadie, S. (ed.), *New Grove Directory of Music and Musicians* (Macmillan, 1980).
Shaoulov, L., *The Bulgarian Theatre* (Foreign Languages Press, 1982).

Sport:
Freeman, S., and Boyes, R., *Sport Behind the Iron Curtain* (Proteus, 1980).
Riordan, J., *Sport Under Communism*, 2nd edn (C. Hurst, 1982).

In addition to the above, the quarterly specialist publication *Survey* published in London contains interesting articles about eastern European cultural life.

7

CONCLUSION

By the early 1980s a remarkable transformation had eliminated the old, peasant world of eastern Europe, which lingered on only in remote corners, of Romania and Yugoslavia especially. In its place there had emerged industrialised societies in which a majority of the workforce was engaged in manufacturing and service industries. Standards of living had risen markedly, as all indices attested, and marked similarities existed between the life-styles and social attitudes of western and eastern Europeans, even if there remained a considerable gulf between their material conditions. In the course of a generation eastern Europe had been revolutionised in an impressive example of the politics and economics of development. There could be no question of a return to the old, pre-communist world.

The political system that had achieved this transformation remained closely tied to the Soviet model, the sole exception being in Yugoslavia. Well designed to meet the requirements of revolutionary change and to mobilise, channel and organise popular activity to transform the economic and social structure, it remained to be seen whether it would adapt to the needs of modernised societies whose principal requirements were steady administration, orderly national life, the guarantee of and respect for the rights of citizens and government in accordance with the due process of law. Without the checks and balances of traditional Western pluralistic parliamentary democracy, the communist political system offered a continual temptation to use power in place of persuasion and to meet dissent or disagreement with repression. The monopoly of power enjoyed by communist parties permitted them the luxury of discounting disagreement, a course not open to Western governments compelled to justify themselves to their electorates, to independent judges and law courts, and to public opinion. It was not inevitable that the communist system would function in this way. In Yugoslavia the necessity of carrying public opinion with government was accepted and a higher level of protection of personal rights and civil liberties acknowledged than elsewhere. Hungary too compared favourably in this respect. But Romania, Bulgaria, the DDR and Czechoslovakia had not developed far along the same path while the convulsions in Poland illustrated the difficulties confronting orderly and peaceful development of the communist system as the heroic period of revolutionary change ended and the need to recognise the legitimate interests of citizens began. It was too easy for communist parties to use force to meet internal changes that they found inconvenient and embarrassing. It seemed probable that the eastern European states would only be able to overcome this problem after the USSR itself had pioneered methods of government that accommodated such pressures.

A further political difficulty arose from the problems of achieving orderly and controlled changes in major policy matters. It was still true by the early 1980s that the communist system was not sufficiently flexible to permit such changes without provoking major crises. As in all governmental systems, policy failure was accompanied by the removal of those responsible, yet personnel changes within the communist system involved massive transfers, promotions and demotions in every aspect of the life of the state, for the operation of the *nomenklatura* ensured that changes at the apex of the political hierarchy would be accompanied by more or less extensive changes in personnel at every level. The communist system had failed to evolve the conception of a neutral civil service and advisory staff or of the legitimate interplay of differences of opinion in every aspect of national 'public' life, such as the media, law courts, education, or police and armed forces. A corner-stone of the system, the operation of the *nomenklatura* ensured that the disruptive effects of changes in personnel at the top of the pyramid of power were transmitted downward; paradoxically, this could weaken effectiveness and produce crises and instability. It remained to be seen whether the eastern European parties would be able to adjust smoothly to a new generation of political leaders whose advent to power could not be long delayed as ageing statesmen neared the end of their careers. Perhaps the most striking demonstration of the inflexibility of the system was its apparent inability to permit the retirement of aged leaders. Political reforms before and the smooth transfer of power after the death of President Tito suggested that the system was capable of development and adaptation, but only in Yugoslavia had real evidence of that been shown.

The most serious political crises arose from economic problems. As with the political system, the communist model had been devised to achieve the transformation of a backward economy into a modern, industrialised one, on the basis of the experiences of the USSR under Stalin. It had been rigorously applied throughout eastern Europe. There too it had achieved its aim of wrenching the area from the traditional world of peasant agriculture. As in the USSR, the process had been accomplished in a remarkably short time. The newly industrialised economies had, however, been based on the favoured heavy industries that formed the backbone of Soviet industrialisation. Iron and steel manufacturing, coal production, the mining and processing of other ores, heavy engineering and shipbuilding formed the basis of the industrial development of every state in the region. Such economic activities had an almost moral dimension, with weight of production being equated with political virtue. However, as had become apparent in the Western world, by 1980 these industries no longer held the key to the industrial future. It was becoming necessary in eastern Europe also to reorientate industry to meet the demands of the newest stages of world industrial development. Microelectronics, computing and information technology, all aspects of electrical engineering, development of bio-logical and chemical engineering industries and modern service indus-tries placed premiums on highly educated and skilled workforces, on elaborate and expensive research institutions, on extensive capital investment, on flexibility of response to change, awareness of new tech-niques and market demands. The two standard elements in communist industrial development had been massive investment of capital and the transfer of labour from agriculture to industry. By the early 1980s the latter possibility had been exhausted, and semi-skilled labour was anyway of no value for modern industry. Capital too was in short supply. The investment made in the first phase of industrial growth had not given an adequate return and required continuing subsidy. All eastern European countries without exception were short of investment capital. Matters were not helped by the uniformity of the region's economies. By basing their industrial development on the autarkic Soviet model they had in effect committed themselves to a style and pattern of economy unsuited to their needs. Greater specialisation and more selectivity in investment would have served the economies of the region better, a lesson learnt by 1980 as increasing efforts to develop industrial specialities showed. The earlier policies had, however, provided the region with too much capacity in heavy industries, often set up without adequate sources of indigenous raw materials, which had to be expensively imported. By 1980 most were operating at a loss and required massive state subsidies. In effect, in eastern as in western Europe, there were problems of adjustment and transition to the latest stages of industrial development which required that declining traditional sectors of industry be phased out. In the east the process was underway before the fruits of the first stage of development had been reaped. The signs suggested that certain states were more successful in reacting to the challenge and found the reorientation easier. The DDR, Bulgaria and Hungary were moving steadily towards greater speciali-sation and selectivity in investment and production. The larger countries were finding the transition more difficult. Both Yugoslavia and

Romania had not yet accomplished the first phase of their industrial development and the problems of transition lay ahead. Czechoslovak industry seemed to be stagnating, while Poland was in the throes of a major economic crisis, associated with the decline in importance of heavy industries which formed the basis of its economy. It was perhaps significant that unrest and disruption centred about the coal-mines and steel-manufacturing centres of south-western Poland and the ship-building yards on the Baltic coast, all engaged in manufacturing processes of declining significance. Given the link between economic difficulties and popular unrest, the implications could be politically serious for other communist states.

Agriculture too was proving troublesome. The difficulties of incorporating largely small-scale, private peasant agriculture into a largely state-owned and controlled economy had not been solved in Poland, where the food crises of 1980 and 1981 were in part at least the result of peasant refusal to market foodstuffs in the absence for purchase of consumer goods and necessary farm equipment. The low productivity of Yugoslav peasant agriculture had been compensated by US food aid during the 1950s and early 1960s, and by food imports subsequently. Elsewhere state-controlled agriculture was proving defective. Despite government efforts during the 1960s and 1970s, eastern European farm output was disappointing. Highly irregular fluctuations hit Five-year Plans, based on assumptions as to the productivity of the agrarian sector which almost invariably proved too optimistic. The deficiencies in collective farm production were to some extent made good by sales of foodstuffs produced on the private plots of collective farmers. These formed a disproportionate percentage of meat, eggs, poultry, fruit and vegetable sales, yet animal products from private plots normally depended on the availability of grain and fodder crops from collective farms.

The maximisation of food production while ensuring market prices that offer a satisfactory return to farmers has always posed problems for industrialised societies. The difficulty lay at the heart of the depressed agriculture of late nineteenth-century Britain, and led successive British governments after 1931 to intervene to secure the price structure of British agricultural production. It also underlay the economic arrangements of the Common Market. In the USA problems arising from the large surplus production of efficient US farmers and ensuing low prices led to the introduction of a significant price support system during the New Deal of President Roosevelt in the 1930s. Similar considerations lay behind the export of substantial quantities of grains and meat which paradoxically by 1980 made the USSR one of the best markets for US agricultural products. The problems posed by agriculture for governments were not unique to eastern Europe. However, by 1980 no eastern European state had devised a satisfactory agricultural system or pricing structure to ensure reliable and steady production and it remained to be seen how the communist economic system could be adapted to achieve this.

By 1980 it was probably true that, Poland apart, communist governments had established their authority and were accepted, occasional upsurges of popular resentment notwithstanding. After all, more or less extensive rioting and destruction was not unknown in the USA, Great Britain, Federal Germany, France and Holland. There were prominent individual critics, but there was little or no evidence that they or the public at large rejected the basic tenets of socialism, and populations accepted and indeed welcomed its social welfare aspects. Free health services, free education, low prices, the elimination of glaring class distinctions and cultural divisions between rulers and ruled were valued everywhere, as was the guarantee of employment that was operative in all states except Yugoslavia. All causes of popular resentment had not of course disappeared. The absence of class divisions, for example, may have removed one cause of social antagonism, but the privileges available to select groups had become an object of sharp resentment. While full employment was welcomed, its consequences – such as continual wage control, shortages in the supply of consumer goods and very slow improvements in real incomes – aroused discontent. In short, in eastern as in western Europe popular approval of some aspects of the economic, social and political system went hand in hand with disapproval of others and public opinion often applauded the ends without appreciating that the means were the price to be paid. Such restlessness did not, however, necessarily signify rejection of the system as a whole. Matters were complicated by the spread of education and the emergence of a new type of society. Despite attempts to stifle comment, by 1980 the public was critical of government and no longer willing to accept dictates and commands in the unthinking way preferred by Stalin, which underlay the command economy and political system he had evolved. As in the West, eastern Europeans demanded the opportunity to consult and take decisions affecting their own lives. Educated, thinking, informed and critical, they were well aware of the limitations placed on the transmission of information. Access to Western broadcasts and the all-pervasive and frequently well-informed rumour machine helped fill the gap, and as eastern Europeans travelled widely within the bloc and increasingly outside it they were exposed to alternative sources of information and were able to make more independent judgements. Not surprisingly they pressed for greater involvement in decision-making affecting their everyday lives. The greatest response had come in Yugoslavia, where the trail was blazed for the rest of the region. The least response seemed to have come in Romania where old-style totalitarianism still largely operated. There was nothing to suggest that it was inherently impossible for communist states to establish popular participation or encourage increasing public involvement in decision-making on local matters and in the discussions prior to policy formulation in social questions. The DDR, Hungary and Bulgaria had all taken substantial strides in that direction. The delicacy of the process was, however, well illustrated by events in Czechoslovakia in 1968 and in Poland after 1980. To be successful and to retain control over the process, it was necessary for the Party to be self-confident and united under appreciative leadership. In the absence of such controlling political direction the process of diversification could become unmanageable and would arouse the suspicions of the USSR. A wide variety of half-submerged complaints, exasperations and animosities normally under strict control might be unleashed. In that respect, too, communist eastern Europe was not so very different.

Further reading

1. *General works:*
Griffith, W.E. (ed.), *Communism in Europe*, 2 vols (Pergamon, 1967).
Mellor, R.E.H., *Eastern Europe, A Geography of the Comecon Countries* (Macmillan, 1975).
Pounds, N.J.G., *Eastern Europe* (Longman, 1969).
Schopflin, G. (ed.), *The Soviet Union and Eastern Europe* (Blond, 1970).

2. *Individual countries:*
Benes, V.L., and Pounds, N.J.G., *Poland* (Benn, 1970).
Bokov, G., *Modern Bulgaria* (Sofia Press, 1981).
Childs, D., *The G.D.R.: Moscow's German Ally* (Allen & Unwin, 1983).
Clissold, S. (ed.), *A Short History of Yugoslavia* (Cambridge University Press, 1966).
Davies, N., *God's Playground. A History of Poland*, 2 vols (Clarendon Press, 1981).
Fischer-Galati, S., *Twentieth Century Rumania* (Columbia University Press, 1970).
Gieystor, A. (ed.), *History of Poland* (PWN–Polish Scientific Publishers, 1968).
Halasz, Z. *A Short History of Hungary* (Corvina Press, 1975).
Hamilton, F.E.I., *Yugoslavia* (G. Bell, 1968).
Ignotus, P., *Hungary* (Benn, 1972).
Kossev, D., *A Short History of Bulgaria* (Foreign Languages Press, 1963).
Leslie, R.F. *et al.*, *History of Poland Since 1863* (Cambridge University Press, 1980).
Mamatey, V.S., and Luza, R., *A History of the Czechoslovak Republic 1918–1948* (Princeton University Press, 1973).
Pamlenyi, E. (ed.), *A History of Hungary* (Collet's, 1975).
Pavlowitch, S.K., *Yugoslavia* (Benn, 1971).
Singleton, F., *Twentieth Century Yugoslavia* (Macmillan, 1976).
Starr, R.F., *Communist Regimes in Eastern Europe* (Hoover Institute, 1982).
Turnock, D., *An Economic Geography of Romania* (Bell & Hyman, 1974).
Wallace, W.V., *Czechoslovakia* (Benn, 1977).

Appendix 1:

CHRONOLOGICAL TABLES

Bulgaria

1944	September	USSR declares war and Soviet troops invade; armistice and Bulgarian declaration of war against Germany.
1946	September	Abolition of the monarchy.
	October	First post-war election: Fatherland Front secures 70.8 per cent of the vote.
	November	Formation of Fatherland Front government.
1946–7		Arrests and trials of non-communists.
1947	March	Currency reform.
	August	Peace Treaty ratified.
	October	Cominform set up.
	December	People's Republic with Soviet-style constitution declared; one-party system formally established; nationalisation laws passed; Soviet troops withdrawn.
1949		First Five-year Plan begins.
	January	CMEA set up.
	March–December	Demotion, arrest, trial and execution of Kostov and other communists: Party purges.
	December	First single-list election.
1952	May	End of food rationing (subsequently reintroduced for short periods).
1953	May	Election of separate Bulgarian Orthodox Patriarch.
1955	May	Warsaw Pact signed.
1959	September	Collectivisation of agriculture declared completed.
1964–5	April–December	Progressive introduction of limited degree of economic decentralisation.
1971	May	New constitution.
1975	June	Appointment of first Roman Catholic bishops to communist Bulgaria.
1978	June	Economic decentralisation of decisions to individual enterprises.

1980	June	Joint ventures with non-communist companies permitted.

Czechoslovakia

1945	April	Establishment of Provisional government at Kosice.
	October	Indirect elections to Provisional National Assembly; introduction of extensive nationalisation programme; currency reform.
	December	Last Soviet and US troops withdrawn.
1946	May	First post-war election: Communist Party secures 37.9 per cent of the vote.
	July	National Coalition government set up.
1947	January	Two-year Plan begins.
	October	Cominform set up.
1948	February	Governmental crisis and mass communist demonstrations in Prague lead to communist *coup* and establishment of purely communist government.
	May	First single-list election.
1949		First Five-year Plan begins.
	January	CMEA set up; nationalisation law passed.
1951	February	Arrest of Clementis.
	November	Arrest of Slansky leading to trials and execution of both him and Clementis.
1953	November	Purges of Party.
1955	May	Collectivisation drive launched; Warsaw Pact signed.
1960	July	New constitution.
1963	October	Release of imprisoned Roman Catholic bishops.
1967	January	Introduction of socialist market economy, first proposed in 1964.
	October	Student demonstrations in Prague.
1968	January	Novotny ousted from Party secretaryship and replaced by Dubcek.
	April	Liberalisation proposals expounded in programme entitled *The Czechoslovak Road to Socialism*.
	June	*Two Thousand Words* manifesto published; Warsaw Pact manoeuvres in Poland and Czechoslovakia.
	August	Last Soviet troops leave Czechoslovakia after Warsaw Pact manoeuvres; invasion by Soviet, Polish, Hungarian, Bulgarian and DDR armed forces.
	October	Federal constitution introduced; formal

agreement to right of USSR to station troops in Czechoslovakia.

1969	January	Self-immolation of Jan Palach.
	April	Dubcek replaced as Party Secretary by Husak.
1977	January	*Charter '77* issued, followed by moves against its signatories.
1978		New experiments in economic decentralisation, extended in 1980.
1979–81	October–December	Trials and sentences for signatories of *Charter '77* and other dissidents.

DDR

1945	May	Formal surrender of German forces and end of Second World War.
1947	October	Cominform set up.
1948		Effective start of nationalisation.
	June	Berlin blockade begins.
1949	January	CMEA set up.
	September	Berlin blockade ends.
	October	Establishment of German Democratic Republic.
1950	February	Creation of secret police.
	October	First single-list election.
1951		First Five-year Plan begins.
1952		First collective farms set up.
1953	June	Riots and demonstrations in Berlin and other cities arising from economic demands and attempts to increase work-loads; suppressed by Soviet troops.
1954	March	End of Soviet occupation regime and Soviet recognition of the sovereignty of the DDR.
1955	May	Warsaw Pact signed.
1956	January	DDR army set up.
1958	June	Food rationing ended (subsequently reintroduced, for short periods).
1960	April	Collectivisation of agriculture declared completed.
1961	August	Berlin Wall constructed.
1963		Economic reforms begin under New Economic System.
1967		Further economic reforms under Economic System of Socialism.
1968	April	New constitution.
1971	September	Signature of Four-Power agreement over Berlin – first official international recognition of the DDR.
1972	April	Nationalisation of the economy declared completed.

| 1973 | June | Regularisation of mutual relations with the Federal Republic of Germany. |
| 1974 | October | Constitutional amendments. |

Hungary

1944	October	Soviet troops enter Hungary.
	December	Provisional National Assembly set up at Debrecen: declares war on Germany.
1945	January	Armistice with the USSR.
	March	Land redistribution begins.
	April	Last German soldiers leave Hungary; secret police set up.
	November	First post-war elections: Communist Party receives 16.9 per cent of the vote.
1946	January	Hungary declared a Republic.
1947–8		Arrest, trial and sentencing of non-communists.
1947	June	Peace Treaty ratified.
1947	October	Cominform set up.
1948	August	Elections: Communist Party receives 21.7 per cent of the vote.
1948–9	December–February	Arrest, trial and imprisonment of Cardinal Mindszenty.
1949	January	CMEA set up.
	May	First single-list election.
1949	June–December	Arrest, trial and execution of Rajk and other communists.
1950		First Five-year Plan starts; beginning of collectivisation of agriculture.
1951	June	Arrest, trial and imprisonment of Archbishop Grosz.
	December	Food rationing ended.
1953	July	Forced collectivisation ended.
1955	May	Warsaw Pact signed.
	July	Cardinal Mindszenty released and placed under house-arrest.
	October	Archbishop Grosz released.
1956	May	Grosz resumes episcopal functions.
	May–June	Promises of democratisation insufficient to stifle growing demands for civil liberties and end of one-party state; increased supplies of consumer goods and amnesties, pardons and rehabilitations of condemned political opponents as crisis grows led to collapse of Party's self-confidence.
	October	Imre Nagy appointed Secretary-General in desperate effort to stem tide; he announces a

programme of free elections, withdrawal from Warsaw Pact and ending of stationing of Soviet troops in Hungary.

	November	Soviet troop build-up leading to use of them to crush resistance in Budapest and elsewhere with heavy casualties; Nagy abducted and taken to Romania after leaving Yugoslav embassy under safe conduct.
	October–December	Intermittent General Strike organised by workers' councils which disbanded in December.
1958		Agricultural collectivisation resumed.
	June	Trial and execution of Nagy.
1961	February	Collectivisation declared completed.
1963	March	Amnesty for many imprisoned after 1956.
1964	September	First agreement with Roman Catholic Church.
1966	June	Acceptance of proposals for economic reform, to operate from January 1968.
1971	September	Cardinal Mindszenty permitted to leave US embassy and retire to Rome.
1975		Continuing improvement in relations with the Vatican leads to nomination of new bishops.
1975–6		Policy of increased co-operation with the West develops.
1978	January	US government returns the crown and regalia of St Stephen.
1980–2		Phasing out of subsidies, moves towards free prices and a fully convertible currency.

Poland

1944	July	Soviet troops enter Poland; Lublin Committee set up.
	September	Land redistribution begins.
1945	June	Government of National Unity established.
	August	Oder–Neisse line agreed at Potsdam Conference as western frontier of Poland.
1946–7		Arrests and trials of non-communists.
1946	January	Nationalisation law passed.
1947	January	First post-war election: government bloc secures 78.9 per cent of the vote – Communist Party allocated 31 per cent of the bloc seats by prior agreement.
	February	Interim constitution adopted.
	October	Cominform set up.
1949	January	CMEA set up.
1949–51		Expulsion, arrest and detention of Gomulka and other communists.

1950		First Five-year Plan begins; collectivisation of agriculture started.
1952	July	People's Republic set up with Soviet-style constitution.
	October	First single-list election.
1953	January	Abolition of food rationing (subsequently reintroduced for short periods).
	September	Cardinal Wyszynski placed under residential restrictions.
1955	May	Warsaw Pact signed.
1956	April	Release and rehabilitation of Gomulka.
1956	June–November	Riots in Poznan, with attacks on police and Communist Party offices, followed by easing of economic policy and promises of more consumer goods; serious tensions and manifestations of anti-Soviet feeling lead to appointment of Gomulka as First Secretary (in October) and announcement of liberalisation programme and of release of Cardinal Wyszynski; secret police placed under jurisdiction of Ministry of the Interior; exploitative coal agreement with the USSR ended (November) and Polish debts to the USSR cancelled; workers' councils legalised.
1964–70		Progressive implementation of economic reform programme.
1968	March	Student demonstrations, officially attributed to Zionism followed by launch of anti-semitic campaign.
	November	'Brezhnev Doctrine' of limited sovereignty of socialist countries if developments within them endanger socialism enunciated at 5th Congress of Polish party.
1970	December	Major food price increases provoke riots in Gdansk and other Baltic coast towns; rises cancelled; Gomulka replaced by Gierek.
1971–5		Rapprochement with the Roman Catholic Church.
1976	June–July	Riots against food price increases, which were then rescinded.
	September	KOR set up to aid those accused of rioting.
1978	October	Cardinal Woytila elected Pope.
1979	June	Pope John Paul II visits Poland.
1980		Major international debt problem revealed.
1980–2	July–December	Increases in food prices produce strikes developing in July–August into demands for establishment of independent trade unions; Gdansk shipyard strike headed by Walesa spreads to other Baltic coast towns and

government agrees to negotiate; produces agreement in August; industrial disputes spread to rest of country and by September unofficial unions established throughout Poland; from October 1980 until March 1981 negotiations over moratorium on debts and extension of new credits with Western countries and USSR and simultaneous expressions of concern at developments by other bloc countries, with Warsaw Pact manoeuvres; political confrontations between Solidarity and government; tension increases during 1981 as continuing slump in economy compounded by food shortages leads to price increases and rationing; September–October 1981: first national congress of Solidarity focuses issue when it elaborates a politico-economic programme covering prices, wages, industrial organisation and the role of workers' councils and the censorship of news; followed by strong reaction by government and by other Warsaw Pact powers, with further military manoeuvres in October 1981; Solidarity announces in December plans for national referendum which is in effect a vote of no confidence in government, and is followed immediately by declaration of martial law and arrest of its leaders; protest strikes largely ended by turn of year; 1982 produces further negotiations with Western states and banks leading to rescheduling of debts in spring accompanied by extension of food rationing, compulsory work decree and abandonment of 1982 economic plan; October 1982: new laws on unions effectively disbanded Solidarity which thenceforth became illegal and was ignored by government; December 1982: lessening in internal tension permits suspension of martial law.

Romania

1944	April	Soviet troops cross frontier.
	September	Overthrow of Antonescu; armistice with the USSR; declaration of war on Germany.
1945	March	Establishment of National Democratic Front government; land redistribution begins.

1946	November	First post-war elections: government bloc receives 68.7 per cent of the vote and Communist Party is allocated seventy-three seats.
1947–8		Arrests and trials of non-communists.
1947	August	Peace Treaty ratified; currency reform.
	October	Cominform set up.
	December	Abdication and flight of King Michael.
1948	March	Elections with Popular Democratic Front securing 90.8 per cent of the vote.
	April	People's Republic set up with Soviet-style constitution.
	June	Nationalisation law enacted.
	August	Secret police created.
1949	January	CMEA set up.
	July	First collective farms formed.
1951		First Five-year Plan begins.
1952	March	Collectivisation of agriculture launched.
	September	New constitution.
1954		Arrest, trial and execution of Patrascanu and other communists.
1955	May	Warsaw Pact signed.
	December	End of food rationing (subsequently re-enacted for short periods).
1958	July	Completion of withdrawal of Soviet troops.
1962	February	Collectivisation officially declared completed.
1963–4	June–August	Breach with CMEA over issue of integration of economies of eastern Europe.
1965	August	New constitution.
1967	December	Adoption of economic reforms.
1969	February	Official repudiation of the 'Brezhnev Doctrine'.
1974	July	Steps taken to recentralise economic decision-making.
1976–7		Moves against Romanian sympathisers with Czechoslovak dissidents and signatories of *Charter '77*.
1980–1		Measures against Romanian supporters of free trade unions.
1981	September	Request for reorganisation of debt repayments to Western states and banks; serious economic problems vitiated by flooding and falls in agricultural output, leading to food rationing and internal disturbances arising from austerity measures.

Yugoslavia

1944	December	Provisional government set up; secret police established.
1945	March	Government of National Unity formed under Tito.
	August	Land reform commences.
	November	First single-list election.
1946	January	People's Republic with Soviet-style constitution set up.
	December	Nationalisation law.
1946–7		Arrests and trials of non-communists.
1947		First Five-year Plan begins.
	October	Cominform set up, with headquarters in Belgrade.
1948	June	Yugoslavia expelled from Cominform.
1949		Agricultural collectivisation begins.
	September	First US credits and first loans from the West.
1950	June	Fundamental Law on Workers' Self-government introduces first steps towards workers' control.
1952		Communist Party reorganised on federal basis and renamed League of Communists.
1953	January	New federal constitution.
	March	Collectivisation ends and existing farms disband.
1956	June	Contact re-established with the Communist Party of the USSR.
1963	April	New constitution.
1964	September	Associated status with CMEA accorded.
1965	July	Economic reforms begin with aim of enhancing role and power of workers' councils and enterprise managements.
1966	July	Dismissal of Rankovic and purge of secret police.
	October	League of Communists reorganised.
1967	December	Constitutional amendments.
1968	October–November	Repudiation of the 'Brezhnev Doctrine'.
1970	October	Stabilisation programme to restrain the economy and prevent it over-heating.
1971	June	Constitutional changes increasing the powers of the federal republics.
1971–2	December–January	Crisis in Croatia arising from dissent from central government economic policies and rise in national feeling, leading to purges of Croatian communists.
1974	February	New constitution.
	December	Nationalist demonstrations by Albanians in Kosovo region.

| 1980 | May | Tito dies. |
| 1981–2 | March onwards | Continuing unrest among Albanian population in Kosovo with concomitant arrests and trials. |

Appendix 2:

HEADS OF EASTERN EUROPEAN COMMUNIST PARTIES, GOVERNMENTS AND STATES, TO 31 MARCH 1983

(*Note:* The titles of the above offices have varied widely. Communist parties have been led by Chairmen, Secretaries-General and First Secretaries; the Head of Government is taken to be the office corresponding to President of the Council of Ministers, while Heads of State are those persons fulfilling the titular duties at the date given, regardless of their actual designation.)

1. Bulgaria

(a) Party:

To July 1949:	G. Dimitrov
July 1949–March 1954	V. Chervenkov
March 1954–	T. Zhivkov

(b) Government:

September 1945–November 1946	K. Gheorgiev
November 1946–March 1949	G. Dimitrov
March 1949–February 1950	V. Kolarov
February 1950–April 1956	V. Chervenkov
April 1956–November 1962	A. Yugov
November 1962–August 1971	T. Zhivkov
July 1971–June 1981	S. Todorov
July 1981–	G. Filipov

(c) State:

September 1946–July 1949	V. Kolarov
1950–November 1958	G. Damyanov
November 1958–April 1964	D. Ganev
April 1964–July 1971	G. Traikov
July 1971–	T. Zhivkov

2. Czechoslovakia

(a) Party:

To September 1951	R. Slansky
September 1951–March 1953	K. Gottwald
March 1953–January 1968	A. Novotny
January 1968–April 1969	A. Dubcek
April 1969–	G. Husak

(b) Government:

June 1945–July 1946	Z. Fierlinger
July 1946–July 1948	K. Gottwald
July 1948–March 1953	A. Zapotocky
March 1953–September 1963	V. Siroky
September 1963–April 1968	J. Lenart
April 1968–January 1970	O. Cernik
January 1970–	L. Strougal

(c) State:

To July 1948	E. Benes
July 1948–March 1953	K. Gottwald
March 1953–November 1957	A. Zapotocky
November 1957–March 1968	A. Novotny
March 1968–March 1975	General L. Svoboda
May 1975–	G. Husak

3. DDR

(a) Party:

To May 1971	W. Ulbricht
May 1971–	E. Honecker

(b) Government:

October 1949–September 1964	O. Grotewohl
September 1964–October 1973	W. Stoph
October 1973–October 1976	H. Sindermann
October 1976–	W. Stoph

(c) State:

October 1949–September 1960	W. Pieck
September 1960–October 1973	W. Ulbricht
October 1973–October 1976	W. Stoph
October 1976–	E. Honecker

4. Hungary

(a) Party:

To July 1953	M. Rakosi
July 1953–November 1953	No head
November 1953–July 1956	M. Rakosi
July 1956–October 1956	E. Gero
October 1956–	J. Kadar

(b) Government:

July 1944–November 1945	Col. Gen. B. Miklos
November 1945–February 1946	Rev. Z. Tildy
February 1946–May 1947	F. Nagy
May 1947–December 1948	L. Dinnyes
December 1948–August 1952	I. Dobi
August 1952–July 1953	M. Rakosi
July 1953–April 1955	I. Nagy
April 1955–October 1956	A. Hegedus
October 1956	I. Nagy
November 1956–January 1958	J. Kadar
January 1958–September 1961	F. Muennich
September 1961–June 1965	J. Kadar
June 1965–April 1967	G. Kallai
April 1967–May 1975	J. Fock
May 1975–	G. Lazar

(c) State:

January 1946–July 1948	Rev. Z. Tildy
July 1948–April 1950	A. Szakasits
April 1950–August 1952	S. Ronai
August 1952–April 1967	I. Dobi
April 1967–	P. Loconczi

5. Poland

(a) Party:

To September 1948	W. Gomulka
September 1948–March 1956	B. Bierut
March 1956–October 1956	E. Ochab
October 1956–December 1970	W. Gomulka
December 1970–September 1980	E. Gierek
September 1980–October 1981	S. Kania
October 1981–	General W. Jaruzelski

(b) Government:

July 1945–February 1947	E. Osobka-Morawski
February 1947–November 1952	J. Cyrankiewicz

November 1952–March 1954	B. Bierut
March 1954–December 1970	J. Cyrankiewicz
December 1970–February 1980	P. Jaroszewicz
February 1980–August 1980	E. Babiuch
August 1980–February 1981	J. Pinkowski
February 1981–	General W. Jaruzelski

(c) State:

To November 1952	B. Bierut
November 1952–August 1964	A. Zawadski
August 1964–April 1968	E. Ochab
April 1968–December 1970	Marshal M. Spychalski
December 1970–March 1972	J. Cyrankiewicz
March 1972–	H. Jablonski

6. Romania

(a) Party:

October 1947–April 1954	G. Gheorgiu-Dej
April 1954–October 1955	G. Apostol
October 1955–March 1965	G. Gheorgiu-Dej
March 1965–	N. Ceausescu

(b) Government:

August 1944–December 1944	General C. Sanatescu
December 1944–March 1945	General N. Radescu
March 1945–June 1952	Dr P. Groza
June 1952–October 1955	G. Gheorgiu-Dej
October 1955–March 1961	C. Stoica
March 1961–March 1974	I. Maurer
March 1974–March 1979	M. Manescu
March 1979–May 1982	I. Verdet
May 1982–	C. Dascalescu

(c) State:

To December 1947	King Michael
June 1952–January 1958	Dr P. Groza
January 1958–March 1961	I. Maurer
March 1961–March 1965	G. Gheorgiu-Dej
March 1965–December 1967	C. Stoica
December 1967–	N. Ceausescu

7. Yugoslavia

(a) Party:

| To May 1980 | Marshal Tito |

October 1979–May 1980	Acting head S. Doronjski
May 1980–October 1980	S. Doronjski
October 1980–October 1981	L. Mojsov
October 1981–October 1982	D. Dragosavac
October 1982–	M. Ribicic

(b) Government:

July 1944–March 1945	Dr I. Subasitc
March 1945–January 1953	Marshal Tito
June 1963–May 1967	P. Stambolic
May 1967–May 1969	M. Spiljak
May 1969–July 1971	M. Ribicic
July 1971–January 1977	D. Bijedic
February 1977–January 1982	V. Djuranovic
January 1982–	M. Planinc

(c) State:

December 1945–January 1953	Dr I. Ribar
January 1953–May 1980	Marshal Tito
May 1980	L. Kolisevski
May 1980–May 1981	C. Mijatovic
May 1981–May 1982	S. Kraigher
May 1982–	P. Stambolic

INDEX

agriculture, 103–11, 190–1
  employment in, 115–16, 140–1
  exports of, 88, 151
  private, 110, 127, 129, 145
  see also collectivisation, land reform, peasantry
alcoholism, 149–51, 171

Bulgaria
  agriculture, 86–7, 88, 104–8, 128–9
  before 1939, 3, 5, 8, 9, 10, 23
  creative arts, 162, 167, 174–5, 178
  economy, 78, 80–1, 97, 100–1
  education, 130, 132, 133, 135
  housing, 138–9
  in Second World War, 12, 17, 20
  population, 6, 25, 115–16, 117, 119–20, 122
  religion, 66–7
  show trials, 22
  social services, 128, 144, 146, 150–1
  society, 117, 128, 135, 142–3, 149–50, 155, 160, 170

Ceausescu, N., 44, 46, 54, 96, 179
censorship, 22, 40, 162–3, 165, 185–6
cinema, 166–9
cities, 116–19, 125, 137, 174
collectivisation, 86–8, 107–11
Comecon (CMEA), 97, 98–9, 103, 189
communist parties
  before 1939, 8–9, 15
  crises within, 35, 39–41, 61
  in Second World War, 15–17
  membership, 29–30, 31, 34, 36, 44
  organisational structure, 34–9
  privileges of, 36, 59, 148–9, 153, 158
  taking of power by, 19, 25–6
constitutions, 28, 54–5, 76, 135, 139
crime, 151, 158–60
currencies, 9, 26, 97
Czechoslovakia
  agriculture, 104–9, 128–9
  before 1939, 2, 8, 10–11, 23

creative arts, 166–7, 169, 171, 173, 184, 185–6
crisis of 1968, 33, 35–6, 41–2, 43, 44, 49, 52
economy, 75, 79, 81, 83, 84, 90, 93, 140
education, 133–5
employment, 140
housing, 137–9, 156
in Second World War, 13, 17, 19–20, 21, 24
population, 6, 25, 115–16, 120, 122
religion, 69
show trials, 22
Slovaks in, 22, 38, 42, 121, 123
social services, 144, 146
society, 141–3, 149–51, 155, 160, 170
sport, 160, 179

DDR (German Democratic Republic)
  agriculture, 87, 104–8, 128
  creation of, 50–2
  creative arts, 163, 166, 169, 172–3, 174, 175, 177
  crime, 159–60
  crisis of 1953, 33, 41, 166
  economy, 52, 79, 81–4, 140
  education, 133–5
  employment, 135–6, 140
  housing, 137–9
  population, 115–16, 119, 120, 122, 139
  religion, 67–8, 70
  social services, 128, 144, 146, 150, 155
  society, 46, 51–2, 142–3, 149–50, 170
  sport, 51, 179, 182
democratic centralism, 33, 40
dissent, 57–8, 59–61, 65–6, 158, 191–2
  in creative arts, 166, 168–9, 171–3, 177, 185–6
Djilas, M., 16, 59–60, 142